D0903726

Beatrice's Spell

Beatrice's Spell

THE ENDURING LEGEND OF
BEATRICE CENCI

B ELINDA   J ACK

OTHER PRESS • NEW YORK

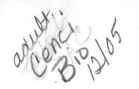

Library of Congress Cataloging-in-Publication Data

Jack, Belinda Elizabeth.
    Beatrice's spell : the enduring legend of Beatrice Cenci / by Belinda Jack.
        p. cm.
    Includes bibliographical references and index.
    ISBN 1-59051-163-8 (pbk. : alk. paper) 1. Cenci, Beatrice, 1577-1599.
2. Cenci, Beatrice, 1577-1599–In literature. 3. Cenci, Beatrice, 1577-1599–Influence. 4. Nobility–Italy–Rome–Biography. 5. Rome (Italy)–History–1420-1798. I. Title.
    DG812.6.C4J33 2005
    364.152'3'092–dc22

                                                    2004021693

For John, Jamie, and Nick

Contents

List of Illustrations   ix

Acknowledgments   xi

Introduction   1

Part I. A True Story
  1 Rome Mourns   13
  2 "No Other Remedy . . . "   21

Part II. Resurrections
  3 Shelley's "Secret Caverns of the Human Heart"   49
  4 Melville: Ambiguous Confession   90
  5 Hawthorne: "The Sins of the Fathers"   120
  6 Harriet Hosmer: Rebellious Innocence   155
  7 The Voyeurs   184
  8 Antonin Artaud: "Unbearable Truths"   199

Afterword   230

Source Notes   238

Index   245

List of Illustrations

—◦◦◦—

1. *Portrait of Beatrice Cenci*, by Guido Reni. Galleria Nazionale d'Arte Antica, Rome.

2. Drawing by A. Sandoz, 1858, after Paul Delaroche, *Beatrice Cenci marchant au supplice*, 1855. British Library.

3. *Percy Bysshe Shelley*, 1819, by Amelia Curran. National Portrait Gallery, London.

4. *Mary Shelley*, around 1814, by an unknown artist. From Eileen Bigland, *Mary Shelley*, 1959.

5. *Claire Clairmont*, 1819, by Amelia Curran. Nottingham City Museums and Galleries (Newstead Abbey).

6. *Byron*, 1818, by James Holmes. National Portrait Gallery, London.

7. Shelley's sketches from his Italian notebook. The Bodleian Library, University of Oxford. MS. Shelly adds. e9, front pastedown-p. i.

8. "Boats attacking whales," from *The Natural History of the Sperm Whale*, by Thomas Beale, 1839.

9. "An Inhabitant of the Island of Nukahiwa," from *Voyages and Travels*, by G.H. von Langsdorff, 1813.

10. "Punishment," watercolor by William H. Meyers, from his
    "Journal of a Cruise on the U.S.S. *Cyane*, 1842–3." Naval
    Historical Center.

11. *Herman Melville*, c.1847, by Asa W. Twitchell. Berkshire
    Athenaeum, Pittsfield, Massachusetts.

12. *Nathaniel Hawthorne*, 1840, by Charles Osgood. Photo-
    graph courtesy Peabody Essex Museum.

13. Harriet Hosmer and her workmen, 1867. Watertown Free
    Public Library.

14. Hosmer working on the clay model of *Thomas Hart Benton*
    in Rome, 1862. The Schlesinger Library, Radcliffe Institute,
    Harvard University.

15. "The Prince of Wales in Miss Hosmer's studio," *Harper's
    Weekly*, May 1859.

16. *Beatrice Cenci*, by Harriet Hosmer, 1856. From the collec-
    tions of the St. Louis Mercantile Library at the University of
    Missouri-St. Louis.

17. *A Study of the Cenci*, by Julia Margaret Cameron, May
    1868. The J. Paul Getty Museum, Los Angeles.

18. Antonin Artaud in his early thirties, playing Frère Massieu in
    Carl Dreyer's film, *La Passion de Jeanne d'Arc*, 1927.

19. Artaud in 1946, aged fifty, two years before his death.

20. Artaud in his production of *Les Cenci*, 1935.

21. Sketches by Artaud, including one of his many self-portraits.

Acknowledgments

I am deeply grateful to Jenny Uglow and Felicity Bryan, both of whom read my manuscript at some stage toward the end of my project. Their advice and enthusiasm were invaluable. If there are any errors that remain, they are my own.

I would like to thank a number of art historians, Italianists, literary critics, cultural historians and Italian friends who supported my researches in numerous ways: Stephen Bann, Emmanuele de Biase Corneli, Anne Jefferson, Dilwyn Know, Francesco Medioli, Martin McLaughlin, Ela Tandello, Marina Warner and Catherine Whistler. Robert di Domenica's willingness to talk about his own (and his wife's) obsession with Beatrice Cenci provided great insight. The friends and colleagues who read or discussed fragments of the book at different points and made useful criticisms or stimulated my thoughts, are too numerous to mention: their contributions are nonetheless much appreciated.

Christ Church has generously supported my research in various ways and numerous Oxford libraries have treated me with enormous patience; their forbearance and expertise are fully appreciated. Libraries abroad have not always responded to the vagaries of my research practices in quite the same way. Nevertheless I am grateful for their support.

Finally I would like to thank my family for their tolerance and encouragement. My husband Allan has lived on the edges of the murky world of Beatrice Cenci for longer than I had planned, but always showed remarkable steadiness and great kindness.

Belinda Jack
OXFORD
SEPTEMBER 2003

There are indeed many wonders, and
With regard to the stories people tell one
Another, it may be
That such tales go beyond the true account
And, embellished with iridescent lies,
Beguile them.

PINDAR

We would connive
in civilised outrage
yet understand the exact
and tribal, intimate revenge

SEAMUS HEANEY,
"PUNISHMENT," 1975

Introduction

—∿∿—

I am setting out to explore a disturbing subject: the response of writers and artists over the centuries to a young woman's life of extraordinary suffering, and the revenge which led to her own violent death. The story of Beatrice Cenci has the atmosphere of a recurrent nightmare, and I have sometimes been tempted to abandon it, worn down by its darkness. Beatrice is at once the ultimate victim, an innocent daughter brutalized by her father, and the aggressor, terrifying in her unhesitating resolve to murder him. At the heart of her life is something emotionally insoluble: we cannot but feel sympathy for her, and yet her capacity for violence is abhorrent. To begin with I was fascinated by the extremes of her life and death, but as I discovered the many guises in which her story has appeared and reappeared, I became intrigued by a parallel story. This book is about Beatrice Cenci but also about the strange lives of those who have fallen under her spell. Many writers and artists have sought to resurrect her, and for those who interest me most it is no exaggeration to say that their fascination cost them their artistic reputations, and many were also spurned by their relatives and closest friends. Their only solace was the knowledge that they had written themselves into a strange fellowship: they were not alone in their infatuation but took their place in a long and very particular tradition. The work they produced under "Beatrice's Spell" was almost invariably their last, their farewell to art, and often to life.

The bare bones of Beatrice's story are these: she was the beautiful daughter of a notorious aristocrat, Francesco Cenci, who imprisoned and brutalized her. In desperation she conspired with her stepmother and brothers who had also been appallingly treated, and in 1598 she organized her father's assassination. After a spectacular trial she was sentenced to death. From the moment of her execution she became a martyr and, to this day, a mass is said for her in Rome on September 11, the anniversary of her death.

Beatrice Cenci's story has a compelling power which explains its survival. Yet it is strangely reminiscent of earlier tales that go back long before her life: the people of Rome must have recognized in the shape of Beatrice's life something already familiar, a reenactment of a particular type of story, in which brutality, incest, torture and murder play prominent roles. These exaggerated forms of human behavior are, of course, what animate many classical myths and Bible tales: wicked fathers and stepmothers, passion, violence and destiny. They are the stuff of folk and fairytales too, those half-remembered stories of "Rapunzel," "Donkeyskin," "Cinderella." Many of these can be traced much earlier, even if we know them from Hans Christian Andersen or the Brothers Grimm, or for that matter Walt Disney. Father–daughter stories in which the father attempts to keep his daughter for himself abound. Remote castles, towers and walled gardens crop up again and again as places of imprisonment where the father can immure his daughter and guard against the penetration of rival suitors. Sometimes the hint of incest lies below the surface, but sometimes it is played out in graphic detail. The bizarre story of Lot's incestuous relationship with his daughters in the cave is related in the opening chapters of the Bible, in the book of Genesis. The incestuous Greek tyrant King Antiochus's relationship with his daughter is picked up by Shakespeare and provides the opening for *Pericles*. Another story is that of Saint Dympna, a seventh-century princess and martyr. She is presumed to have been the daughter of a Celtic chieftain who developed an "unlawful passion" for his daughter after his wife's death. The official *Vita*, the life of Saint Dympna, was written in the thirteenth century, hundreds of years after she lived and some three centuries before Beatrice Cenci, but her tale was retold by the Jesuit Pedro Ribadeneyra, and published in Latin in 1624 only twenty-five years after Beatrice's execution. It may be that Ribadeneyra saw the parallels between Dympna and Beatrice's lives—and violent deaths. Unlike Beatrice, Princess Dympna escaped her father with the help of her confessor, but her father's feelings were so strong that her absence only fueled his desire. He tracked her down in Geel, near Amsterdam, and when she refused to marry him he ordered his men to kill both his daughter and the priest. They killed the priest, but could not bring themselves to kill Dympna, so her father beheaded her himself. A further aspect of Saint Dympna's life is relevant to Beatrice. There are often peculiar reasons why a particular saint should become patron to this group or that. Dympna became the patron saint of the insane. In the medieval mind at least, incest was inextricably linked with madness, and this association continues to play a peculiar role in the tellings and retellings of the life of Beatrice Cenci. Her story has provided many with a smokescreen, an opportunity to explore areas that remain forbidden.

There are, of course, variations in the endings of these incest stories and one of the most disturbing undercurrents is also

treated differently: that is the degree of the daughter's consent
or collusion. There is often a suggestion that however odious the
perpetrator, the object of passion also shares some responsibility. Very occasionally the "victim" of incest is not a victim at
all, but a scheming "perpetrator." In the Old Testament, Lot's
daughters set about seducing their father with cool deliberation:
"Come, let us make our father drink wine, and we will lie with
him, that we may preserve the seed of our father" (Genesis 19.28).

There are other more recent parallel stories. Sigmund Freud
had a good deal to say about Oedipus and his mother, and he
had things to say about fathers and daughters too, but he wasn't
altogether prepared to come clean. In *Studies on Hysteria*, published in 1895, Freud included the case of "Katerina." Her real
name was Aurelia Kronich and a good deal of meticulous research claims to have authenticated the case. Many scholars,
however, remain deeply skeptical and maintain that Freud's accounts are based almost exclusively on his own fantasies. Aurelia
was, according to Freud, the daughter of an employee in the al-
pine inn where he was staying one summer. They got to know
one another and when she spoke to him about her "nervous attacks," Freud suggested that the root cause of her anxiety might
have been something she had witnessed in the past. Aurelia recalled that years earlier she had caught sight of her father lying
on top of her cousin. Seeing this had made her ill; she had vom-
ited for three days. Freud probed further and Aurelia remembered
that her father had done this to her too, some years earlier. Re-
calling and articulating her experiences brought about an instant
cure, or so he reports. The case was crucial in his development
of a theory in which sexual experience, repressive memory and
hysteria were linked. His therapeutic process allowed the patient
to find a way out of a vicious circle. In many of the representa-

tions of Beatrice's story she is described or depicted as being unable to relate what it is that her father has done to her. His crime is literally "unspeakable." Beatrice's sense of shame has to do with her intimate involvement with an ultimate transgression, which frequently results in her exhibiting something akin to a kind of madness.

The really odd thing about Freud's account of "Katerina" is that he originally described the molesting figure not as her father but as her "uncle." It was a quarter of a century later that he "admitted" (in a footnote) that it was Aurelia's abusive father who had incestuously raped her. Freud himself admitted to feeling a deep and complicated yearning for his youngest daughter, Anna. Clearly Freud himself had some difficulty telling the true story in "Katerina" and perhaps one or the other or both versions were invented. The fear of incest and similar veiled admissions of incestuous desire emerge in the uses and abuses of Beatrice's story.

Beatrice Cenci has seen many resurrections in paintings and sculptures, late Renaissance manuscripts, plays, poems and novels, operas and songs. These have been produced all over the world, in many languages including Italian, English, French, German, Spanish, Swedish, Polish and Japanese. What intrigues me particularly is what I see as the "dangerous," as opposed to the "safe," tradition amidst these retellings. Beatrice's story has often been plundered; many have flirted with it, or engaged with it simply to exploit it, and have then abandoned it, apparently unaffected by their encounter. This is the "safe tradition" where the artist has walked away unscathed. Those who belong to the "dangerous tradition," on the other hand, contract the full-blown "Cenci disease" and never recover from it. This line begins with the English poet Percy Bysshe Shelley, and continues with the American writers Herman Melville, author of *Moby-Dick*, and

Nathaniel Hawthorne, famous for his exploration of adultery in *The Scarlet Letter*. It is maintained in the work of the little-known American neoclassical sculptor, Harriet Hosmer and is dramatically evident in relation to the last writer I treat at length, Antonin Artaud, the French *avant-garde* dramatic theorist and playwright. His suffering and madness were part of his mythical status and they were played out on a remarkably public stage. When he died in 1948 he was, like Beatrice, quickly proclaimed a martyr.

A mysterious, late sixteenth-century portrait which prompted a vast number of reproductions did a great deal to keep Beatrice's story alive. There are numerous mostly eighteenth- and nineteenth-century copies of this Baroque painting, and even canvases which tell the story of the painting of the painting. The original portrait came into the possession of the Barberini family toward the end of the eighteenth century: its whereabouts during the previous two hundred years are disputed. It is first mentioned in a "Catalogue of Paintings" drawn up in 1783: "Picture of a head. Portrait, believed to be of the Cenci girl. Artist unknown." A few years later, a copy, dated 1794, attributes the original painting to Guido Reni. The copyist, unlike the author of the catalogue, may have known the historian Lodovico Antonio Muratori's retelling of the Beatrice story in his twelve-volume *Annali d'Italia* (1749), which includes a description of Guido's introduction into the prison on the eve of Beatrice's execution. Other eighteenth-century reproductions indicate that her reputation was already becoming international. There were printed reproductions including one by Clemente Kohl from a drawing by Linder (1789), and another by L. Legoux under the direction of Bettellini. Nineteenth-century paintings and engravings depicting Guido in Beatrice's cell, or Beatrice's last meeting with her stepmother, or her last confession, or of her on her way to execution, came thick and fast. But, bizarrely, the original portrait that gave rise to all these representations is in fact almost certainly not a portrait of Beatrice at all—indeed, many art historians dispute its attribution altogether, although others have pointed out its similarity with other heads by Guido, particularly those of sibyls, or seers.

At some point, perhaps in the eighteenth century, perhaps much earlier, the portrait "became" Beatrice. That it turns out to be a projection is all the more significant because it suggests a need, a hunger, for a tangible link, an iconic representation. During the Cenci trial conversations in Rome were dominated by discussion of her likely fate. Her execution gave her story a dramatic ending and became one of the great stories of the oral tradition of Rome. When the portrait was "discovered" in 1783, there was a great will to identify—in what turns out most probably to be the face of a prophetess—the beautiful Beatrice Cenci. From the late eighteenth century, and still more so during the nineteenth, huge numbers of people sought out the painting, as they continue to do today. It was bought by the Galleria Nazionale d'Arte Antica in 1934 and hangs in the Palazzo Barberini. Despite professional art historical judgment the label simply has a query beside both the names of the artist and subject, while guide books still describe it as the "Head of Beatrice Cenci."

The art historian who undertook to discover the true details of the portrait, the highly respected Italian scholar Corrado Ricci, was drawn into something murkier and more time-consuming than he had anticipated. Initially he simply wanted to know whether or not the painting was of Beatrice, and who it was by. He must have resolved these questions quickly, or at least he must have soon realized the limits of what it was possible to establish. But Ricci, like so many others, became increasingly drawn into her story and in the end he virtually abandoned his art historical researches in favor of investigating the true historical facts, the catalyst for so much artistic creativity. His work was based on a slim historical account by Antonio Bertoletti, who published *Francesco Cenci e la sua Famiglia* (1879), based on a manuscript found in the Vittorio Emanuele Library in Rome among other documentation, but he went on to spend five years examining vast numbers of manuscript sources, pamphlets, articles and books. He also recorded some of the curious details of the contemporary oral tradition still surviving in La Petrella where Francesco had been murdered hundreds of years earlier. In one version, he was told that her torturer hung her by her flaxen hair, which reached her knees. In the foreword to his massive two-volume work, *Beatrice Cenci* (1925), he claims, in a tone which either infuriates or charms:

> Passion and bad faith . . . began their work of deforming truth on the very day the fate of the Cenci was decided. Neither by those who championed her cause nor by those who made themselves the apologists of her judges does the slightest attempt at impartiality ever seem to have been made. Rulers, prelates, ambassadors, nobles and populace rush into the fray on one side or the other, each striving to surpass the other in violent partisanship.

Ricci nobly confronted the "evil fertility of error" in the literature that quickly grew up around the Cenci case, guided in his labors by the "precept of the mighty Dante": "The truth no lie shall plunder of its due."

Ricci undertook remarkably extensive research. He gained access to the secret archives of the Vatican, and the records of the confraternities of San Giovanni Decollato, of the Crucifix and of the Stigmata. The Cenci-Bolognetti, princes of Vicovaro, also showed him remarkable documents in their private collection, including an autograph letter of Beatrice, written on August 22, 1599, twenty days before her execution. Ricci's bibliography (included in the Italian edition but not reproduced in the English translation) is evidence of his thorough knowledge of the field, but he is guilty of the same lack of impartiality as those he criticizes. Take his line on incest, for example, a subject that was vital to Beatrice's defense. Ricci denies that there is any "evidence" to support the accusation of incestuous rape. He then categorically asserts that Francesco did not sexually abuse his daughter:

> The lack was not due to any scruples in his character, but to the fact that even in the most vicious there often exists a natural and general repugnance to "fusion with one's blood" which preserves brothers and sisters, parents and offspring, from incestuous contacts, and saves humanity from physical, intellectual and moral ruin.

He provides a footnote to this, in which his own personal anxieties seem to play a part:

> We have paid much attention to the opinion of illustrious jurists and psychiatrists on this subject. They have confirmed our statement that were it not for such an instinctive repugnance this crime would assume an appalling frequency, disastrous for humanity, on account of the constant stimulus to sexual relations and the facilities for our secret cohabitation within families.

Ricci is more preoccupied by the fear of the moral and social collapse that would result, in the absence of what he calls "natural," or "instinctive repugnance," than in openly engaging with the possibility that the experience of incestuous rape, or at least the fear of its happening, played a determining role in Beatrice's actions. For Ricci, the charge of incest seems too ghastly to imagine, so it becomes unimaginable, and therefore cannot have happened. He does not pronounce on the "consequences for humanity" of Francesco's known and well-documented other practices: sodomy, the entertainment of prostitutes—both women and boys—in his palace, and the simultaneous involvement in his sexual relations with his wife. For Ricci, Beatrice's story had dangerous depths that he was afraid to plumb. The charge of incestuous rape needs to be reconsidered, both as a matter of historical fact, likelihood or possibility, and as a haunting echo in the retellings and representations of Beatrice Cenci. Within the "safe tradition" it has sometimes been silenced, displaced, played down or crudely amplified, but within the "dangerous tradition" its reverberations continue to disturb.

PART I

A True Story

—⁓—

CHAPTER I

Rome Mourns

The voice of Rome is the consent of the people.
BEN JONSON, *CATELINE*, 1611

Everyone in the city was there. They had been drawn in their thousands to take part in the closing scene of a tragedy. Flowers piled up in massive brightly colored banks as the immense procession, filling the breadth of the streets, made its way past. Candles, and little crosses, some homespun and rustic, others ornate and valuable, were also left in great numbers by a steady stream of mourners determined to pay their last respects, however slow the progress of the crowd, however stifling the heat. An eyewitness account, dated a few days later, reports that several hundred people collapsed in the crush and that seven or eight people were believed to have died as a result. One person wrote simply, "All the populace ran to weep over the body until midnight, and to put lighted candles round about it." The numbers were more astonishing than anyone had predicted. Every social group from the poorest to the grandest, and of every age, race and religion was there: travelers too, who happened to be in the city, paid homage to the young woman. They came to mourn, but at the same time, by dint of their participation, they protested, no doubt unconsciously, against all manner of things: the cruelty of personal relationships, or society in general, the structures of power, the authority of the Church, the vagaries of justice.

Others died with her, but it was Beatrice who became the object of intense emotion and compassion. The people's loyalty to her had been evident during the preceding months, but the scale of public mourning was nevertheless a surprise. Contemporary commentators emphasized her beauty, her strength of character, and the vulnerability, and powerlessness, associated with her age and sex. Her status as defenseless victim was thrown into relief by the power and connections of the family. She could hardly have come from a wealthier or more influential background. She was admired for her aristocratic bearing, her seemingly effortless self-control displayed with a childish modesty. What moved the people, according to another who was there, was "the death of a young girl who was of very beautiful presence and of most beautiful life." These two attributes—outer beauty and inner goodness—were emphasized again and again, irrespective of her wrongdoings. Her grace, they said, was childlike, unaffected and beguiling. It led many to describe her age as much younger than it actually was. Her physical courage was also read as evidence of an essential inner goodness, and this seems to have carried more weight than knowledge of her crime. She was described as "bold," "constant," "of great heart," even "virile" despite her femininity. No sooner had she died than commentators began to analyze her relationship with the people of

Rome. A steady stream of written accounts appeared at the end of the sixteenth century, and books followed. The volume of material has become as phenomenal and controversial as its subject.

In the months of investigations leading up to her trial for patricide in 1599, Beatrice Cenci had suffered atrocious tortures "most bravely." This included bearing *la corda*: the victim's arms were tied behind the back and then twisted by mechanical process to force the shoulders out of joint, causing such agonizing pain that most victims gave in and accepted the allegations made against them. The people of Rome said that Beatrice, like the first Christians, had shown extraordinary strength in the face of her suffering and proclaimed her a martyr.

At times the accused were treated well. The last entry in the *Record of Victuals Supplied* lists their final meals. Just before hearing their sentences Beatrice and her stepmother Lucrezia were given supper. The two women were served fish, claret, fruit, eggs, bread and salad. Shortly after, Cristoforo, the Pope's courier, arrived with the sentence. In it, Francesco Cenci, Beatrice's father, and one of Rome's wealthiest and most influential aristocrats, was described as the victim of an atrocious crime. No mention was made of the numerous "unnatural vices" for which he had been previously tried and sentenced, or of the suffering to which he had subjected Beatrice and the rest of the family. On the contrary, because of his children's guilt and the guilt of his wife, Francesco was described as "a most wretched father" and "most unhappy husband." The sentences, it was said, were necessary to prevent the accused from boasting about their monstrous wrongdoing. Their punishment would serve as a terrible example to any who might consider patricide.

For his part in the conspiracy Giacomo, Beatrice's older brother, was to be transported through Rome on a cart to the place of punishment. His flesh was then to be torn into strips with red-hot tongs. On arrival at the scaffold the executioner was to beat him to death with a mallet in order that his soul be "separated from the body." His corpse was then to be dismembered and the pieces hung on hooks. Bernardo, Beatrice's younger brother, was spared. But clemency, in his case, was of a horribly twisted sort. Firstly he was to accompany Giacomo and witness his brother's death, and then the executions of both Lucrezia and Beatrice. Afterwards he was to return to prison for a further year before being sent to row in the galleys for the rest of his life. All this was carefully calculated with the intention that "life may be a torment and death a solace."

On the morning of September 11, 1599, according to an account written by Vannini, one of the Comforters of the Company of St. John the Beheaded, a charitable brotherhood that attended executions, "Signor Giacomo and Signor Bernardo were taken by ministers of justice out from the Tordinona [Prison]." Giacomo was bare to the waist, unprotected against the red-hot pincers which tore at his flesh, while Bernardo was wrapped in a black cloak. The young men were carried through the streets in open carts. From the Tordinona the procession made its way across Rome to the Via Santa Maria di Monserrato where the cortège halted. Lucrezia and Beatrice were then summoned from their prison and went on foot to the Piazza Ponte Sant'Angelo where the punishments were to be administered. Neither woman was bound and they were wearing mourning garments. The streets through which they passed were among the grandest in Rome, lined by large palaces and magnificent houses.

I have walked the route and a grandeur remains above the level of the first stories, despite all the signs of urban modernity—

the advertisements, the Coca-Cola cans, cigarette ends and used chewing gum, the constant scream of Roman traffic. Many of the façades are as impressive today as they were in the sixteenth century: very early in the morning, when the streets are empty you can still imagine the whole of Rome flooding toward the city's most notorious public execution on that September day.

In every doorway and window, and on every balcony, people waited to see the cortège pass. Others descended into the streets to join the river of people flowing in its wake. The procession moved at a slow walking pace, eventually reaching the Ponte Sant'Angelo. In the center of the open space a high scaffold had been built and foot soldiers and papal agents were assembled at its base. Every vantage point around the square was occupied, and people had even climbed on to the parapets of the bridge itself, undaunted by the fear of falling into the river. In the event a number were jostled and did fall from the considerable height of the bridge. Some were saved, others drowned. All around and in the distance, every rooftop, bastion and tower was peopled with onlookers. Commentators recorded the loud noise of women wailing and sobbing, and of men shouting and cursing, before the cortège arrived. But as soon as the two women became visible at the head of the procession silence spread wave-like through the crowds and out into the streets behind and beyond the place of execution. The vast crowd was moved to complete quiet.

Beatrice and Lucrezia were taken to the little chapel to the right of the bridgehead, reserved for those condemned to death. They had a right to enter and pray in the coolness and in private. Giacomo's lacerated body was carried in after them. Bernardo joined the group and they apparently said mass together. They were even given a little time to speak to one another. Then they reemerged, one by one, into the sultry September morning. Bernardo was brought out first, to be positioned on the scaffold in accordance with his sentence. Lucrezia was then escorted out of the chapel: her face was white with terror, her legs trembled. In the end the Comforters of St. John the Beheaded, their faces hidden by black hoods, carried her in a half-swoon on to the scaffold. By the time her head was in position she was unconscious and when the blade fell it severed the neck cleanly.

Beatrice was next. The silence was briefly broken by gasps and stifled sobs. When Beatrice climbed swiftly but calmly on to the scaffold a hush fell again. Although her head was tipped slightly forward there was apparently nothing submissive in her posture. She did not for a moment falter and approaching the block she leaned forward without hesitation. The axe fell; then came the thump of her severed head. Giacomo was then brought to the scaffold. His body was already torn, disfigured and gushing with blood. But he managed to speak and proclaimed the innocence of his young brother, in a voice that echoed round the open space. He then approached the block and in an instant was bludgeoned to death. His body slumped and then his neck was cut, his trunk quartered and the pieces hung, butcher-fashion, on the hooks of the scaffold.

A number of accounts were written on the day, including one by the Venetian Ambassador Giovanni Mocenigo, who wrote to his lord:

> This morning they put the Cenci to death, convicted of having procured the death of their father. The elder son was torn and then clubbed to death; the heads of mother and daughter were taken off. And because a younger brother learned of the matter after the deed and did not reveal it, his Holiness willed that he

go free from death, but that he be present at all these tortures, on the same platform; and there he swooned several times, as the last dues were rendered to God by these unfortunates.

Now that Pope Clement's wishes had been carried out, most of the civic and religious officials disappeared. Bernardo was escorted back to the Tordinona and a few Brothers waited with the bodies. An *avviso*, a report sent from Rome by Ambassadors of other kingdoms, informing their rulers of events in the papal dominion (*avvisi* were also sold on the streets of Rome) reads, "The corpses were left . . . to the public view, that is the women each on a bier with torches lit around about them, and Giacomo hanging in quarters." Gradually all those who had been unable to make their way into the Piazza del Ponte at the time of the executions were able to see the remains.

Eventually leave was granted for the removal of the corpses to their graves. Three cortèges formed. The Company of Pity of the Florentines laid out Giacomo's fragments *in figura*—that is in the shape of a reassembled body—and took him to the Church of St. John the Beheaded. In the evening his dismembered corpse was returned to his relatives who, in accordance with his last wishes, brought it to San Tommaso ai Cenci. Lucrezia was taken to one of the many churches in Rome dedicated to Saint Gregory. It may well be that her remains are in San Gregorio della Divina Pietà, a church near the Cenci Palace.

The great funeral was Beatrice's. The crowds which had dispersed after the executions reassembled and the piazza was full once again. Confraternities, monks, aristocrats in their carriages, visitors to Rome, everyone in the city joined the torch-lit procession that accompanied Beatrice's body from the Piazza to its final resting place in the Church of San Pietro in Montorio. The route followed the Via Giulia, straight as a die, crossed the Tiber and led up the winding, tree-lined Via del Gianicolo to the church. There the great mounds of flowers accumulated and the church was lit by hundreds of candles left by the mourners. The distinctive smell of candle wax must have mingled with the perfume of heaped flowers.

It was not until the middle of the night that the number of mourners began to dwindle, and in the early hours of the morning the Brothers of the Sacred Stigmata and the minor canons of the Osservanti (Franciscan Observants) attended to her burial. Beatrice would have been comforted had she known that among the canons was Father Andrea Belmonte, her own confessor. The body was gently lowered into the apse. Her severed head was placed on a silver platter beside her body. The stone that was lifted over her to seal the grave bore no inscription.

Beatrice had cast her spell during the weeks and months of her grueling trial. Who was this beautiful daughter of a Renaissance Roman aristocrat? And what had been the nature and motive of her crime? Who was her father, Francesco Cenci, and what of his "unnatural and unspeakable vices"? Her grave was unmarked but she had conquered Rome, where her memory would live on, to captivate the imaginations of artists and writers for centuries to come.

CHAPTER 2

—⁓—

"No Other Remedy . . ."

He had us put in a room nailed up by certain joiners.
BEATRICE CENCI'S DEPOSITION, FEBRUARY 12, 1599

Almost forty years before these dramatic events, on May 20, 1562, within the gloomy Cenci Palace in Rome, Beatrice Cenci's grand-father was dying. Monsignore Cristoforo Cenci was the head of a now rich and powerful family. The Cenci were an ancient noble family, but probably not as ancient as Francesco Cenci boasted. He presumably had the ancient Roman tombstone of Marcus Cincius Theophilus built into the façade of the Church of San Tommaso ai Cenci, near his palace, to substantiate his claim. Most certainly the family had long been powerful and included three cardinals and even a tenth-century pope. Since that moment of greatness the family had acquired a brutal and anti-papal reputation which no doubt played a part in the fatal outcome of the trials of Beatrice, her stepmother and brothers.

Through various dishonest practices, and without the slightest show of shame, Cristoforo had built up a vast family fortune as one of the chief comptrollers and collectors of finance in the Papal Court. Most of his wealth was by now safely invested in property—palaces, castles, and extensive farms. Knowing that he was about to die, he had summoned his mistress, Beatrice Arias, with whom he had had a son, Francesco, aged twelve, whom he had recently recognized legally, and who would eventually inherit his vast fortune. On his deathbed Cristoforo regularized his relationship with his mistress who had recently been widowed and was thus free to marry her lover. Cristoforo was too weak to participate in the ceremony and his hands, twisted by gout, lay bandaged in front of him. He was unable to sign the contract nor could he place the ring on his wife's finger, but the marriage was duly recorded, with the notary acting as proxy for the dying man.

Soon after Cristoforo's death his widow Beatrice remarried, further strengthening her financial and social position. This, her third marriage, was to a man of law, Evangelista Recchia. Equally shrewdly she arranged for the marriage of her sister, Lucrezia, to Stefano Guerra, notary to the Papal Court of Justice, or *Ruota*. Cristoforo and Beatrice can be described as a dishonest accountant and a gold-digging, serial bride. And these, of course, were Beatrice's grandparents.

Francesco's inheritance was immense: two vast palaces in Rome, landed property on the outskirts of the city, and further estates in the Abruzzi, the Kingdom of Naples. He frequently displayed the temper and strong will of a spoiled child—or perhaps of one who was little loved. He was only eleven when he attacked one Quintilio da Vetralla "with loss of blood" and the first of an endless string of lawsuits was brought against him.

Francesco apparently also showed precocious sexual interests. His tutor, Francesco Santacroce, consulted with his mother and it was decided that he should be married at the earliest opportunity so as to avoid "solitary excesses" and dangerous contact "with courtesans." This may, of course, have been a ruse on Santacroce's part to give his own family a stake in his employer's wealth: at fourteen Francesco married his tutor's niece, Ersilia, who was the same age. The marriage took place in November 1563, but whatever Francesco's sexual precocity, Ersilia did not bear her first child until 1567, a son, Cristoforo, who lived only three years. In 1571 Giacomo was born and of the ten or eleven children that followed six more survived. Beatrice was the fifth and Bernardo the youngest.

Francesco's desires were not satisfied by marriage and the record of his frequent convictions and appearances before the *Ruota* makes lively reading. His crimes were of two types: acts of extreme violence and of "sexual abnormality." The former were often perpetrated against servants for alleged insubordination.

The first record of Francesco's involvement in the courts as an adult dates back to 1566 when he was involved in an attack on his cousin Cesare Cenci. The documentary evidence describes the crime and sentence, but the motive for the attack remains obscure. Francesco was found guilty and charged with the crime but, thanks to his stepfather Evangelista Recchia's interventions, he was bailed to his mother's house rather than being imprisoned in the Castel Sant'Angelo. He had to remain there and to present himself, whenever summoned, under forfeit of 10,000 gold *scudi*, a significant sum although far from crippling for Francesco. The value of a *scudo* is difficult to estimate exactly but the annual rental income for two shops which he owned and left in his will was approximately 120 *scudi*.

In April the following year, Francesco was again in court. There had been a peasant uprising in the Nemi region some thirty kilometers northeast of Rome and a delegation had arrived in the city "bearing complaint to the Pope" against their lord Francesco Cenci. He had disappeared in order to escape justice but the Papal Court nevertheless brought an action against him and had him tracked down. An *avviso* reads, "The Signor Francesco Cenci has been brought a prisoner to Nemi and held there . . . It is said that he caused a vassal of his to be hanged on the gallows." At first Francesco was ordered to pay a fine of 10,000 *scudi*, but he agreed only to 8,000. Meanwhile other allegations of cruelty were made against him, and further complaints alleging the innocence of the man he had caused to be hanged. The *avviso* claimed that he would now have to pay 21,000 *scudi*. In the event he paid only 5,000.

In October of the same year, 1567, he was once more tried for cruelty against one of his employees, this time a muleteer, but the young man in question, Lorenzo d'Assisi, was so terrified by Francesco's threats of retribution that it was not until October 22, 1568 that he finally plucked up courage to lodge a formal complaint.

In January 1570 Francesco was tried for sodomy for the first time. Through the intercessions of Cardinals Farnese and Santacroce, he was freed and there is no actual record of a fine having been paid. That same year Francesco returned to Nemi where he was again involved in protracted lawsuits with the peasantry who accused him of repeated acts of brutality. His guilt seemed to be confirmed by his sudden flight to Aquila, northeast of Rome, and under the instructions of Pius V he was arrested, taken to the Viceroy of Naples, and then to Rome where he was imprisoned in the Castel Sant'Angelo.

In order to raise sufficient funds to buy his way out of prison, and aware that the "insurgence" of the Nemi peasantry was likely to continue, he set about selling his lands there. A letter dated March 25, 1571, to Marcantonio Colonna, with the Castello given as the address, begs him to buy the Nemi from him. The following year he sold his estate to Muzio Frangipani, and at last had the wherewithal to buy his freedom.

A little over a year later Francesco was imprisoned for "unnatural vice." The bail was set at some 50,000 *scudi*, a vast sum but one which he would nevertheless have been able to pay. Less than a year later, on August 6, 1572, he was jailed once more, again for a violent assault on a servant. After his release some months later, Francesco threw himself into an act of ostentatious piety and set about restoring San Tommaso ai Cenci, a church that nestles close to the Cenci Palace near the banks of the Tiber. Such contradictory behavior, alternating lawbreaking and pious display, was not untypical of his class; many Roman aristocrats behaved similarly.

A not unusual example of Francesco's cruelty is provided by the case of Maria, a Milanese, daughter of Filippo, a perfumer. On June 6, 1577, she brought a case against her master and, although mice have gnawed the documents in the archives, there is still enough material to follow her story. Apparently Francesco sent for Maria and asked her to fetch a key. She left to do as she had been asked but returned empty-handed because "his boys" had taken it. Francesco, perhaps enraged at his sons' interference with his keys, lost his temper, seized a broom handle and beat Maria. He did not, however, completely lose self-control. But that evening he summoned the terrified Maria and this time asked that she "go and see what Domenico, his clerk, was doing." This she did, but she did not ask Domenico to come to his master because she had not understood that to be his request. Domenico then left the house whereupon Francesco, hearing that Maria had "failed to do as she had been asked," flew into an uncontrolled rage and beat Maria with the broom handle as hard as he could, until she was bleeding profusely and severely bruised. Two other women servants witnessed the attack, perhaps to teach them a lesson in the merits of obedience to their sadistic master. In her statement Maria claimed, "He struck me many times, and I fell repeatedly, and he kicked me also. He left me on the ground, assuming that I was dead for there was blood coming out of my mouth." The notary verified the bruises which she still had. She also alleged that "for three days I was in so much pain that I was unable to eat, drink or speak." There is no record to tell how the case was settled but it is likely that Maria was pacified by a few *scudi*, like so many women in her position.

Marriage to Ersilia Santacroce had done little to pacify Francesco, and his acts of violence and infidelity had been many. Ersilia died two days after giving birth, on April 16, 1584. The baby was a girl, Francesca, who lived barely five days. After her death his brutality and loose living became all the wilder.

The following year Sixtus V was elected to the papacy. He was a man determined to deal with corruption, insisting that justice be done and be seen to be done, and that wrongdoers be punished irrespective of social position. At this point Francesco drew up his will, hoping to secure the family's position in the event of his death. His testament is dated November 22, 1586. It opens philosophically: "Fearing that I may die at any hour, and death being the one thing that is certain." He then asks that he be buried in the Chapel of St. Francis in San Tommaso ai Cenci at one o'clock in the morning in the presence of assistants, monks, friars and his own orphans with seven torches and nothing more elaborate. He leaves money for hospitals and for dowries for marriageable girls and sees to the needs of his own daughters, legitimate and illegitimate, including a certain Lavinia. His principal heirs are named as Cristoforo, Rocco, Bernardo and Paolo and others that may be born should he remarry. To Giacomo he left the minimum allowed by law, evidence of his dislike of his eldest son. The inclusion of various formulae such as "to Our Lord God and His Glorious Mother and to Saint Francis and to all other Saints of the Celestial Court" has led some people to claim that Francesco "was not therefore such an evil father nor atheist nor misanthrope as people would constantly have us believe, but quite obviously an excellent head of family."

Francesco continued to vent his anger against various members of his extended family. His stepfather, the advocate Evangelista Recchia di Barbarano who was employed essentially as an estate manager, allegedly slandered his stepson and threatened to kill him. Francesco managed to have Evangelista's entire library of four hundred legal tomes sequestered, claiming, "Evangelista was my mother's husband and thus my stepfather, and he managed my property for a long while, and when I wanted to review the accounts and required him to pay what he owed me, his hatred for me was aroused." His relationship with his sons also deteriorated rapidly after his wife's death. According to his cousin Cesare Cenci, he was unwilling to accept any responsibility for them: "He would not receive them in the house . . . nor send them to school, much as they wished to study. . . . He was never willing to do anything for them."

Virtually all his fortune had been inherited from his father, Cristoforo, and Sixtus V was well aware that much of that wealth had been acquired through embezzlement from the papal coffers. On February 25, 1590, the Pope initiated proceedings against

Francesco Cenci intent on stripping him of his inherited fortune.
Bartolomeo Cesi, Francesco's representative, was instructed to
return "the fruit of illicit negotiations carried on contrary to the
constitution of Pius IV." His property was to be sold "for such
prices which to you seem proper; and the moneys from these sales
paid into the hands of our General Depository."

Francesco clearly knew that evasion of any sort was point-
less. Instead he confronted the drama head-on and sought an audience early in April 1590. A letter from the Pope to Monsignore
Cesi survives and offers interesting insights into the pragmatism
of papal authority at the time:

> Since we wish to act toward him with kindliness, we order you
> that, when our said Francesco shall have paid into the hands of
> our General Depository or to whomsoever you should designate
> 25,000 *scudi* in the manner and on the terms that you shall agree
> upon, free and clear, however, of every title and twentieth part
> of the Commissario, you shall revoke every attachment, stay and
> impediment and accord him every right and action . . . And make
> to him an instrument of cession, liberation and general quittance
> in such sort that neither Francesco nor his heirs may ever again
> in the future be on this molested.

The sum that Francesco paid was considerable, but significantly
less than the amount he might have had to hand over. It was
clearly in his interests to settle for good and once the moneys
had changed hands he received what is, in effect, an extraordinary receipt. It details his father Cristoforo's wrongdoings, both
financial and carnal, and his administrative abuses, his adulter-
ous relations with Beatrice Arias are alluded to, and doubts are

cast on the validity of their subsequent marriage and thus Francesco's legitimacy. But the papal decree ends, at least, on a rather different note. The payment made by Francesco has, it seems, regularized the sins of the father and the document closes with decrees of absolution and benediction.

Francesco's sense of horizons widening once again was further enhanced by Sixtus V's death. Over the next two years popes followed one another in such quick succession that instability reigned, as it had before Pope Sixtus's accession. The underdogs of Renaissance Rome were quick to take advantage: the gates of the city were no longer secure and bandits had easy access. Prisons released their charges without recourse to the law so as not to have to bother with them. Antisocial behavior of all kinds went unchecked; it was an atmosphere well suited to Francesco Cenci's lifestyle, and not surprisingly, during this period of widespread criminality and debauchery, his relations with his family deteriorated still further.

Tensions between Francesco and Giacomo were aggravated by the latter's marriage in 1591. It may be that Francesco was jealous. After Giacomo married Lodovica Velli, a distant cousin, and settled into an apartment within the Cenci Palace on the Monte di Cenci, Francesco soon moved out. He took up residence in another Cenci palace, on the banks of the Tiber. But he did not want to live alone and so he withdrew his two daughters, Antonina and Beatrice, from their convent to keep him company. Rocco also moved with his father but Cristoforo stayed with Giacomo, and Paolo and Bernardo were sent away to school in a neighboring district. At this point Francesco's thoughts seemed to have turned to his own widowed position and he started to consider the possibility of remarrying. The widow of a distant relative, Lucrezia Petroni, seemed an appropriate choice.

She had two sons and four daughters and she needed greater
financial support. She was plump and rather matronly, but only
thirty-eight and not unattractive, and she was weak willed and
somewhat feeble minded. Francesco's sexual activities were no
secret and his convictions and legal wrangles were well known.
Lucrezia must have felt in a precarious position and so quickly
consented to marriage. Francesco had agreed to see to the education of her younger children, a promise which he never fulfilled. The nuptial agreement was made on November 27, 1593.
The very next day an illegitimate daughter of Francesco's was
baptized, Caterina, born to Secondina Vincenzo, a young
woman with whom Francesco continued his affair, although
Lucrezia did refuse to allow Secondina to live with them in a
ménage à trois.

Not long after his marriage, fuller details of the life that
Francesco had been living during the preceding months suddenly
became public. In March 1594 Matteo Bonavera, who had been
in Francesco's service since June 1593, stole a black serge cape
from a man in the street. He was caught by the police and during questioning let slip a cryptic phrase about his master's unwillingness that he speak of him. When he was asked why a
worthy and noble man should fear being spoken of, he began to
tell of the extraordinary acts that he had seen his master performing, as had numerous other servants in his house. Francesco's
young sons, Matteo claimed, had witnessed them too.

The transcription of the trial that followed gives graphic details. Bonavera testified that Francesco Cenci had frequently tried
to persuade him, in conversation and by physical approaches,
to satisfy his sexual desires. When Bonavera refused Francesco
would turn to "boys whom he took from the stable." Maria of
Spoleto was also mentioned as a mistress of Francesco's. Two

stable hands and Maria were then arrested and questioned. Initially Maria confessed only to having had "natural relations" with him. She added by way of defense for these extramarital encounters, "I had no husband and he no wife." But she later related more complicated goings-on which had occurred at the time of the carnival in 1591. She was in the kitchen with Margherita, the cook, when Francesco summoned her. She mounted the stairs to Francesco's room where both he and a "bad young fellow" were waiting. Francesco expressed his desire to have them both together, at which point Maria started to scream and made to escape: she succeeded but the boy was promptly locked in with Francesco. On another occasion she saw the same boy leaving Francesco's apartment. The older man kissed the boy "there in the doorway and then sent him off, and he asked that the boy leave via the coach-house." Maria seemed not so much surprised or disturbed by her master's activities as simply jealous. It was also said that during his encounters with boys he would inflict minor injuries, sometimes scratching their faces.

In her first examination Maria had alleged that her relations, although extramarital, were not otherwise irregular, rather "such as plenty of respectable men have." But when reexamined on June 2, 1594, she broke down and spoke of Francesco's violence against her if she refused to consent to his requests. She also alluded to other sexual activities with Francesco: "I know the penalty that is put upon those who do things like these and have them done to them . . . but now I have thought that the honorable Senator and Your Lordship might still have compassion, knowing what little I could do, a poor woman and a servant of Signor Francesco, while I was in his power." Clemente Anai, one of the boys questioned, claimed that Francesco "kissed me with those bristly hairs, and said to me 'stay still you beast!'" Bernardo, aged only twelve, was aware of his father's activities and expressed his regret at his father's behavior.

Francesco was finally arrested and imprisoned awaiting trial. During the court proceedings allegations were made and denied, counterallegations were made and refuted. There seemed to be little evidence other than the statements of those involved. The accusations of sodomy were the most serious; it was not unusual for those convicted to be burned at the stake. Fortunately Francesco had an expert lawyer in Emilio Morea, who had married Lavinia, Francesco's illegitimate daughter. Emilio was employed by the Papal Court of Justice and thanks to his skillful advocacy Francesco was eventually released from prison though with a large fine: 100,000 *scudi*, a significant part of his fortune, to be paid to the Papal Exchequer.

Francesco's arrest and conviction provoked him into further attacks on his family. He accused Giacomo of conspiring to have him imprisoned in order to get his hands on his money, and also claimed that Giacomo had confided in others that he wanted to murder his father. The force of Francesco's accusations was so strong that Giacomo sought the Pope's protection.

By the spring of 1594 Francesco was also openly at war with his eldest son Cristoforo and then, on March 11, Rocco, his second son, was killed in a duel, a not altogether uncommon happening. It may be that Francesco, knowing the strength of Cristoforo's hatred for him, feared for his life. In any case he wanted to leave Rome at the earliest opportunity but was obliged to stay within the papal dominions until his whole fine had been paid. This he finally achieved in March 1595 and early that April he set out with his wife Lucrezia, and his eighteen-year-old daughter Beatrice, to the remote castle of La Petrella in the Abruzzi Mountains a hundred miles northeast of Rome. He had many properties of his own but most were in a poor state of repair so he arranged to borrow the castle of La Petrella in the precipitous village of the same name, from his friend Don Marzio Colonna, a celebrated military commander. La Petrella was two days' journey from Rome, on the road between Rieti and the Abruzzi, and accessible only by mule track. The township cowers beneath an outcrop and above it, on the rocky cliff, the fortress-like castle sits proudly. For Lucrezia and Beatrice it served as a prison. Today its ruins are overgrown and look more like picturesque broom-covered rocky crags than the remains of a building.

The castle was looked after by Olympio Calvetti who lived there with his mother, his wife Plautilla, and two children, Vittoria and Prospero. Olympio was a handsome man, dark-haired, bearded with a fine moustache, an accomplished horseman, tall and strong. He was charged with the care of Lucrezia and Beatrice when Francesco returned to Rome to sort out his financial affairs. Soon after this Francesco learned of Cristoforo's death. He had been involved in an argument over a well-known courtesan and his death had been violent. No one, except Beatrice, grieved for Cristoforo, whose reputation was not unlike his father's.

Back at La Petrella, Lucrezia and Beatrice endured their imprisonment. Beatrice's only solace was Vittoria, Olympio's little daughter, whom she adored. When Francesco returned, Lucrezia and Beatrice suffered his brutality, his cruelty and other humiliations and abuses. At one point Paolo and Bernardo, the two youngest Cenci boys, were brought to the castle, which must have been a great joy for Beatrice, but such was the grimness of life at La Petrella that both boys escaped. They returned to Rome where Paolo died, and after that Bernardo took refuge with Giacomo.

During the summer of 1597, abandoned at La Petrella, Lucrezia and Beatrice, now twenty, started to discuss how they might free themselves from Francesco's clutches. At least initially, it was an escape that they meditated, not Francesco's murder. Olympio was drawn into these discussions and acted as a go-between, traveling from La Petrella to Rome to discuss plans with Giacomo. Whether Olympio's feelings for Beatrice made him an interested party no one will prove without unequivocal, or at least without substantial, evidence.

The reality of the two women's lives is plain from contemporary accounts:

> He [Francesco] had little vents put over the windows, and he had the windows closed in such a way that one could not lean out there, and he had the entrance-door of the rooms locked, and he had a wicket made in the door where Santi [the servant] put in the food; and to this wicket there was a keyhole, and in this keyhole was a key, and it was kept locked by Santi, and at night he locked this wicket with a key.

Beatrice's deposition, made on February 12, 1599 during the trial, confirms these details of their domestic imprisonment as unwilling anchorites:

> When our father was away for about two years and went to Rome, besides leaving Santi de Pompa [in effect as their jailer], he also closed all the windows of the hall and of the chambers, and he had us put in a room nailed up by certain joiners, and then he had a cutting made above these windows, that is in the frame of the windows, and he had a lantern-window made so that we might have light, and he left matters thus. We could

approach and look out of the windows left open in this way, but we had to stand on a chair, or stool. . . . We had our food and drink through the door, from the hands of . . . Santi.

Further confirmation of the circumstances in which the two women were held was given by Girolama, a widow of Antonio of Capranica, and Calidonia Lorenzini, of Siena, who were both persuaded to go to La Petrella as ladies-in-waiting. In her deposition Girolama stated:

> When I arrived at La Petrella, I found there the ladies locked in with four keys, and the windows barred and nailed up with certain lantern-windows overhead, and the key was kept by a certain Santa de Pompa, and when I went in Santa opened the door to me, but afterwards I had to stay locked up as the ladies were, and there I aged ten years, in the year and a half that I was actually there.

During the summer of 1597 a young man, Marzio Catalano, returned to his native village of La Petrella and was employed for a period in the castle. In his deposition he provides a succinct and clear account of Beatrice's state of mind that summer:

> She was determined not to lead that life any longer, and since no one thought of trying to get her wedded, neither her father nor her brothers, if she found no other remedy she was ready to kill herself with her own hand.

In the months that followed, Beatrice had Marzio deliver letters to her brothers and other relatives in Rome. She told them how her father treated her and begged for their help. Then, one of her letters fell into her father's hands and when he returned to La Petrella in December 1597 he was intent on punishing Beatrice both for daring to write, and for the scandalous accusations she had made against him.

Francesco Cenci left Rome on December 11: Beatrice was to be subdued once and for all. The journey to La Petrella was slow because of deep snow in the mountains and he arrived on December 13, the feast of Santa Lucia, but Francesco was in a far from festive mood. Moments after his arrival he had his daughter brought out to him. Beatrice was terrified by her father's mood and simply denied having written the letter, but Francesco pulled it out and flourished it in her face, shouting in anger. He then reached for a bull-pizzle—the penis of a bull used as a whip—that hung on a hook in his room and lashed her with it uncontrollably. Beatrice put out her hands to protect her face but her hands were badly lashed—the scars never had time to heal fully. Girolama gave a description of Francesco's attack on his daughter:

> He took a bull-pizzle which he kept there, and he thrashed her horribly with it, saying that she had written to Rome and had also sent a petition and Beatrice denied these allegations and he kept her shut in her bedroom for two or three days, and he himself brought her food, and he would open the door of the bedroom, and put it on the floor and then he would go away at his good will.

The precise nature of the punishment she suffered when he visited her remains unspoken. The expression "he would go away at his good will" suggests that he was with her for a purpose and left her only when fully satisfied.

During those bleak days her resolve strengthened. Her step-mother reported Beatrice's first words when she was released: "I intend to make Signor Francesco repent of the violence that he has done to me." One other incident was also reported by the two ladies-in-waiting, Girolama and Calidonia. Lucrezia, late one evening, apparently arrived very distraught in the other two women's bedroom and flung herself on Girolama's bed. The two women watched perplexed until Francesco appeared and summoned her back into their bedchamber where Francesco had been with Beatrice. Girolama also explained how she had erected a screen between Beatrice's bed and her parents "so that the girl would not be able to see when Signor Francesco had to do with his wife."

Beatrice cannot, at this point, have been sexually naïve. On the one hand there is the allegation of incest committed by her father, and on the other considerable evidence that Francesco's sexual activity was carried on, if not publicly, at least without any effort of secrecy. A letter survives, written by Baldassare Paolucci, written on August 14, 1599, to Cardinal d'Este, summing up the sweeping movements of the Cenci trial itself. He told of Beatrice's extraordinary courage in the face of torture and of how she finally broke down:

> The accomplices set before her, and unable to resist the great tortures any longer, she said that God could no longer suffer her iniquities, and so she wished to die with the others. And by the crime and parricide she had committed, she confessed that, through her will to kill her own father she had [compassed] her own death and (what afflicted her more) she had thereby lost

her virginity, reft from her by the one who did the deed; a thing
not known heretofore.

This refers to relations she is alleged to have had with Olympio.
Six witnesses testified to Olympio and Beatrice's "intimate relations" and their allegations were made in total twenty times. But
the matter can be seen from various points of view.

In the first place, Beatrice's "admission" to relations with
Olympio was made while suffering extreme physical torture. It
may well be that the Papal Court, aware of the public sympathy
for Beatrice, sought to disgrace her by having her declare herself
to be someone quite different from the innocent virgin that the
people of Rome were coming to love so ardently as the details of
her case emerged. Or it may be that Olympio's price, if he was
to be persuaded to conspire to murder Francesco, was intimacy
with Beatrice. There have also been suggestions that the "poor
boy," one of numerous benefactors mentioned in a codicil to
Beatrice's will, may have been her son by Olympio. This is pure
speculation and no one who has suggested this has considered
that the child could equally have been the result of Francesco's
incestuous relationship with his daughter.

There is no doubt that Beatrice and Olympio spent time alone
together discussing the ways in which Beatrice might be saved
from her father and her imprisonment—and later on discussing
Francesco's murder. The first conspiracy was arranged in Rome.
Olympio had traveled there at Beatrice's request and met Paolo
and Bernardo, and Giacomo, now the eldest of the brothers. The
plan was to attempt to poison Francesco. Olympio returned to
La Petrella with a phial containing some lethal fluid. But when
he got back he was met not with a delighted Beatrice, but a disappointed one. Because Francesco feared for his life he had, for

some time, insisted that Beatrice and Lucrezia act as tasters, sampling every foodstuff and drink. Some other means of murder needed to be devised. Olympio was fearful of acting alone and enlisted Marzio Catalano's help.

Round about the time of these discussions Francesco was laid low by an attack of gout and confined to bed; the accomplices could pick their time. On the morning of September 7, 1598, Olympio and Marzio entered his bedroom but fear drove them back. In the adjoining room, where Beatrice was waiting, she expressed her dismay at their cowardice and declared that if they were unwilling to do the deed that they had been planning for so long, she would murder her father with her own hands. Humiliated by Beatrice's resolve, Olympio and Marzio went back into Francesco's bedroom and bludgeoned him to death. To cover their tracks they then clothed his large, limp body, dragged his corpse out on to the balcony and humped it up over the railings to plunge into the "warren." This was an area of scrub below the castle rock, some thirteen meters deep, which was used as a rubbish tip. So as to make it look as though he had fallen through the floor, they dislodged a number of planks. But the deception was carried out too hastily, and this would be part of the conspirators' downfall. Lucrezia and Beatrice hurriedly disposed of the bloody sheets and bedding, but again too little care was taken.

As previously planned, Olympio leaked news of Francesco's "fatal accident" to the town, but Marzio's nerves got the better of him and he fled panic-stricken out of the castle and away. The two women called for help from within the castle grounds and a crowd soon formed, discussing ways in which Francesco's body might be lifted out. Three or four men, assisted by ladders, climbed down into the pit. The heavy corpse, roped to one of the ladders, had to be lifted up over the wall. The women explained that

Francesco had ventured out on to the half-rotten gallery against their advice and had fallen through the floor, and the injuries to his head were explained by the fall. The deep gash in his eye-socket was said to be the work of an elder branch that had caught him on the way down.

At this point there seems to have been no suspicion of foul play and Francesco's body was carried to the castle pool to be washed and laid out in readiness for burial. Beatrice was asked for instructions for the burial rites and requested that these take place as soon as possible. But neither Beatrice nor Lucrezia attended, which encouraged gossip. Meanwhile they waited impatiently for Giacomo and Bernardo to arrive from Rome. Entombed in the Church of Santa Maria in La Petrella, the body was no longer available for public scrutiny but the wound to the eye was much discussed: a branch, people argued, would not have caused such a deep wound as the body fell. Olympio's wife, Plautilla, who had not been drawn into the conspiracy and who may have been jealous of the attention that her husband had shown Beatrice, had seen the bloody bedclothes. The hole in the floor of the balcony, others whispered, was surely too small to have allowed such a large man to pass through in the manner that the two women had described. Soon there was a general consensus that Francesco's death had not occurred as the two women had alleged but that a violent crime must have been committed.

Marzio returned to claim payment for his part in the crime and Giacomo and Bernardo arrived with their cousin, Cesare Cenci. Giacomo took possession of his father's property and two days later the entire party returned to Rome, Beatrice, her two brothers, Lucrezia, the two murderers, Olympio's daughter, and various servants. In their absence the people of La Petrella talked more and more openly and before very long accounts of these speculations reached the papal authorities in Rome.

The journey back from La Petrella was an agonizing one, particularly for Beatrice. Giacomo apparently talked about their crime in a way which gradually directed increasing blame toward his sister. When they reached Rome Lucrezia and Beatrice were finally separated, after years of confinement almost exclusively in each other's company. Their parting was a rehearsal for a more terrible separation which would take place not so many months later. Beatrice—who took charge of little Vittoria—had no choice, it would seem, but to return to the Cenci Palace, protected by the unpredictable Giacomo. Tensions ran high.

Rumors from La Petrella had reached Rome quickly. By November 5 an investigation into Francesco Cenci's death was underway. Initially the family was treated with the degree of delicacy appropriate to their social standing. Giacomo was the first to be questioned, at home, on November 14. Beatrice was next. Giacomo claimed that he had heard of his father's death by letter and had immediately traveled to La Petrella to support his sister and stepmother. As to how his father had died he simply stated, "They say that he fell against an elder tree, that his head collided with it, and that one of those great spines must have entered his temple." Giacomo was then compelled to take an oath pledging to remain in detention in his own house, under a forfeit of 50,000 scudi.

Beatrice's first response was feigned dismay that an examining judge should want to speak to her about her father's fatal accident. She calmly explained that he had fallen from a balcony which, because of rot, had collapsed beneath him. Her stepmother alerted her and she ran to look, unaware as to his condition. She acknowledged that she had not attended the burial but she had arranged that his remains be accorded due ceremony. Whether she had not attended the burial out of a fear that she might break down and reveal her guilt or whether out of a desire to avoid the extreme hypocrisy it would have represented, we will never know. She was detained in the palace on the same basis as her brother.

On Monday, November 16, Lucrezia was questioned and her story in no way contradicted the two which the examining magistrate had already heard. Lucrezia was similarly confined to the house, but bound over not to leave the room in which she slept. Presumably the magistrate had some suspicion that a woman as obviously weak-willed as Lucrezia was unlikely to be primarily responsible for any crime, and this may explain why her bail was only 5,000 *scudi*.

At this stage no investigations had yet taken place at La Petrella but when the coachman there was questioned, the examining magistrates must have felt a growing sense of purpose. The servant, because of his humble status, had been arrested, imprisoned and interrogated, although he had in fact played no part. He was asked at length about other members of the Cenci household, in particular about Olympio, and his answers bore out the rumors: Olympio, he alleged, although a mere servant, had been drawn into the Cenci family and had established an intimate relationship with Beatrice. We cannot know under what duress his statement was made.

Meanwhile, Olympio was on his way to La Petrella, possessed by the knowledge that various things needed to be concealed before any visit by officials. He arrived on November 17 or 18. Although he was well aware of the accusations being made against him locally he nevertheless set about making things look a little better. He demolished more of the balcony and had a local mason, Lattanzio d'Alessandro, wall up the balcony door through which Francesco had been dragged. Meanwhile, Plautilla removed the bloodstained mattresses from the scene of the crime but, rather than burning them, or disposing of them properly, set about concealing them. It seems that she considered destroying them a waste.

Searches of the castle of La Petrella began in earnest some days later, under the direction of Biagio Querco, auditor. The bloodstained mattresses were soon discovered and the people of La Petrella were keen to inform him of the alterations Olympio had recently made, and of the obvious motivation behind these. Querco also gained expert advice about the exact nature of Francesco's injuries. Unsatisfied in various respects he ordered that the body be exhumed. It was soon confirmed that Francesco's head injuries were the work of human hands, wielding a hatchet-like tool.

A formal proclamation was made against Olympio, Marzio, Lucrezia, Beatrice, Giacomo and Bernardo. The official document declared that they had either committed, or conspired to have committed, the murder of Francesco Cenci. The people of La Petrella had been outraged as much by the conspirators' confidence as by their crime. The Cenci may have counted on the people of La Petrella saying nothing because of their own loathing of Francesco or out of fear of the family's power, but as one Francesco Giucciardini succinctly declared, "the common people feels itself less offended by a breach of liberty than by a breach of justice." The people of La Petrella were determined that the guilty be punished, but the people of Rome would respond with enormous compassion when it came to the fate of Beatrice. Their sense of outrage at the breaches of liberty and justice was very different.

Olympio's behavior from the moment of the murder had been characterized by extreme arrogance. Marzio Catalano, on the

other hand, had tried to keep out of the way, but his whereabouts
were known. Before long he was arrested and taken to the
Tordinona prison. In his deposition he confessed to having received payment from Beatrice and to have talked of poisoning
Francesco. This was enough for the Papal Court to order the
immediate arrest of Giacomo and Bernardo. Olympio promptly
fled. The Chief Constable and *sbirri* (policemen) arrived at the
Cenci Palace and arrested the two brothers in the presence of
Beatrice.

Chilling records have survived detailing the questioning of a
long series of witnesses and the use of torture to elicit informa-
tion, a common practice in the proceedings of the Papal Court.
As well as the documents relating to the trial, there are substantial numbers of contemporary *avvisi*.

Olympio remained the greatest danger to the Cenci, and
Giacomo was determined that his evidence never be heard.
Beatrice and Lucrezia were apprised of the plan, and begged
Giacomo to drop it, as they had begged him to abandon an earlier plan to do away with Marzio. Giacomo, meanwhile, incarcerated in the Tordinona, needed an ally and found one in the
unlikely figure of Monsignore Mario Guerra, cleric, representative at the Papal Court, and loyal friend of the Cencis. Guerra
was protected by one of the cardinals and seems to have oper-
ated as though he was above the law. A price was placed on
Olympio's head and Cesare Bussone, one of the Cenci servants,
and Marco Tullio Bartoli of Terni, were employed to do the deed.
Eventually they found Olympio at Lake Piediluco with his wife
and family, near the beautiful waterfall of Terni. The assassins
then persuaded him to follow them to a nearby inn and not long
after, the authorities were informed of the discovery of a head-
less body.

Cesare Bussone returned to Rome to inform the Cencis of Olympio's murder and soon news of the crime, which Giacomo had naturally wanted to be kept secret, spread up through the social hierarchy to the Pope himself. Bussone was arrested and police were dispatched to Piediluco. This was to prove catastrophic for the Cencis, as Plautilla, Olympio's wife, was brought back with the authorities to Rome. The Cencis were then required to answer to each of Plautilla's penetrating accusations. Monsignore Guerra, whom they counted on for support, had for some reason left the city. But even without his influence the Cencis would not have anticipated having to face torture. Noble families as powerfully connected as theirs would not normally be subjected to the ignominy of torture, except with the personal approval of the Pope himself, but this he immediately granted.

Pope Clement VIII, either because of a genuine fear of increasing violent crime among the wealthy, or because of greed (he stood to benefit directly from the Cenci conviction through fines or seizure of assets), or because of a fear of women's violence, or because of the whole heady mix, ensured that the Cenci trial moved rapidly toward its inevitable conclusion.

The accused eventually confessed although Giacomo tried to shift the entire blame on to his younger sister and Lucrezia also claimed that Beatrice had been the moving force. But support for Beatrice was immediately evident from large numbers of friends and relations who called to visit her, and prominent lawyers came forward keen to be involved in her case. Prospero Farinaccio, whose own reputation was not unsullied—he had previously been prosecuted for sodomy—represented the Cenci family. A larger than life figure in Rome at the time, his portrait can be seen both in a monument over his tomb in San Silvestro del Quirinale in Rome and in a portrait by Cavaliere Cesare d'Arpino. And it was Farinaccio who, in one of the many myths about Beatrice's last days, supposedly arranged for Guido Reni to enter Beatrice's cell to paint the famous portrait.

No suggestion had been made by the prosecutors alleging that the conspirators, in seeking to do away with Francesco, were driven by an impatience to inherit the aristocrat's wealth. Some motive for the crime needed to be proposed and Farinaccio quickly set out to show how Beatrice and Lucrezia had been intolerably treated by Francesco, imprisoned by him at La Petrella and tormented with threats of violence. They had also been made to witness repeated acts of indecency, thereby being forced to collude in his peculiar erotic life. Furthermore Farinaccio alleged that Francesco had attempted, and no doubt succeeded, in committing incestuous rape against his daughter, Beatrice.

Pope Clement, who was supreme judge in his own court, was unmoved by Beatrice's defense. The case had had to be drawn up hastily and Farinaccio's reputation did little to ingratiate him to the Holy Father. The common view during that summer of 1599 was clearly swaying toward a belief that nothing could now spare Beatrice. Finally, on the evening of September 10, the papal messenger arrived bringing their sentences.

PART II

Resurrections

—⁓—

CHAPTER 3

Shelley's "Secret Caverns of the Human Heart"

Whence are we, and why are we? Of what scene
The actors or spectators?

PERCY BYSSHE SHELLEY

Percy Bysshe Shelley first saw the famous Guido Reni portrait said to be of Beatrice Cenci at the end of April 1819. He was spellbound:

> There is a fixed and pale composure upon her features . . . Her head is bound with folds of white drapery from which the yellow strings of her golden hair escape, and fall about her neck. The moulding of her face is exquisitely delicate; the eyebrows are distinct and arched; the lips have that permanent meaning of imagination and sensibility which suffering has not repressed . . . . Her forehead is large and clear; her eyes, which we are told. were remarkable for their vivacity, are swollen with weeping

and lustreless, but beautifully tender and serene. . . . Beatrice
Cenci appears to have been one of those rare persons in whom
energy and gentleness dwell together without destroying one
another.

Shelley was in his mid-twenties, despairing at his life as a little-
known poet of doubtful reputation. He was living in Italy, essentially in exile. The vagaries of his relationships with women,
which had become steadily more unconventional, and the scandalous elements of his poetry, which was considered ungodly,
politically subversive, sexually perverted, sometimes all three,
caused him to be spurned by English society. Where some artists ignore, or even derive satisfaction from public condemna-
tion, Shelley deeply regretted his public image and was hoping
to transform his reputation both as an author and as a man.
He longed to be recognized as a great artist, not by some elite
minority, but by a broad audience and he was looking for a
popular subject on which to base his next work. He had learned
of Beatrice Cenci's story some months earlier, but the painting, and the complexity of character visible in her features combined with her unusual and mesmerizing beauty, convinced him
of her tragic power. He was more forcibly struck by her looks
than he had been by any living woman. She was more sensitive, more beautiful and more mysterious than any of the real
women whom he had loved. He may have seen something of
himself in Beatrice's life of suffering and injustice and he was
also convinced that her story would exert a chilling power over
his audience. His encounter with Beatrice Cenci prompted him
to believe in a double resurrection: of the condemned woman
and of himself, the condemned artist.

A few days later, on May 11, he visited the Cenci Palace with its barred windows and dim courtyard and experienced at first hand the lingering presence of the family's ghastly history:

> The palace is situated in an obscure corner of Rome, near the quarters of the Jews, and from the upper rooms you see the immense ruins of Mount Palatine half hidden under their profuse overgrowth of trees. There is a court in one part of the Palace (perhaps that in which Cenci built the Chapel of San Tommaso ai Cenci), supported by granite columns and adorned with antique friezes of fine workmanship, and built up, according to the ancient Italian fashion, with balcony over balcony of open-work. One of the gates of the Palace formed of immense stones and leading through a passage, dark and lofty and opening into gloomy subterranean chambers, struck me particularly.

He was in awe of the ruined extravagance of the palace and its atmosphere of Gothic decay. In it he recognized the arrogance and fake grandeur of institutional wealth and power, combined with disturbing traces of evil and suffering. The young woman was long dead and yet the building had triumphed over the natural forces of weather and time, and over successive political periods.

Shelley was convinced that the plight of Beatrice Cenci was not confined to sixteenth-century Italy but transcended time and place. Throughout his adult life he had come back to the question of whether or not the individual should simply accept fate, or take the law into his or her hands when subjected to extreme provocation or in other rare circumstances. He was very aware of the political connotations of Beatrice's story. In 1793, Charlotte Corday had murdered Marat in his bath because she considered him the bloodiest of the patriarchs of the French

Revolution, responsible for the progress of the Terror: she had been guillotined. Beatrice and Charlotte had both sought revenge against men who behaved as though above the law and who committed appalling violent crimes. The full weight of the law then fell on both women. But Shelley did not condone their actions. Like Cyntha in his *The Revolt of Islam* (in part a reflection on the French Revolution), his Beatrice is motivated by self-contempt to despise:

> . . . Hate—that shapeless fiendly thing . . .
> Whom self-contempt arms with a mortal sting.

Shelley's encounter with the long-departed Beatrice came at a crucial moment, when he was trying to make some sense of the disasters that had marked both his private life and his career as a writer. He had worked determinedly and the previous years had been productive, but his publishers had rejected the bulk of what he had written and the likelihood of critical acclaim seemed as remote as ever. He wondered at his failures and could not but compare himself with a close contemporary, Lord Byron, whose *Childe Harold's Pilgrimage*, published in 1812, had made him the darling of London society. A few years later Byron was suspected of an incestuous relationship with his half-sister, and left for Europe. He became friends with Shelley in Italy, and in August 1818 they spent time together in Venice. Shelley was fascinated by Byron's resilience, his love of life, his contempt for his critics and his creative energy, but he found it difficult to understand why Byron's sense of selfhood and even his reputation as a poet had been seemingly unaffected, even heightened, by the scandals of his private life.

A few weeks before seeing the Beatrice portrait for the first time, Shelley was musing on their differences: Byron's attitude to fate was playful, Shelley's was earnest. He saw himself as the unhappy but ever-heroic optimist, bravely living in accordance with his own conscience, buffeted by the hostile attitudes of the society around him, suffering, misjudged, but resolute. The parallels between his own life and Beatrice's were striking. Byron, on the other hand, was the bold cynic, shrewd and strong. Byron seemed happy and was loved but Shelley was on the verge of despair. He immersed himself in a strange dialogue based on their conversations in Venice.

Shelley's publishers were used to being shocked by the manuscripts which they received from Italy, and most of what was accepted for publication was sternly edited before seeing the light of day, but even today we are startled by his dramatic poem, "Julian and Maddalo: A Conversation," which he was working on that spring. In it Shelley explored questions of amorous and erotic disappointment and the psychological repercussions of rejection. His encounter with Beatrice would prompt him to chart still more intractable questions of the relationship between abuse and madness, but the seeds were sown in "Julian and Maddalo."

Count Maddalo (based on Byron) is a wealthy Venetian nobleman, a genius capable of redeeming his degraded country if he could be bothered. But he is proud, and his awareness of his own superiority leads him to dwell on the nothingness of life around him. He is a skeptic, snatching life's pleasures, arguing that chance and circumstance reign supreme, and that the individual is driven by mysterious passions, rather than by reason or conscience. Julian (based on Shelley), on the other hand, is an Englishman of good family, and remains determinedly hopeful,

convinced that life can be improved and that humans exert a
degree of control over their own and others' destinies. The involvement of a third figure in the work, the Maniac, who is less
a character in the poem than a part of the two other men, transforms what might have been an abstract philosophical dialogue
into something more real, and murkier. Shelley describes this
third player rather cryptically in the preface:

> Of the maniac I can give no information. He seems by his own
> account to have been disappointed in love. He was evidently a
> very cultivated and amiable person when in his right senses. His
> story, told at length, might be like many other stories of the same
> kind: the unconnected exclamations of his agony will perhaps
> be found a sufficient comment for the text of every heart.

The Maniac has suffered, and the suffering has gone so deep as
to rob him of his sanity. Maddalo considers him lost, while Julian
is haunted by the idea that the Maniac might yet be saved:

> *But I imagined that if day by day*
> *I watched him, and but seldom went away,*
> *And studied all the beatings of his heart*
> *With zeal, as men study some stubborn art*
> *For their own good, and could by patience find*
> *An entrance to the caverns of his mind,*
> *I might reclaim him from his dark estate.*

What he dreams of is akin to the therapeutic relationship "discovered" years later by Freud. Julian also believes that his devotion to
the Maniac will "make me know myself." This idea of daring to
follow others into deep mental abysses in an attempt both to res-

cue a tortured soul, and to gain self-knowledge, haunted Shelley and broke in again and again, both in his life and in his writings.

Maddalo accompanies Julian when the two of them visit the Maniac in his asylum, "a great palace": his monologue is one of the most haunting passages that Shelley ever wrote, filled with shattered images of sadism and masochism, of suggested but unspecified tortures and suicide. He speaks of tearing out "The nerves of manhood by their bleeding root/ With mine own quivering fingers" and suggests a necrophiliac voyeurism:

> *I haste, invited to the wedding ball*
> *To greet the ghastly paramour, for whom*
> *Thou hast deserted me . . . and made a tomb*
> *Thy bridal bed . . . But I beside thy feet*
> *Will lie and watch you from my winding sheet.*

Maddalo's angelic daughter explains that the Maniac was visited, in the end, by his former lover—and then died. The final lines are superbly inconclusive, yet soothing. The girl speaks:

> *"Ask me no more, but let the silent years*
> *Be closed and ceared over their memory*
> *As yon mute marble where their corpses lie."*

And Julian lays the poem to rest:

> *I urged and questioned still, she told me how*
> *All happened—but the cold world shall not know.*

"Julian and Maddalo" was deemed unpublishable and remained unpublished until after Shelley's death. Its explorations of the psychosexual mania brought on by unrequited love bordered on obscenity and certainly transgressed contemporary notions of what was proper in poetry. While finishing this poem, Shelley's commitment to telling Beatrice's story, of impressing it on "the cold world," strengthened. Shelley had invented the Maniac's story but Beatrice's was true, and in many ways it plumbed the same depths. Francesco, like the Maniac, is driven by sexual passion. Beatrice is the victim of her father's sadistic and incestuous desires and no one can rescue her from the madness that overcomes her as a result of Francesco's abuses. Shelley could return to "caverns" of the mind so reminiscent of the Maniac's, and to the "dark estate" of the Cenci family. His lifelong preoccupations about the nature of intensely private tragedy (Beatrice's) and political tragedy (the Cenci family representing society) could all be written into the work. This coincidence of the private and public was particularly appealing to the Romantic imagination.

Shelley had a small copy of the Beatrice portrait propped up in his rooms in the Via Sestina and he was delighted and encouraged when his servant recognized Beatrice. He noted that "the story of the Cenci was a subject not to be mentioned in Italian society without awakening a deep and breathless interest"; Beatrice always stirred up romantic pity and protestations of her innocence. The resilience of her story, and the people's continuing devotion to her, confirmed his feelings that he had found what he was looking for. He had long considered writing a play as a means of reaching a different public and of exciting the very different and immediate responses that are part of theater. *The Cenci* is his only completed play.

During the spring of 1819 he threw himself into his extraordinary work, and at the same time commissioned a portrait of himself by a friend also living in Rome, Aemilia Curran. Her painting, which was never finished but nevertheless remains the most important portrait of him, bears striking resemblance to the portrait of Beatrice. A year later Shelley commissioned Curran to copy the Cenci portrait to be used as a frontispiece to the first edition of his play, *The Cenci* (1820). Comparisons between the two Curran portraits, of Shelley and Beatrice, reveal the prominent cheekbones that throw the large almond-shaped eyes and cheeks into shadow, resulting in a shared look of simultaneous vulnerability and defiance. Both are disquietingly androgynous figures.

The coexistence of physical and psychological strength or weakness, and the way these are played out in relationships, lies at the heart of Shelley's play. He sought to explore and expose the effect of evil actions on the mind. In his preface he described the story as "eminently fearful and monstrous." The story might be extreme, exaggerated, remote, but it was an enlightening story, one from which everyone could learn: "If told so as to present to the reader all the feelings of those who once acted it, their hopes and fears, their confidences and misgivings, their various interests, passions and opinions acting upon and with each other, yet all conspiring to one tremendous end, would be as a light to make apparent some of the most dark and secret caverns of the human heart."

Shelley's Francesco represents unmitigated moral depravity, seeking to establish absolute control—physical and psychological—in order to satisfy his own desires. He is the archetypal sadist deriving heightened pleasure from the suffering caused by his own gratification. Beatrice is a strong and vital character who is gradually driven to counter evil with evil. Her progress is from virtue to vice, from the pitiable girl of Act 1 to the resolute woman who

contrives to have her father murdered and finally to the tragic
victim calmly awaiting her execution. She is unhesitating and is
not moved to counter oppression with pity and love. She lives in
a real world, in which corruption and decadence reign, and in
which evil must be dealt with in a practical fashion. Her intelligence and insight are emphasized early on: "Her subtle mind,
her awe-inspiring gaze / Whose beams anatomise . . . nerve by
nerve." The change in her personality is brilliantly exposed: her
father's violation of her causes a kind of madness and she con-
templates suicide. Ironically she rejects this idea as forbidden by
God and it is then that the thought of murder comes to her, as
though from outside herself:

> What is this undistinguishable mist
> Of thoughts, which rise, like shadow after shadow
> Darkening each other?

Beatrice becomes chillingly single-minded and, still more disturb-
ingly, she transforms the act of murder in her mind into "a high
and holy deed," one which will rid the world of evil.

Shelley's play exposes his understanding of violence, of the
power that one person can exert over another and the tangled
motivations and results of such actions. He identifies the corrupting effects of violence on both the aggressor and victim, and al-
ludes to the complexities of power that work themselves out in
sexual passion and sexual acts, and the strange collusion of the
victim that may be a part of it. He exposes hypocrisy, and the
individual's capacity to deny double standards that stare him in
the face. He acknowledges the shadows of guilt that lurk all
about, ignored, or half-glimpsed, but never fully acknowledged.
All this he recognized in the Cenci story, and in the lives of people

around him. His own life had been an endless quest to root them out, and expose them. But how well did he know himself? What dark experiences and tortured self-knowledge did he bring to his *Cenci* play? Was Shelley's fascination exclusively bound up with Beatrice, or did he also catch terrifying glimpses of himself in her male tormentor, Francesco? What were the strange passions that had played themselves out in his relationships with women and how much of them were written—consciously or unconsciously—into his play?

Shelley had no brothers, only adoring sisters who willingly submitted to his often peculiar and passionate desires. Where he might have had a more physically combative relationship with brothers, his relationship with his sisters was based on heightened sensation of an imaginative, or psychological, even paranormal, kind. Of his three sisters, Elizabeth (b. May 1794), Mary (b.1797) and Hellen (b.1801), he was closest to Elizabeth. She was the great friend of his childhood and separation from her, when he was sent away to Syon House Academy, between 1802 and 1804, greatly added to his unhappiness at the school. His first publication was co-authored by Elizabeth and many of the women he would go on to love were writers, creators of alternative worlds.

At the Shelleys' childhood home, field Place, with its ample attics and unused corners and spreading gardens, there was plenty of scope for games of make-believe. Shelley was mainly in charge, Elizabeth in second command. What mattered to Shelley, above all, was to elicit a peculiar kind of fear from his sisters. His sister Hellen recalled, a long time afterwards:

> The tales to which we have sat and listened evening after evening,
> seated on his knee, when we came to the dining-room for dessert,

were anticipated with that pleasing dread, which so excited the mind of children, and fastens so strongly and indelibly on the memory.

His compulsion to provoke extreme fear never left him, surfacing in relationship after relationship.

Years later a copy of "Monk" Lewis's *Tales of Terror* was found in the children's library in field Place. In the margins Shelley had sketched grotesque horned creatures and devils. This was a practice that he continued as an adult in his working notebooks. His sisters worshipped him, but they also feared his obsessions and the dark world of his imagination. He would have them follow him into a darkly magical world "dressed . . . in strange costumes to personate spirits or fiends, and Bysshe would take a fire-stove and fill it with some inflammable liquid and carry it flaming into the kitchen and to the back door."

Shelley's Gothic imagination matured over the years and his pyromaniacal tendencies became more ambitious. At Syon House Academy his schoolfellows recognized his "violent and extremely excitable temper." They too felt a secret fear and the result was to make him the object of bullying. Shelley tried to distance himself:

He was known as "Mad Shelley";—and many a cruel torture was practised upon him for his moody and singular exclusiveness. Shelley was my senior; and I, in common with others, deemed him as one ranging between madness and folly . . . Like Tasso's jailer, his heartless tyrants all but raised up the demon which they said was in him. I have seen him surrounded, hooted, baited like a maddened bull,—and at this distance of time I seem to hear ringing in my ears the cry which Shelley was wont to utter in his paroxysms of revengeful anger.

Shelley's behavior, when victimized, was very often sensational and has never been forgotten by those who witnessed it. There are innumerable accounts of his fits of temper and despair. He refused to submit and railed against the injustice of powerlessness.

When he returned to field Place for the holidays, he was even more domineering with his sisters and his "experiments" became more dangerous. Now only Elizabeth participated willingly in what their parents called Shelley's "pranks." This may have been a euphemism chosen in order to deny a more worrying truth. There is something wonderfully overearnest about Hellen's account. And yet:

> When my brother commenced his studies in chemistry, and prac-
> tised electricity upon us, I confess my pleasure in it was entirely
> negatived by terror at its effects. Whenever he came to me with
> his piece of folded brown packing paper under his arm and a
> bit of wire and a bottle . . . my heart would sink with fear at his
> approach; but shame kept me silent, and, with as many others
> as he could collect, we were placed hand-in-hand around the
> nursery table to be electrified.

Hellen remained ever apologetic. But when Shelley claimed that he could cure their chilblains by electrification his sisters' "terror overwhelmed all other feelings."

Shelley's persecution continued at Eton where practices were institutionalized. "Nailing" involved picking a boy out to be the target of a muddy football which was shot at him as violently as possible. Shelley was frequently "nailed" and his reactions to this and other torments were spectacular to the point of further encouraging his tormentors: "The result was a paroxysm of anger which made his eyes flash like a tiger's, his cheeks grow pale as

death, his limbs quiver, and his hair stand on end." Throughout
his life Shelley deplored extreme violence, but it was part of his
own make-up. At Eton he was provoked into stabbing a boy
through the hand, pinning him to a desk. The school left him with
a deep loathing of organized authority and of social conformism.

More sophisticated versions of much of the equipment of
Shelley's childhood accompanied him in 1810 to University
College, Oxford, where his undergraduate career would come
to an abrupt halt a few months later. A fellow student, Thomas
Jefferson Hogg, who became one of Shelley's lifelong friends,
described his companion's rooms:

> Books, boots, papers, shoes, philosophical instruments, clothes,
> pistols, linen, crockery, ammunition, and phials innumerable,
> with money, stockings, prints, crucibles . . . were scattered on
> the floor in every place. . . . An electrical machine, an air pump,
> the galvanic trough, a solar microscope, and large glass jars and
> receivers, were conspicuous amidst the mass of matter. . . . Upon
> the table . . . were . . . books . . . and a handsome razor that had
> been used as a knife.

The move from Eton to Oxford was a shock. Shelley reveled
in the freedom, but felt suffocated by the quasi-monastic life of
the college and the intellectual conformism of the university. There
was a mediocrity about the lives of most of his fellow students,
and the dons were overwhelmingly reactionary, clerical, uninspir-
ing, often hypocritical. Shelley used to make a spectacle of himself leaving chapel at the earliest opportunity in order to retreat
to his own rooms. He was quickly rewarded by being considered
a heretic. Although Shelley participated as little as possible in the
organized teaching of Oxford, leaving lectures only minutes after

they had begun, and seeing as little as possible of his tutors, he read voraciously, debated heatedly with Hogg, who was also something of an atheist, and a number of others—and he wrote.

As with his other childish interests, rather than growing out of them they became exaggerated later on. At Oxford a simpleton son sometimes accompanied the woman who saw to his rooms. Shelley would make toward him with his "philosophical apparatus" threatening in half-jest that he was about to electrify the boy, who "roared aloud with ludicrous and stupid terror." Shelley was turning the tables in order to look back through some sinister glass on his own unpredictable behavior as a boy. The sadistic abuses that he had suffered as a child encouraged a sadistic streak of his own.

Although Shelley and Hogg's conversations often ranged widely over abstruse, abstract areas of speculation, they spent a good deal of time discussing political theory. Hogg had read a good deal and he and Shelley were soon discussing British, continental and American radical thinkers including Gibbon, Voltaire, Rousseau, Paine, Franklin, Godwin and Adam Smith, the political economist. What interested Shelley above all were the implications of these men's thinking for the rights of the individual. He delighted in their penetrating attacks on public authority and he began systematically to think through, and discuss, the relationship between private morality and public codes of conduct. He considered the ancient story of Antigone's burial of her brother Polynices' body in defiance of an edict of her uncle, the King of Thebes. She was condemned to death but was she immoral, Shelley wondered? "Did she wrong when she acted in direct noble violation of the laws of a prejudiced society?" Shelley made up his mind: "Political ideas are quite distinct from morality." When he discovered Beatrice Cenci she confirmed his conviction that stories of this kind were not exclusively the stuff of myth but continued to be lived out.

Shelley was living in a flurry of intellectual excitement. He had also become accustomed to an idiosyncratic daily pattern, often sleeping a good deal in the day and rising at night. This did little to calm the bizarre dreams which terrified him throughout his life. He persuaded Hogg to court his sister, Elizabeth, initially by correspondence. Shelley considered Elizabeth too much in their father's control. She was the first of many women whom he sought to "save" from paternal power: years later he would delight in his discovery of Francesco Cenci, whose character vindicated Shelley's deep suspicions about the motivation of fathers in relation to their daughters. When he returned to field Place Shelley spoke to Elizabeth at length about Hogg. She seemed uninterested and Hogg, while no doubt curious about Shelley's sister, was obviously far more enraptured by his extraordinary friend, relishing his memories of Shelley's displays:

> He then proceeded, with much eagerness and enthusiasm, to show me the various instruments, especially the electrical apparatus; turning round the handle very rapidly, so that the fierce, crackling sparks flew forth; and presently standing upon the stool with glass feet, he begged me to work the machine until he was filled with the fluid, so that his long, wild locks bristled and stood on end.

Shelley had clearly electrified Hogg. But Shelley's father, Sir Timothy, somewhat ironically, considered Hogg to be a dangerous influence on his son. Hogg had written an ideological novel, *Leonora*, and Shelley's publisher, John James Stockdale, who read the manuscript, quickly wrote to his friend Sir Timothy to warn him of his pernicious influence. Father interviewed son at field Place and though their discussions of atheism and conformism were civil, Sir Timothy and his wife Mary were both clear that airing ideas such as Shelley's would lead to social ostracism at best, prosecution at worst. In the early nineteenth century atheism was indissolubly associated with immoral behavior, rejection of class (immediately resulting in a social slide), even the rejection of all patriotic commitment, perhaps treachery. Shelley's parents also knew of his powerful influence over his sisters. He wrote triumphantly to Hogg: "My mother fancies me on the High Road to Pandemonium, she fancies I want to make a little coterie of all my little sisters." This was indeed his intention and soon he was advertising that he had designs on other people's little sisters too.

During the winter of 1811, Shelley was subdued by the news that his childhood love, Harriet Grove, his cousin and senior by one year, was engaged to be married. Shelley's pride was wounded and he made much of Harriet's rejection of him, claiming unrealistically that he had been abandoned solely because of his anti-religious views: he had been a martyr to his convictions, his atheism had caused him grievous suffering, the loss of the great love of his life. His commitment to atheism would now have to be all the more wholehearted—in line with his great sacrifices.

A few weeks later, a pamphlet was published and distributed, co-authored by Hogg and Shelley. Although published anonymously, it soon became public knowledge that the authors of *The Necessity of Atheism*, almost the first serious defense of atheism to be published in England, were the two young undergraduates of University College. After being summoned before the Master and Fellows, Shelley and Hogg were soon packing their bags.

Shelley was feared for more than simply his "pranks." There was a general anxiety among those who knew him about the power of some of his beliefs and the energy with which he was prepared to expound and promulgate them. Joseph Merle, who would later become a prominent journalist and newspaper editor, remembered Shelley's outbursts from his Oxford days:

> On all other subjects he was one of the mildest and most modest youths I have ever known; but once let religion be mentioned, and he became alternately scornful and furious. If his opinions were contradicted, he contented himself in the first instance with jeers on the weakness of the person who dissented from his views. If the contradiction was kept up, and his adversary became animated in his defense of revealed religion, his countenance underwent a fearful change, and his eye became one of fire.

Merle went as far as to suggest that Shelley was, in some ways, a "dangerous member of society." He was outstandingly clever, and was embarking on adult life with both social standing and reasonable wealth. But an obsession had taken hold of him, and he would try to impose it on others, if necessary by the power of fear:

> Overstudy had made him mad on religious subjects; and as on all others, his mind was fresh and vigorous, he was in the position of a monomaniac who is incurable, because his insanity is concentrated in one faculty.

Shelley's abrupt departure from Oxford in March 1811 was the beginning of a series of expulsions in his life which pushed him into ever more distant states of exile, that would eventually become difficult to bear. And he started to associate solitude with a recognition of personal evil:

> Solitude is most horrible. . . . Not with my own good will can I endure the horror the evil that comes from self in solitude . . . what strange being I am, how inconsistent, in spite of all my boasted self-hatred of self—this moment thinking I could so far overcome Nature's law as to exist in complete seclusion; the next shrinking from a moment of solitude, starting from my own company *as if it were that of a fiend*, seeking anything rather than a continued communion with *self*—Unravel this mystery—but no. I tell you to find the clue which even the bewildered explorer of the cavern can never reach.

Shelley was fascinated and terrified by the workings of his own mind. Self-consciousness, our capacity both to think and be the subject of our thinking, became crucial to his poetry. But solitude brought him close to a kind of madness and he recognized that imprisonment, incarceration, solitary confinement, were about removing the dangerous individual from society, but also, and more importantly, about requiring him to live (sometimes exclusively) in his own fearful company, at the mercy of the mysterious influences of the self—on self. In *The Cenci* it is Beatrice's incarceration at La Petrella that encourages "thoughts . . . sick with speed."

In the wake of Shelley's expulsion, Sir Timothy's relationship with his son deteriorated and Shelley began, more and more, to associate paternal authority with public authority and organized religion, his two great bugbears. Shelley's atheism was strengthened by his belief that he had lost Harriet Grove because of his anti-religious feelings: now he confused his feelings for another

Harriet, this one Westbrook, with his growing loathing of paternal power. But he did not question the nature of the control he himself exerted over the women he claimed to be liberating.

Shelley had turned to the Westbrook sisters during the months of loneliness that followed his departure from Oxford. Harriet, the youngest, had been a school friend of his sisters. Their lives were sheltered and they had been brought up to high standards of self-discipline, hard work and self-denial. Shelley broke in on Harriet's life like a streak of lightning and she was duly lit up but also deeply disconcerted. She had little confidence and saw life as a battle against fears, against inhibitions born of repression, against evil. Shelley was attracted to her, but the challenge of liberating her from the physical and mental incarceration into which he decided she had been thrown by her father was equally seductive. This was something of a fantasy on Shelley's part, or at least there was nothing remarkable, within the contemporary social context, in the Westbrook sisters' upbringing. Shelley wrote heroically, and fanatically, to Hogg:

> I almost despair—you have not only to conquer all the hateful prejudices of religion, not only to conquer duty to the father, *duty* indeed of all kind—but I see in the background a monster more terrific. Have you forgotten the tremendous Gregory: the opinion of the world, its myriads of hateful champions . . . Yet *marriage* is hateful detestable—a kind of ineffable sickening disgust seizes my mind when I think of this most despotic most unrequired fetter which prejudice has forged to confine its energies. Yet this is Xtianity—& Xt *must* perish before this can fall.

For all Shelley's brilliant insights into people and the world, and despite his acute self-consciousness, he could be stupendously blind to his own motives. He failed to see the effects of his own influence on those around him. Shelley was blind to the fact that he was projecting a good deal of his own neuroses on to Harriet and thereby drawing her into them. In the same way he was blind to the fact that an educational experiment which he proposed to Merle around this same time might have damaging effects on the lives of those involved. No doubt inspired by Rousseau's claims for the beneficial effects of a natural childhood and Thomas Day's social experiments in the 1770s, Shelley made a bold request to Merle:

> I wish to find two young persons of not more than four or five years of age; and should prefer females, as they are usually more precocious than males. . . . I will withdraw from the world with my charge, and in some sequestered spot direct their education. They shall know nothing of men or manners until their minds shall have been sufficiently matured to enable me to ascertain, when brought into play, what the impressions of the world are upon the mind when it has been veiled from human prejudice.

Merle wrote back in dismay:

> The idea of a youth of twenty shutting himself from the world with two females until an age when, without religious instruction, they should have no other guarantee for their chastity than the reason of a man who would then be in the summer of his life, with all his passion in full vigour, was more than absurd— it was horrible.

The power he would wield over the girls' emotional education, or more particularly their erotic development, was not something that Shelley discussed, however quick he was to see, or imagine, the dangerous inequalities in the power relations between fathers and daughters.

Determined that his estrangement from his family should not affect his ties to his little sister Hellen, he appealed to her loyalty and continued his old game of frightening her just a little:

> Because everybody else hates me, that is no reason that you should. Think for yourself my dear girl, and write to me to tell me what you think. Where you are now you cannot do as you please.—You are obliged to submit to other people.—They will not let you walk and read and think (if they knew your thoughts) just as you like tho' you have as good a right to do it as they.— But if you were with me you would be with some one who loved you, you might run and skip read write think just as you liked . . . . Nobody can suspect you, you may easily write and put your letter into the Summer House where I shall be sure to get it. I watch over you tho' you do not think I am near, I need not tell you how I love you.—I know all that is said of me—but do not believe it. You will perhaps think *I'm* the Devil, but no, I am only your brother who is obliged to be put to these shifts to get a letter from you.

When one of the servants informed Sir Timothy of Shelley's approaches to his sister, he was infuriated; indeed it is difficult to think that Shelley was acting in his sister's interests. What he wanted was to capture a hostage from among his father's loyal and submissive camp; in fact a few years later Shelley actually considered a plan to kidnap both Hellen and Mary.

Shelley married Harriet Westbrook in 1811, against all his principles. After Harriet had written to him that summer, claiming that her father "persecuted her in the most horrible way," they eloped and married. But Shelley was soon writing to J.H. Lawrence to congratulate him on his four-volume *The Empire of the Nairns; or the Rights of Women*. Having finished it, Shelley "retained no doubts, as to the evils of marriage." The power he wielded as a husband, combined with the sexual freedom denied him, explain much of the abhorrence he expressed toward the institution of marriage.

One other woman was to be drawn into Shelley's life during this period: Elizabeth Hitchener, a young self-educated woman who had risen to a position of respect as local schoolmistress. She and Shelley entered into an intense intellectual relationship and she helped Shelley to refine some of his political, philosophical and religious ideas, and his more detailed ideas for social reform, including his plans for a radical community, a new microcosmic political order. But he had by no means grown out of his tendency both to draw women under his influence and then to ask them to collude in something acutely psychologically disturbing. By January 1812 Shelley's conversations with Elizabeth became increasingly ghost-ridden and his plans for an ideal society took a phantasmagoric twist. He wrote to Miss Hitchener explaining:

> I shall try to domesticate in some antique feudal castle whose mouldering turrets are fit emblems of decaying inequality and oppression. . . . As to the ghosts I shall welcome them, altho Harriet protests against my invoking them, but they would tell tales of old, and it would add to the picturesqueness of the scenery to see their thin forms flitting thro the vaulted charnels.

The Cenci Palace which he visited a few years later would be strikingly familiar to him. Shelley cast himself as the patriarchal figure presiding over the "antique feudal castle," not unlike Francesco at the castle of La Petrella, where Beatrice and her stepmother were imprisoned.

A few months after his marriage, Shelley fell in love with Mary Godwin, daughter of William Godwin and Mary Wollstonecraft. After Mary's death Godwin had married Mrs. Clairmont, a widow, but remained closest, however, to his daughter Mary. During Mary's adolescence their relationship was intense and this, once again, made her curiously attractive to Shelley. The strength of Godwin's paternal hold over both Mary, and Jane Clairmont, her stepsister, was something he had to challenge.

By the summer of 1813 the various projects for radical political communities that Shelley had dreamed up since leaving Oxford had come to little, and his relationship with Harriet had far from calmed him. That summer, according to Hogg, Shelley claimed to have caught elephantiasis:

> His imagination was so much disturbed, that he was perpetually examining his skin, and feeling and looking at that of others. One evening, during the access of his fancied disorder, when many young ladies were standing up for a country dance, he caused wonderful consternation amongst these charming creatures by walking slowly along the row of girls and curiously surveying them, placing his eyes close to their necks and bosoms, and feeling their breasts and bare arms, in order to ascertain whether any of the fair ones had taken the horrible disease. He proceeded with so much gravity and seriousness, and his looks were so woebegone, that they did not resist, or resent, the extraordinary liberties, but looked terrified and as if they were about to undergo some severe surgical operation at his hands.

Shelley could provoke astonishing passivity in women, a response to his ability to stir up fear. In *The Cenci* he would have Francesco say:

> *All men delight in sensual luxury,*
> *All men enjoy revenge; and most exult*
> *Over the tortures they can never feel—*
> *flattering their secret peace with others' pain.*
> *But I delight in nothing else. I love*
> *The sight of agony.*

Harriet, pregnant with their second child, knew of Shelley's infatuation with Mary Godwin but hoped that his passion would pass. In the meantime Shelley devised a plan and on the morning of July 28, 1814, at 4 a.m., he waited at the corner of Skinner Street for the chaise that he had ordered. Soon two small figures appeared, clutching bundles, their eyes staring in response to the early hour and the sleeplessness of the night before. Then Shelley and the two half-sisters, Mary, aged sixteen, and Jane, aged fifteen, headed for Dover, and the Continent. Jane looked out of the carriage window, her eyes filled with tears, and Mary slept, propped between Shelley's knees.

Six weeks later they were back in England. Shelley's letters to Hogg that autumn were frank and full: he described his love for Harriet as a burden that had sapped his energy and diverted him, he now claimed, from the proper course of his life. He came very close to blaming the failure of his marriage exclusively on the institution itself. Marriage, he wrote, was "a gross and despicable superstition." He felt the reverse of guilt: having identified the emptiness of his commitment, he felt regenerated, optimistic and open to life once again. The fact of Harriet's pregnancy added no further complications, or feelings of regret. All that mattered, he believed, was that his wife be reassured by the services of a first-class doctor. Mary, on the other hand, had "ennobled" him and her smile, in particular, continued to seduce him: "how persuasive it was, and how pathetic!" Beatrice's expression would be described later in very similar terms.

Shelley delighted in involving Mary and Jane in macabre readings. Often Mary would retire quite early, and Jane and Shelley would continue to work on each other's terrors. A typical entry from that autumn in Shelley's diary (which Mary was privy to) reads:

> Shelley, unable to sleep, kissed Mary and prepared to sit beside her and read until morning, when rapid footsteps descended the stairs. Jane was there; her countenance was distorted most unnaturally by horrible dismay—it beamed with a whiteness that seemed almost like light; her lips and cheeks were of one deadly hue; the skin of her face and forehead was drawn into innumerable wrinkles—the lineaments of terror that could not be contained; her hair came prominent and erect; her eyes were wide and staring, drawn almost from the sockets by the convulsion of the muscles; the eyelids were forced in, and the eyeballs, without any relief, seemed as if they had been newly inserted, in ghastly sport, in the sockets of a lifeless head.

The writing could equally be Mary's sketch of Frankenstein's monster, the famous creature of her invention. Or it could be Shelley's description of the physiological changes that occur to a young woman's head, at the moment of execution. There is something pathological about Shelley's desire to describe Jane's looks and behavior in fantastic detail. The entry continues:

This frightful spectacle endured but for a few moments—it was displaced by terror and confusion, violent, indeed, and full of dismay, but human. She asked me (Shelley) if I had touched her pillow (her tone was that of dreadful alarm). I said, "No, no!" ... She told me that a pillow placed upon her bed had been removed, in the moment that she turned her eyes away to a chair at some distance, and evidently by no human power. ... We continued to sit by the fire, at intervals engaging in awful conversation relative to the nature of these mysteries. ... Our conversation, though intentionally directed to other topics, irresistibly recurred to these. Our candles burned low, we feared they would not last till daylight. Just as dawn was struggling with moonlight, Jane remarked in me that unutterable expression which had affected her with so much horror before; she described it as expressing a mixture of deep sadness and conscious power over her. I covered my face with my hands, and spoke to her with studied gentleness. It was ineffectual; her horror and agony increased even to the most dreadful convulsions. She shrieked and writhed on the floor.

These scenes happened frequently during the autumn of 1814 and they are connected with a change in Shelley's writing. Up until this point his poetry had been inspired primarily by ideological or essentially political convictions. Now it begins to be animated by a recognition of darker inner psychic forces and journeys into the shadows of the self.

At about the same time as Shelley's account of Jane's "spectacles" she changed her name to Claire, and it is as Claire Clairmont that she is known. Shelley had been encouraging her to re-create herself in part in accordance with his own bizarre image of who she truly was. The relationship between Mary and Claire was, needless to say, strained by Shelley and Claire's closeness. Meanwhile Shelley was busily planning yet another alternative community, writing excitedly to interested parties, and Hogg joined them in their search for a London address that was large enough for the growing community. On February 22, two months prematurely, Mary was delivered of a tiny baby girl. To everyone's astonishment it looked as though she would survive: she suckled well and started to put on weight. The baby's resilience stood, in some way, for the resilience of Mary and Shelley's relationship. But Mary was depending more and more on Hogg, and Shelley on Claire. Then on 6 March Mary awoke to find the baby dead, its little body contorted and wracked, as though it had suffered convulsions. Mary was beside herself with grief and turned to Hogg: "My dearest Hogg my baby is dead—will you come to me as soon as you can—I wish to see you. . . . Will you come—you are so calm a creature & Shelley is afraid of a fever from the milk—for I am no longer a mother now."

Mary fell pregnant once again. Both worked hard, Mary studying the Latin authors while Shelley refined his reading of Greek, devouring the tragedies of Aeschylus and Euripides. In his work questions of public law and natural justice, personal honor and heroic action drew him back to areas that had first engaged him at Oxford—and would captivate him in Rome.

By late spring 1816, Shelley had allowed himself to be persuaded to join Claire in her pursuit of Byron to Geneva. Mary's energies were taken up by her new baby, a boy at last, William. Shelley was delighted. But his primary interest was now to establish a closer association with Byron. Before long it would emerge that Claire was pregnant and neither man was wholly convinced as to the baby's paternity.

Soon life in Geneva became virtually impossible for the little community that had gathered. There is something absurdly indignant in Shelley's recollections of the social ostracism they had experienced:

> The natives of Geneva and the English people who were living there did not hesitate to affirm that we were leading the life of the most unbridled libertinism. They said that we had found a pact to outrage all that is regarded as most sacred in human society. Allow me, Madam, to spare you the details. I will only tell you that atheism, incest, and many other things—sometimes ridiculous and sometimes terrible—were imputed to us. The English papers did not delay to spread the scandal, and the people believed it.

The Shelley household traveled back to England. Claire's affair with Byron had come to an abrupt end but her spirits gradually lifted; and there was the baby to look forward to. Shelley, on the other hand, was about to face one of the most traumatic periods of his life. Unbeknownst to him, Harriet had left the children with their grandparents the previous September, and had taken lodgings in Chelsea, giving her name as "Harriet Smith." By November 9 she had disappeared and a month later, on December 10, 1816, her body was discovered in the lower reaches of the Serpentine. *The Times* described the young woman as in a late stage of pregnancy. Harriet was still, of course, Shelley's wife and he was plunged into despair. Yet he denied any responsibility for Harriet's suicide. A letter to Mary reads:

> It seems that this poor woman [Harriet]—the most innocent of her abhorred and unnatural family—was driven from her father's

house, & descended the steps of prostitution until she lived with
a groom of the name of Smith, who deserting her, she killed
herself.

Shelley blamed paternal neglect, if not abuse, and Harriet's "unnatural and abhorred" background.

A month later Claire gave birth to a baby, Alba, and Byron,
who had always accepted paternity, asked that they call her
Allegra. It had been agreed that the little girl would be handed
over to Byron as soon as she was out of infancy. Meanwhile,
Shelley escaped into his work, treating disturbing subjects. He
wrote enthusiastically to Byron, "I have been engaged this summer, heart and soul, in one pursuit." This was *Laon and Cythna,
or, The Revolution in the Golden City* in which his hero and heroine were brother and sister—and lovers. Both Laon and Cythna
survive unlikely adventures, including incarceration leading to
madness. Cythna suffers fearful hallucinations in which she is
raped, gives birth and is forced to eat what she believes are bits of
Laon's body. In a preface to the poem Shelley argued that the theme
of incest was intended to shock the reader, to awaken him to the
fossilized nature of institutions. He knew what the public reaction was likely to be, but he didn't care. In the same letter to Byron
he declared, "It is to be *published*—for I am not of your opinion
as to religion, etc, and for this simple reason, that I am careless of
the consequences as they regard myself. I only feel persecution
bitterly, because I bitterly lament the depravity and mistake of
those who persecute. As to me, I can but die; I can but be torn to
pieces, or devoted to infamy most undeserved."

Incest, in particular, would continue to preoccupy his thoughts,
and in his poetry he continued to use it as a means of exposing

the backwardness of "institutions." In *Rosalind and Helen*, which he started some time later, Rosalind's story concerns an incestuous love affair and a tyrannical father. The Cenci story would provide an extraordinary opportunity to explore these dark preoccupations in dramatic form, and with dramatic results.

While Shelley reeled in dismay at the critical reception of his work, he suffered searing criticism of his personal conduct. A couple of years later, the poet Robert Southey, formerly a close friend, would articulate the view of the majority of Shelley's friends. In part perhaps because Southey had himself given up a great deal for his family at the expense of his professional life, he criticized Shelley's private life mercilessly: "Ask your own heart," he wrote in relation to Harriet's suicide, and with a sermonizing tone, "whether you have not been the whole, sole and direct cause of her destruction. You corrupted her opinions; you robbed her of her moral and religious principles; you debauched her mind."

Harriet had committed suicide in late 1816. In 1818 Shelley and Mary suffered the loss of Clara. Despite the tragedies, 1818 was one of Shelley's most productive years. The immediate fate of his work, however, in terms of publication, remained bleak. Even *Prometheus Unbound*, his most famous poem, which he started in September 1818, failed to secure immediate publication. "Julian and Maddalo," also begun that year, was not published during his lifetime. By April 1819, Shelley was seriously considering the story of the Cenci. Shelley, Mary, Claire and little "Willmouse" (William) were all back in Italy, in Rome. The seed for the play had been sown some months earlier, in Livorno, where the Renaissance story had been circulating among the English. The Shelley household had rented the Casa Bertini for the season and that May Mary was passed a manuscript of the

Cenci tale and translated it into a little calf-bound notebook. The
story begins boldly: "Sodomy was the least and Atheism the
greatest of the vices of Francisco [Cenci] . . ." The first "vice"
was one for which Shelley had the deepest abhorrence, considering it an "operose and diabolical machination." "It is impossible," he wrote, "that a lover could usually have subjected the
object of his attachment to so detestable a violation or have consented to associate his own remembrance in the beloved mind
with images of pain and horror." Atheism, on the other hand
was one of Shelley's own most celebrated "vices." The combi-
nation of identification and revulsion would prove irresistible.
But neither Shelley nor Mary was yet committed to the Cenci
story. That would take Shelley's encounter with another man's
resurrection of her: he fell in love with the portrait.

Shelley and Mary debated at some length as to who should
write a Cenci work. Mary's interest in monsters, in incest, in
domination and liberation, and in strong women, naturally drew
her to Beatrice, and although in the end they agreed that Shelley
should take the Cenci on, Mary did write Beatrice into her novel
Valperga (1823), the successor to *Frankenstein*. The novel is set
in fourteenth-century Tuscany, but one of its two heroines,
Beatrice, is presented as a forerunner of Beatrice Cenci, blessed
with "exquisite and almost divine beauty":

> Her deep black eyes, half concealed by their heavy lids, her
> curved lips, and face formed a perfect oval, the rising colour that
> glowed in her cheeks which, though her complexion was pure
> and delicate, were tinged with the suns of Italy, formed a pic-
> ture such as Guido has copied from life when he painted the
> unfortunate Beatrice Cenci.

The manner in which Shelley worked on his new project was unlike any other: Mary and Claire were both involved. At one point Mary recorded: "Shelley's imagination became strongly excited, and he urged the subject to me as one fitted for a tragedy. More than ever I felt my incompetence; but I entreated him to write it instead. . . . This tragedy is the only one of his works that he communicated to me during its progress. We talked over the arrangement of the scenes together."

By this point Shelley was showing consumptive symptoms and there was much discussion about where the healthiest place to live in Italy might be. That May in Rome little Willmouse also fell ill. After a brief recovery he was overcome by convulsions and Mary watched horrified as his body twisted and bent like little Clara's. Shelley stayed up for three consecutive nights, desperate that his son survive. On June 7, 1819, days after the illness's second onslaught, William died, quietly, as though accepting his fate. The Shelley household was childless once again. Claire had lost Allegra (who had been handed over to Byron), Mary had lost Clara, and Shelley had now lost his favorite: his four-year-old son. He thought he would never recover. In a letter he announced William's death: "You will be kind enough to tell all my friends. . . . It is a great exertion to me to write this, and it seems to me as if, hunted by calamity as I have been, that I should never recover any cheerfulness again."

Shelley may well have been grieving not only for his beloved Willmouse. It is very likely that he also had a brief affair, during 1818, with his maid, Elise. A baby was born on December 27, 1818 and christened on February 27, 1819, Elena Adelaide Shelley. The day after Elena was baptized the entire Shelley household left Naples, never to return. Elena was left with Elise.

December 27 was also a significant day in Claire's life. She too may well have lost a baby on that date, through miscarriage. Shelley chose December 27 as a crucial day in his Cenci play. On that day Francesco summons his friends to a banquet in morbid recognition of his sons' deaths, sons that he has come to hate:

> . . . *Rocco*
> *Was kneeling at the mass, with sixteen others,*
> *When the church fell and crushed him to a mummy,*
> *The rest escaped unhurt. Cristofano*
> *Was stabbed in error by a jealous man . . .*
> *Which shows that Heaven has special care of me.*
> *I beg those friends who love me, that they mark*
> *The day a feast upon their calendars.*
> *It was the twenty-seventh of December.*

The choice of December 27 can be read as an ambiguous secret confession. How at ease was Shelley with his promiscuity and how did he feel about the deaths of his babies? Nor would this have been the first time that Shelley slept with two women more or less at the same time. Harriet and Mary's babies were born at only a two-and-a-half-month interval in the winter of 1814–15. Given that Mary's baby was born some two months prematurely, it is likely that his relationships with the two women all but co-incided. Written into Shelley's *Cenci* is a fundamental despair at life—Shelley's own, and indeed Mary's. Shelley blamed the insidious force of patriarchal influence. Mary blamed Shelley.

During that 1819 summer, a summer of great sorrow, Mary wrote to her friend Marianne Hunt: "We came to Italy thinking to do Shelley's health good—but the Climate is not any means warm enough to be of benefit to him and yet it is that that has destroyed my two children." Italy had not been good to Mary: "if I would write anything else about myself it would only be a list of hours spent in tears and grief."

That same summer Shelley returned to his *Cenci.* He distanced himself from Mary, reasoning that her despair was something that she could only overcome alone. In a fragment of a poem, he wrote, "Wherefore hast thou gone, / And left me in this dreary world alone? [. . .] For thine own sake I cannot follow thee / Do thou return for mine." And in his play he wrote:

> *'tis a trick of this same family*
> *To analyze their own and other minds.*
> *Such self-anatomy shall teach the will*
> *Dangerous secrets . . .*

Did Shelley know that any attempts he might make to understand Mary's despair would lead her openly to condemn him? The play continues:

> *[Such self-anatomy] . . . tempts our powers,*
> *Knowing what must be thought, and may be done,*
> *Into the depth of darkest purposes:*
> *So Cenci fell into the pit . . .*

That summer Shelley wrote on, alone in a high, glazed room, atop the Villa Valsovano, in Livorno. He brooded too, and had his Beatrice ask, in the final act of the play:

> *If there should be*
> *No God, no Heaven, no Earth in the void world;*
> *The wide, grey, lampless, deep, unpeopled world!*

In the absence of a God, Beatrice considers that her father's
power, from beyond the grave, may be all that exists:

> *If all things then should be . . . my father's spirit,*
> *His eye, his voice, his touch surrounding me;*
> *The Atmosphere and breath of my dead life!*

The identification between God and the Father is complete—and
he is terrifying:

> *If sometimes, as a shape more like himself,*
> *Even the form that tortured me on earth,*
> *Masked in grey hairs and wrinkles, he should come*
> *And wind me in his hellish arms, and fix*
> *His eyes on mine, and drag me down, down, down!*

Beatrice may voice an agnosticism closer to Shelley's beliefs at
this stage of his life than the atheism of his youth. One of the
few substantial differences between Shelley's sources and the play
is bound up with questions of religious or theological conviction.
The opening lines of Mary's transcription of the Italian manuscript begin with Francesco's "sodomy and Atheism." But the
Francesco of Shelley's play does not share the ideological position that Shelley espoused so vociferously. It may be that he chose
to change Francesco's convictions in order to discourage possible comparisons between Francesco and the playwright. Shelley
chose to render him the ultimate religious hypocrite in order to
demonstrate that "the most atrocious villain may be rigidly de-
vout." He was fascinated by the coexistence of profound faith,
and the endless repetition of acts which arouse guilt. He explains
this by dramatizing the relative positions of Catholics and Prot-

estants, a device which obscures his own ambiguous religious beliefs:

> To a Protestant apprehension there will appear something un-
> natural in the earnest and perpetual sentiment of the relations
> between God and man that pervade the tragedy of the Cenci. It
> will especially be startled at the combination of an undoubting
> persuasion of the truth of the popular religion with a cool and
> determined perseverance in enormous guilt.

For all his avowed atheism, Shelley was a convinced pacifist of a strikingly Christian kind. He believed it the duty of the victim of even "the most enormous injuries" to seek to convert "the injurer from his dark passions by peace and love." "Revenge and retaliation" were, he claimed, "pernicious mistakes." "If Beatrice," he wrote, "had thought in this manner she would have been wiser and better; but she would never have been a tragic character."

In Shelley's play there is no one to teach Beatrice "peace and love." The absolute control of mind and body, of the religiously hypocritical society in which she finds herself, successfully corrupts her. The force of the play becomes more political than moral as she comes to be seen as the tragic victim of a corrupt and corrupting society. What the play ultimately criticizes are the repressive forces which stifle individual conscience.

By August Shelley had finished the manuscript and sent it off to England. Mary was still struggling in vain to free herself from the depression that had pulled her so low. While Shelley waited for news of his *Cenci*, he was confident that it would soon be performed and that he would soon win the wide critical acclaim for which he longed. He wanted a Miss O'Neil to play Beatrice and admitted that he would be unable to witness her performance because the experience would quite overwhelm him: "It would tear my nerves to pieces."

In his Preface to *The Cenci* Shelley spelled out what he thought most compelling about Beatrice's story. He was experienced enough to guard against possible misunderstanding: he emphasized the moral complexity of Beatrice's story and its power to provoke the reader, or spectator, into seeking some kind of moral resolution:

> It is in the restless anatomizing casuistry with which men seek the justification of Beatrice, yet feel that she has done what needs justification; it is in the superstitious horror with which they contemplate alike her wrongs and their revenge; that the dramatic character of what she did and suffered, consists.

When Covent Garden rejected the manuscript of *The Cenci*, and Drury Lane likewise, Shelley was taken aback. And when it was finally published in a small edition, he was dismayed by its reception. One critic praised Shelley's dramatic powers while deploring "the wickedness of their perversion," and another claimed that incest was not the stuff of tragedy but rather "a morbid and maniac sin of rare and doubtful occurrence." "Of all the abominations," wrote one of Shelley's most vociferous critics, "that intellectual perversion, and poetical atheism have produced in our times, this tragedy appears to us to be the most abominable." His old friend Southey drew harsh parallels between Shelley's life and the events of the Cenci story:

> You have reasoned yourself into a state of mind so pernicious that your character, with your domestic arrangements, as you

might term it, might furnish the subject for the drama more instructive, and scarcely less painful, than the detestable story of the Cenci, and this has proceeded directly from your principles . . . . It is the Atheists Tragedy.

One of the least critical reviewers wrote, "This tragedy is the production of a man of great genius, and of a most unhappy moral constitution" (*London Magazine*, May 9, 1820). Shelley considered that the review had been written with "great malignity," a poignant indication that Shelley cared much more about his reputation as a man than simply as a writer, but he now knew that a triumphant return to England would never take place.

That spring of 1822 Shelley had to break the news of little Allegra's death to Claire. Byron had had her incarcerated in a convent at the age of four and just over a year later she died, possibly of consumption.

By the summer Shelley's periods of despair had become a continuum. He wrote to an old friend requesting a lethal dose of "Prussic Acid, or essential oil of bitter almonds." He insisted that he was not preoccupied by thoughts of suicide, "but I confess it would be a comfort to me to hold in my possession that golden key to the chamber of perpetual rest." One of his last poems, "To the Moon," conveys a bittersweet mood of alienation from others, and fatigue at the world:

> *Art thou pale from weariness*
> *Of climbing heaven, and gazing on the earth,*
> *Wandering companionless*
> *Among the stars that have a different birth,—*
> *And ever changing, like a joyless eye*
> *That finds no object worthy of its constancy?*

Shelley had been missing for ten days before his body, together
with those of his two companions and the boat boy, was washed
up on the beach between Massa and Viareggio, at the end of
July 1822. He had not yet turned thirty. His exposed flesh had
been eaten away, but he was easily identified by his distinctive
clothing: nankeen trousers, white silk socks and boots. In his
breast pocket, and doubled back as though stowed away in
haste, was a volume of Keats's poems. His yacht, the *Don Juan*,
had gone down in a summer storm in the Gulf of Spezzia. The
boat had been under full sail as it sank. Not long before, an
Italian captain had bravely gone alongside amid tremendous
waves to warn Shelley, the reckless skipper, to abandon ship
or at the very least to persuade him to reef the sails. In response
a figure had been seen attending to the rigging but another man
seized him by the arm, as though in anger, and pulled him away
from the sails. Shelley had diced with death, and he took three
others with him.

When news of his drowning reached England, his religious
iconoclasm dominated discussion. An article in the *Courier*
began: "Shelley, the writer of some infidel poetry has been drowned;
now he knows whether there is a God or no." Mary and Claire
mourned. They were aged twenty-five and twenty-four.

A few days after Shelley's death, Byron sent a letter to the
writer Tom Moore in London, a friend they had shared: "there
is thus another man gone [,] about whom the world was ill-
naturedly, and ignorantly, and brutally mistaken." Shelley had
questioned his class, abandoned its values and behaved according to his own ideas and convictions. Beatrice's life and death
moved him to explore an intractable—and true—story. And
Beatrice's final speech echoes Byron's words. He spoke of un-
kindness, stupidity, and above all injustice in the world's treat-

ment. Beatrice, in the closing scene of Shelley's play, speaks to her younger brother, the only Cenci to have been spared execution:

> *One thing more my child,*
> *For thine own sake be constant to the love*
> *Thou bearest us; and to the faith that I,*
> *Though wrapped in a strange cloud of crime and*
> *shame,*
> *Lived ever holy and unstained . . .*

Shelley, like his ambiguous, tragic character Beatrice, lost all faith in the world's judgment. The same "cloud of crime and shame" hovered over his name: his commitment to a dramatic resurrection of the martyred Beatrice had led inexorably to his own critical martyrdom.

—◠◡◠—

CHAPTER 4

Melville: Ambiguous Confession

There is an unseemly exposure of the mind, as well
as the body.

WILLIAM HAZLITT

Herman Melville, like Shelley, had his own copy of the portrait
of Beatrice and he gave it an important role in his novel, *Pierre*.
The portrait's presence goes way beyond the merely decorative:
it is the catalyst for a tragic moment of recognition that a sexual
relationship between the hero and heroine would be incestuous.
Melville's readership recognized in *Pierre* an author they abhorred, or feared, maybe both: he misjudged the reception of the
book as spectacularly as Shelley misjudged the reception of his
Cenci play. *Pierre* was Melville's last novel.

   In 1852, Melville, then a little-known American author, wrote
to his English publisher, John Murray, convinced that he had
embarked on a truly popular novel. His tone is strikingly reminis-

cent of Shelley's description of the material of his Cenci play: "here now we have a *new book* . . . possessing unquestionable novelty, as regards my former ones, treating of utterly new scenes and characters;—and, as I believe, very much more calculated for popularity than anything you have yet published of mine—being a regular romance, with a mysterious plot to it, and stirring passions at work." Melville insisted that whatever the reception of earlier works, *Pierre* would finally satisfy his publisher's financial worries. Like Shelley he desperately wanted to believe that with this latest work he would gain the recognition and acceptance for which he yearned. At the climax of *Pierre*, the characters of the novel are unexpectedly faced with a reproduction of the Beatrice Cenci portrait which focuses in dramatic fashion the threads of incest, innocence, guilt and murder that lie at the heart of her story—and that of the novel's hero. Parallels between Pierre and Melville are unmistakable and although the novel is set in Melville's own time and place, there are also some bizarre parallels between the Cenci story and Melville's experience. Shelley had set out to dramatize a late Renaissance story but revealed a good deal of himself in the telling. Melville, on the other hand, embarked on an autobiographical novel set in his own period but the events of Beatrice's life and its tragic darkness are the stuff of both her life and the author-protagonist's.

John Murray's father was Byron's publisher and Shelley had hoped that Murray might take him on, but he was turned down. Murray *fils* also rejected Mary Shelley's *Frankenstein* and he was far from convinced about Melville and was growing weary of losing money on his novels. These writers' lives and preoccupations made them high-risk propositions.

Pierre was a hopeless last-ditch attempt on Melville's part. It charts the intractable decline of an author's life and work and it exposes Melville's sexual inhibitions and frustrations. The novel was written in a state of exhaustion in the wake of *Moby-Dick* (first published in 1851 as *The Whale*), and when it was finished Melville withdrew from society and fell into a long, isolating depression. Then in 1856 he rallied, and set out on another journey not to the South Seas which he knew so well, but east, to the Middle East and Europe. But even the scale and mysteries of the Pyramids triggered no emotion equal to that stirred by the mighty whale which had inspired *Moby-Dick*. He returned via Italy. There he saw the original of the Beatrice Cenci portrait that he had written into *Pierre*, and he jotted some notes about Beatrice's city:

> Rome fell flat on me. Oppressing flat . . . Tiber a ditch, yellow as saffron. The whole landscape nothing independent of association. St Peter's looks small from tower of Capitol . . . Dome not so wonderful as St Sophia's . . . Went to Baths of Caracalla. Wonderful. Massive. Ruins form as it were natural bridges of thousands of arches. There are glades and thickets among the ruins—high up.—Thought of Shelley. Truly, he got his inspiration here. Corresponded with his drama and mind. Still majesty and desolate grandeur.

Melville's problems with organized religion, with all forms of authority, with punishment, with power, with the forbidden (particularly in sexual relations), his quest to explore the landscape of the mind through an exploration of the real world, the weight of some mysterious guilt, the anguish of regret, all these are the stuff of his fiction. The same preoccupations resurface in the poetry he wrote in his last years. Above all he recognized that much of experience can only be half-glimpsed and so remains "unspeakable." Just before his death, in 1891, he published *Timoleon* at his own expense in an edition of just twenty-five copies. Many of the poems express his vision of the mysteries and darkness of the human consciousness. "In a Church in Padua" likens the religious building to some piece of massive underwater apparatus. The lines confuse land and sea, what is visible and what is hidden, and they ultimately point to the impossibility of being washed clean of guilt:

> *Dread diving-bell! In thee inured*
> *What hollows the priest must sound,*
> *Descending into consciences*
> *Where more is hid than found.*

In Rome, Melville saw the match between the majesty and grandeur of the city and the drama of Shelley's mind. The Englishman's excitable behavior as a child, his lurid fantasies, his sadism, his fascination with fear, all pointed toward the man he would become: the appeal of the Cenci story to him was fully understandable. Melville, however, was a very different child born into a very different society. Until the age of thirteen there was nothing much to distinguish him from thousands of other comfortably off American children except perhaps a tendency to ill health and hypochondria, which turned him into a reader. But when family tragedy struck, his life, and perspective on life, changed dramatically.

He was born in New York on August 1, 1819, the year that Shelley wrote his Cenci play. Change was coming and America was opening up. During the year of his birth, the Erie Canal was dug, an inroad into America that largely explains why New York pulled ahead of other ports. Although Melville was born in New

York, he often stayed in the country with his numerous landed relatives: at Gansevoort, near Saratoga, with his Grandfather Peter and Uncle Herman, at Albany with Uncle Peter and over to the east, in the Berkshires, on Uncle Thomas Melville's farm. The Gansevoorts, on his mother's side, were of Dutch origin, a large and established American family. On his father Allan's side there were titled Scottish cousins still living at the original Melville seat at Carnbee, in Fife, whom Allan had visited a year or so before Herman's birth. All in all it was a wealthy and apparently secure background. The crafts mattered more than the arts but food and physical exercise mattered most, and the joys of Herman's childhood were largely those of the outdoors: rivers and boating, woods and forests, horses and companions. His future looked confidently charted.

Herman's father, Allan, was an importer of French goods and he was careful in his business and strict with his family. He was something of a pedant and married a woman who agreed with him about almost everything. Hers was also a wealthy and re-spected family, so he had taken very few chances. Maria's life was dominated by an obsessive sense of pride: everything and everyone had to be correct, and as a mark of the family's status things tended to be ridiculously overformal. Religious observance and regular dinner parties shaped the week with a "good" pew as important as the right guests. But everything was invested in the material; a good deal remained unspoken and repressed.

Herman was the third child, following an older brother and sister. His mother went on to have five more children and he may well have longed for more maternal affection: in *Pierre* his hero is an only child living alone with a fine-looking widowed mother. When Herman was five the Melvilles moved two miles uptown to Bleecker Street, which was then close to open country. He was a sickly child and in 1826 was sent to stay with the Gansevoorts at Albany in the hope of building him up. His father described him in a letter to his wife's relatives as "backward in speech and somewhat slow in comprehension," but, he continued, "as far as he understands men and things" he is "both solid and profound and of a docile and amiable disposition." A year later he was sent to the Broadhall, near Pittsfield, to stay with Uncle Thomas. These two families—the Gansevoorts and Uncle Thomas Melville and his wife—introduced Herman to different worlds. The Albany family were country people and the food was rich and plentiful. Uncle Thomas had married a French woman and when the two of them spoke in this mysterious language, Herman was seduced by its mellifluous sounds and excited by the secrets that it expressed. Perhaps this is where his longing for adventure began—in language—and real voyages, when they came, would lead him back to words and their power to travel beyond the known. Allan had traveled extensively and Herman was intrigued and proud, even estimating the miles his father had covered: "by land 24,425 miles, by water 48,460 miles."

Stimulated by the books of prints and drawings that Allan had brought back from his travels, Herman dreamed of faraway cities: London, Paris, Rome, cities that had been built before Columbus had even sailed to America. He was sustained more and more by a life of the imagination just as the reality of his father's life was about to change dramatically. Allan's business went from bad to worse and a rapid slide landed him in bankruptcy: he became mentally ill and died in 1832, to the horror and deep shame of the family. Herman was thirteen, an age when things can go one of two ways: the dead can be condemned or deified. Herman had not yet recognized his father's humanity. He was young enough still to regard him as unimpeachable: death exaggerated his greatness. His mother, on the other hand, showed her all-too-human frailty and looked to Herman for comfort. His older brother Gansevoort was expected to do his best to provide for them economically; Melville was expected to provide emotional support and his relationship with his mother became one of stifling mutual dependence. There was some help from the extended family but not enough. Herman saw that his cousins' lives would now be very different from his own, and that adult life would bring still greater differences: he began to rail against the injustice of fate.

At the age of fifteen Herman entered the dull world of adult employment: his Uncle Peter was one of the trustees of the New York State Bank and strings were pulled to get him a job there as a clerk. His ambitions of travel, of seeing something of the world like his father, or of marrying a Frenchwoman like his uncle, or of rising to the rank of general in the army like his Grandfather Peter, seemed an impossible vision. He was desperate to break free from his immediate family and in the autumn of 1835 left the city to work in the hayfields near Pittsfield. When the harvest was in he taught the local children who were no longer needed in the fields. He also attended the Albany Classical School and on September 1, 1836 returned to the Albany Academy until March 1, 1837. It was a patchy education although books and knowledge and particularly the fascination of civilizations more ancient and complex than America had taken hold of Herman as a child. He decided to head for Europe and to educate himself along the way. What he did not foresee was that he would learn less about the outside world in the sense his father might have construed it, and a great deal more about life—in its coldest and darkest regions.

In 1838 Melville signed up to work his passage on the *St. Lawrence*. The chaste society of Lansingburgh was rather different from the society he joined and his ambiguous social position made matters worse. The captain could disingenuously assume that his family would provide him with money to make the voyage comfortable, and so withheld his pay. The family's shabby pride was such that they did nothing to disabuse the captain. Herman had little experience of the kind of men he was now working with, an intimacy that is never greater than at sea. His escape from the dreariness of life at home was replaced by a brutal existence with uncertainties lying in store on foreign shores.

The captain seemed affable and decent enough on land but became vicious and wholly unprincipled at sea, and Jackson, the first mate, a monstrous figure more depraved, more inhumane, than anyone Herman had ever previously encountered or even read about, took control whenever the captain turned his back. The rhythm of most of the crew's lives—work, drunkenness, prostitutes—came as a shock to a nineteen-year-old member of the Juvenile Total Abstinence Association and the Anti-Smoking Society: early on he witnessed a crew member wracked by delirium tremens throwing himself overboard. The work was hard and strange, the names of every rope and knot unheard of before. As he cleaned out the animals aboard, greasing the pulley mechanisms, the smells turned his stomach. "Miserable dog's life is this of the sea: commanded like a slave and set to work like an ass: vulgar and brutal men lording it over me, as if I were an African in Alabama." He was learning a great deal about real people and the philosopher, the poet, the visionary within him, was simultaneously receiving vital stimulus. Later other words came too:

> I was first conscious of a wonderful thing in me, that responded
> to all the wild commotion of the outer world, and went reeling
> on and on with the planets in their orbits, and was lost in one
> delirious throb at the center of the All. A wild bubbling and
> bursting at my heart, as if a hidden spring gushed out there.

For all the powerlessness of his position Melville was not to be
broken. What he witnessed at sea were the extremes of human
experience lived out in a microsociety. He was aware of the in-
justices and the sadism of the men over him and saw that the
civilized airs of the captain stood for a wider class hypocrisy
which he would later write into his fiction.

Liverpool was another rude awakening, a far cry from the
settled civilization of the European ports he had seen pictures of
in his father's books. The ship docked early in the morning on
July 4 and, like the narrator of one of his later books, *Redburn*,
Melville took "a vast deal of lonely satisfaction in wandering
about, up and down, among out-of-the-way streets and alleys."
The beggars, the drunks, the prostitutes, the thieves, the poverty
shocked him, and the papers were full of stabbings and fatal
drunken accidents. Some of these he noted in his journal: particularly bizarre was the account of an infanticide, at Carlton,
near Worksop. The story began with a double incest: a brutal
father, Thomas Pye, had impregnated his two daughters. When
one later delivered a baby, her sister killed it on the other's behalf. Beatrice's murderous resolve, when he learned of it, was
very believable and Francesco Cenci might be an amalgam of the
incestuous Thomas Pye, the sadistic Jackson and the shamelessly
hypocritical captain of the *St. Lawrence*.

When the six weeks were up Herman had seen life in the raw
and the shock went deep. Intellectually he understood much

better what it was to be a man in society, an individual swept up in the rapidly transforming urban conglomerations, the human whirlpools of the mid-nineteenth century. In Liverpool he had met men and women making their way to America—from Ireland mostly, but also from Scandinavia, Germany and other European countries. In the Brunswick Dock, one of numerous new docks that lined the Liverpool riverfront, he counted the black steamers and noted: "Here you see vast quantities of produce, imported from starving Ireland."

On his return he taught again at Greenbush (now New Albany). He read widely: the English classics, Shakespeare and Milton, and the Romantics, including Byron and Shelley; he read Scott and Coleridge. But he also read his contemporaries. The publication of two works of fiction was of particular significance to his ideas about the direction in which his life might move. In 1839, in the magazine *The Knickerbocker*, a story appeared by Jeremiah N. Reynolds. It told of the taking of a great white sperm whale in the Pacific. The whale was called Mocha Dick. The following year an autobiographical novel by Richard Henry Dana Jr.—*Two Years Before the Mast*—was published. Years later Melville wrote to Dana, describing the deep impression the book had made:

Those strange, congenial feelings with which after my first voyage, I for the first time read "Two Years Before the Mast," and while so engaged was, as it were, tied and welded to you by a sort of Siamese link of affectionate sympathy.

In the year that Dana's account was published, at the end of December 1840, Melville made his way to New Bedford, in New England, the center of the whaling industry. Here Melville joined the crew of the *Acushnet*; the master, Valentine Pease, was a harsh skipper. The ship stopped at Rio de Janeiro, the Galapagos Islands, and probably on the Peruvian coast. He was in tough company and later he would learn of the fates of his shipmates: suicide, murder and death from syphilis. But Melville also experienced the joys of leaving behind an icy New England winter for the brightness and color of the Pacific. And he was mesmerized by the world of whaling: from the excitement of the chase, the fleshy excesses of cutting up whale blubber to the delicate expert crafts associated with whalebone: the carving and whittling of ornaments and charms. On deck, in moments of solitude, he contemplated the vastness and mysteriousness of space. Whaling, the purpose of being there, the pursuit and killing of that vast and powerful creature, became an intimate and inalienable part of the philosophical and spiritual experience that he underwent: "If, at my death, my executors, or more properly my creditors find any precious MSS. in my desk, then I prospectively ascribe all the honor and the glory to whaling; for a whale ship was my Yale College and my Harvard." Crews lived in cramped quarters with no privacy and forced together for months on end they got to know one another well. Stories were exchanged, usually describing gory disasters, near-death experiences, mutinies or lunatic skippers. The horrors of late Renaissance Italy, when he learned of them, were already familiar.

Melville endured a year and a half aboard the *Acushnet* and then considered his position. Whale trips sometimes lasted as long as five years. When they reached Nukahiva Island naked women swam aboard in the port and offered themselves to the sailors. The scenes may have startled Melville but they beguiled him too, as his novel *Typee* shows.

The landscape about the port had a mesmerizing pull: densely wooded valleys and dramatic mountains behind. Melville and his close friend Toby Green were both struck by the extraordinary beauty of the place, yet both knew that in the hinterland the natives were reputed to be cannibals. In Green's account of their adventures he evokes a youthfully feminine space: the surface of the water is soft and smooth, the entrance tantalizingly concealed, the soft growth luxuriant. Melville's description, by contrast, dwells on an aggressive penetration of what lay before them. His words suggest that possession, whether personal or imperialistic, involves aggression:

> Towards noon we drew abreast the entrance to the harbor, and at last we slowly swept by the intervening promontory, and entered the bay of Nukahiva. No description can do justice to its beauty; but that beauty was lost to me then, and I saw nothing but the tri-colored flag of France trailing over the stern of six vessels, whose black hulls and bristling broadsides proclaimed their warlike character. . . . The whole group of islands had just been taken possession of by Rear Admiral Du Petit Thouars, in the name of the invincible French nation.

He saw the phallic weaponry "bristling" from the sides of the ships and the flags as symbols of domination and possession. Unlike Greene's romanticized description, Melville's shows his reluctance to separate beauty from the bleak reality of its social, political and historical context. His reading of the landscape is like Shelley's vision of the half-hidden realities among the ruins of Renaissance Rome. For both, sex and power operate privately— and reveal themselves in public and political manifestations.

Melville and Toby decided to escape; they were both twenty-one. On July 9, when they were ashore with other crew members, and sheltering from torrential rain in a canoe house, an opportunity presented itself. The first night was hard as the temporary shelter that they tried to erect was quickly torn apart. The following day they struggled on through dense terrain and one of Melville's legs began to cause him unbearable pain. On the evening of July 13, they looked down the final steep descent to their chosen valley. They "stood on the brink of a precipice over which the dark stream bounded in one final leap of full 300 feet."

Despite Toby's companionship, Melville felt a sense of utter desolation:

> During the whole of this night the continual roaring of the cataract—the dismal moaning of the gale through the trees—the pattering of the rain, and the profound darkness, affected my spirits to a degree which nothing had ever before produced.

The sense of foreboding written into this part of Melville's story is bound up with what followed. When, more dead than alive, they finally made their way down to the village, they were taken in to one of the largest bamboo buildings where they were inspected by successive groups of natives, filing through in a remarkably orderly way: "Was it possible that, after all our vicissitudes, we were really in the terrible valley of Typee, and at the mercy of its inmates, a fierce and unrelenting tribe of savages?" The name "Typee" means "eater of men." By now Melville's leg had become seriously infected and on July 27 or thereabouts Toby left in the hope of finding medical help. He did not return. Melville was left alone, worried about Toby's safety—and his own. He had no way of knowing whether the natives' treatment of him was proof of extraordinary hospitality and courtesy, or whether he was being fattened for some ritualistic slaughter come the appropriate religious season. He had ample time to observe the calm and settled life of his carer-captors:

> There were none of those thousand sources of irritation that the ingenuity of civilised man has created to mar his own felicity. There were no foreclosures of mortgages, no protested notes, no bills payable, no debts of honor in Typee; no unreasonable tailors and shoemakers, perversely bent on being paid; no duns of any description; no assaults and battery attorneys to foment discord, backing their clients into a quarrel, and then knocking their heads together; no poor relations everlastingly occupying the spare bed-chamber and diminishing the elbow-room at the family table; no destitute widows with their children starving on the cold charities of the world; no debtors' prisons; no proud and hard-hearted nabobs in Typee; or, to sum up all in one word—No Money! That "root of all evil" was not to be found in the valley.

"Civilization," whether that of the ancient cities of Europe or a rapidly modernizing America, revealed itself in a very different light when compared with the ways of the Typee. Accompanying the differences in their material and social life were psychological differences which were of particular interest to Melville: "Blue devils, hypochondria, and doleful dumps all went and hid themselves among the nooks and crannies of the rocks."

By August 9 Melville was aboard the *Lucy Anne*, an Australian whaler, having been exchanged with the Typee for what he described as "suitable items of traffic." The precise nature of his experience during the preceding fortnight when he was alone with the Typee is difficult to ascertain with any degree of certainty: *Typee* is, after all, a fictionalized account. But there is no ambiguity about Melville's views of what was wrong with mid-nineteenth-century America: the growing materialism, conformism, divisions between rich and poor in the cities, the anonymity of urban life, the narrow doctrines and religions. All the unnecessary complexities and the hypocrisy of so-called civilization struck him forcibly while the leisure, the lack of physical inhibition, the relaxed sexual ways: all this seemed like an Eden. He was particularly drawn to Fayaway and he bathed with her and her friends in the river, or paddled idly upstream in a canoe with her. Whether Melville was able to overcome his inhibitions seems unlikely and in *Moby-Dick* he has Koheleth advise, "Be not righteous overmuch: why should thou destroy thyself?" For Melville sex was a hopeless double-bind: a choice between guilt and shame or frustration and misery.

By 1843, after a long period of wandering in Polynesia, Melville was on his way home, aboard the U.S. frigate *United States*, and he quickly fell in with the naval routine. The crew was large and the ship was well run, leaving him spare time to meditate on the extraordinariness of his months in the Polynesian islands. But there were aspects of the ship's discipline which he abhorred: flogging, in particular. The sadistic pleasure enjoyed by the floggers, and the sexual satisfaction that some of them obviously experienced, filled him with disgust. He would recognize similarly arbitrary punishment in the summary and brutal torture masquerading as the meting out of justice in the Cenci tale.

Having been starved of books for many months, Melville was much cheered by the ship's impressive library. He measured his own experience against that of other travelers: Walpole's *Letters*, *The Jew of Malta*, *Volpone*; Morgan's *History of Algiers*, Knox's *Captivity in Ceylon*. He read Elizabethan drama and seventeenth-century travel writings. But while his reading nourished his individual perspective on life's big questions, the institutional context within which he was living punished his independent spirit. He was deeply disturbed by an edict requiring all seamen to shave their beards, seeing that the obligatory removal of hair, or the act forcefully of removing it, was humiliating. Melville's indignant protests were crushed.

Melville had left America as a young man of little experience. His ideological commitments—insofar as he had properly allied himself—were largely those of his family or immediate social milieu. His experiences whaling, traveling the South Sea Islands, and on a U.S. naval frigate had been varied and formative. His body had changed shape—he was muscular, tanned, toughened, but his mind had not yet had sufficient space to reassemble his diverse experiences into any kind of shape.

He arrived in Boston in 1844, but his job opportunities remained as limited as before. Although American society was beginning to modernize, to mechanize, to loosen socially, to question certain ideologies and institutions more bravely than before, none of this meant that Melville, with his limited formal education, could assume any kind of role of responsibility or creativity. Writing about his adventures was a practical solution: it would fill up his days and, with any luck, provide some sort of financial return.

Melville moved to Manhattan during the winter of 1844–5 and embarked on *Four Months in the Marquesas among the Typees*, published in America under the more eye-catching title,

Typee: A Peep at Polynesian Life. He had actually only spent a
couple of weeks, as opposed to "four months," among the Typee
and this might lead one to question how truthful his account is.
Melville's brother Gansevoort was working in London as a minor
diplomat and he had secured an advance from John Murray on
Melville's behalf. When it was published, in 1846, missionaries
denounced the truth of Melville's story. His account of the detri-
mental effects of missionary penetration caused outrage, and the
dishonesty of what the missionary bodies had to say in their defense pushed Melville into a more vociferously anti-Christian position than would otherwise have been his instinct. He had seen
the collusion of missionary and colonial forces and bemoaned the
destruction of indigenous, "purer" ways. His problems with Christianity were bound up with a number of things: the arrogant superiority of so many who purported to be its followers, the oppressive
power of religious institutions, the self-righteous certainty—and
equally hypocrisy—that marked many Christian individuals and
organizations. But neither was Melville an out-and-out Atheist.

Typee does not propose a simple argument for the superiority of the so-called primitive over the so-called "civilized" but
invites a questioning of the nature of human happiness, the purpose of individual and collective life, the appropriateness of
committed sexual relationships, the nature of human needs in
terms of the material, and the spiritual. Amid the furor that
followed his publication, Melville felt somewhat at sea. He was
taken aback by the extreme response to his descriptions of the
free sexual lives of the Polynesians, and although he was amazed
and delighted to be a published author he found the publicity
disturbing. He also had to contend with his brother's decline:
Gansevoort had been suffering from severe depression. On
April 4, 1846, in one of his last letters home, he wrote:

> The climate is too damp and moist for me. I sometimes fear that
> I am gradually breaking up. If it be so—God's will be done. I
> have already seen as much of London society as I care to see. It
> is becoming a toil to me to make the exertion necessary to dress
> to go out. . . . My circulation is languid. My brain is dull. I nei-
> ther seek to win pleasure or avoid pain. A degree of insensibil-
> ity has been stealing over me, and now seems permanently
> established, which to my understanding is more akin to death
> than life. Selfishly speaking I never valued life much—it were im-
> possible to value it less than I do now.

At no point in his correspondence did he mention any physical
disease. His depression seems inexorably to have worsened. On
May 12, he died; he may well have committed suicide. There
had been some gossip among political acquaints in London about "mental derangement." Gansevoort's death hit the
family hard and prompted two strong feelings in Melville—guilt
that he had not done more for his brother and anxiety for the
shape of his own life.

By the time he came to write *Mardi*, his third book, Melville
was married. He had made his commitment to Elizabeth Shaw,
the daughter of Judge Shaw, and they had married in August
1847. It was a perfectly reasonable marriage, but the people of
Mardi, its heroine in particular, suggest that the domesticity and
repression of mid-nineteenth-century middle-class American life
was all too much of a compromise. *Mardi* is a fantasy in which
the hero's commitment is to a goddess-like figure more like an
exalted Fayaway (the beautiful young woman he had met among
the Typee) than the daughter of a respectable man of law. And
in *Pierre* Elizabeth seems to be the origin for the steady but un-
exciting Lucy, rather than for the seductive Isabel.

In February 1849 his son, Malcolm, was born, bringing disruption to his writing life at home and exacerbating his financial anxieties. He had to write quickly and he had to write for a decent-sized audience. He fell back on autobiography and produced *Redburn*, an account—with extensive reflections—of his first eighteen years. Melville was not impressed with his own work: "When a poor devil writes with duns all around him, and looking over the back of the chair, and perching on his pen, and dancing in his inkstand—like the Devils about St. Anthony—what can you expect of that poor devil? What but a beggarly Redburn?"

White-Jacket, which Melville embarked on while *Redburn* went to press, is a more mature work, but also a more straightforward one. By now Melville was thirty and, with three books behind him, knew how to make an account of life on a man-of-war compelling, vivid, a subject for debate. *White-Jacket* is full of criticism, but this is done with a satirical lightness of touch.

Melville had produced two books in the space of a few months. Feeling that he needed a break, in October 1849 he set off for London in order to negotiate with John Murray. Away from home he was able to brood undisturbed about his next book and he considered something more substantial, more all-embracing, more profitable, a kind of sum of all that had come before.

By the spring of 1850 any doubts that Melville may have had about the difficulty of writing with integrity *and* finding a decent-sized audience were dispelled by the laudatory reception of Nathaniel Hawthorne's *The Scarlet Letter*. And Melville's response to reading it was to dare to conceive of *Moby-Dick*—and to long to know the author of *The Scarlet Letter*.

During the summer of 1850 Melville had his way, meeting Hawthorne at a publisher's gathering in Stockbridge. The circumstances might have been described by Melville during one of his unrestrained romantic moods; the party climbed a local mountain, were caught in a summer storm and Melville and Hawthorne, sheltering together under an outcrop of rock, were encouraged, as is traditional, to exchange confidences that they might otherwise have uttered only after years of more cautious conversation. Melville's feelings of identification with Hawthorne could not have been stronger, as his extraordinary language demonstrates:

> Whence came you, Hawthorne? By what right do you drink from my flagon of life? And when I put it to my lips—lo, they are yours and not mine. I feel that the Godhead is broken up like the bread at the Supper, and that we are the pieces. Hence this infinite fraternity of feeling.

The relationship that developed meant more to Melville than to Hawthorne although the Hawthorne children were devoted to him, and to his dog who was large enough for the children to ride. Sophia Hawthorne was nevertheless much struck by Melville, and her description of him is knowing:

> A man with a true warm heart and soul and an intellect—with life to his finger-tips—earnest, sincere and reverent, very tender and *modest*—And I am not quite sure that he is not a very great man—but I have not quite decided upon my own opinion—I should say, I am not quite sure that I *do not think him* a very great man—for my opinion is of course as far as possible from settling the matter. He has very keen perceptive power, but what astonishes me is that his eyes are not large and deep [as her husband's were]—He seems to see every thing very accurately and how he can do so with his small eyes, I cannot tell. . . . His

nose is straight and rather handsome, his mouth expressive of sensibility and emotion—He is tall and erect with an air free, brave and manly. When conversing he is full of gesture and force, and loses himself in his subject—There is no grace or polish— once in a while his animation gives way to a singularly quiet expression out of these eyes, to which I have objected—an in- drawn, dim look, but which at the same time makes you feel— that he is at that instant taking deepest note of what is before him—It is a strange, lazy glance, but with a power in it quite unique—It does not seem to penetrate through you, but to take you into himself. I saw him look at Una so yesterday several times.

Among the children Una was Melville's favorite. She was six at the time Sophia was writing, and Melville was entranced by her look of vulnerability oddly combined with precocious self-assur- ance. She joined the ranks of Melville's "forbidden" women: his mother, Fayaway, Una.

The relationship which Melville longed to establish with Hawthorne was not going to mature, although Melville had plumbed depths of human experience and Hawthorne recognized his bravery. While Hawthorne had journeyed into not dissimi- lar regions in his writings, he was a writer, not a talker. Melville longed for an intimate friendship in which no subject would be taboo. Hawthorne's writings dared to embrace questions which mattered desperately to Melville: questions of sexual anxiety and sexual subversiveness. What Melville wanted was a reciprocal relationship in which each could assume the role of both psy- choanalyst and patient. On June 29, 1851, Melville wrote: "Let us speak though we show all our faults and weaknesses, for it is a sign of strength to be weak, to know it, and out with it, not in a set way and ostentatiously, but incidentally, and without pre-meditation." Hawthorne did not, or could not, live up to Melville's hopes. It may be that his relationship with Sophia served him much better than Melville's with Elizabeth. Sophia's description of her husband's "great, genial, comprehending silences" suggests that although he was sometimes aloof, they were contented. He may also have feared exposing himself to the knowing Melville.

Melville journeyed on alone through the Dantesque labyrinth of *Moby-Dick* "whose waters of deep woe are brackish with the salt of human tears." The story of *Moby-Dick* is a parable on the mysteries of evil, a force that is at once part of the inner reality of our humanity and out there in the elemental world to be visited, randomly, on us. The teller of the tale, Ishmael, is one of the assorted crew members who set sail under Captain Ahab's command. When the captain first emerges from his cabin Ishmael is appalled: "Reality outran apprehension . . . He looked like a man cut away from the stake, when the fire has overrunningly wasted all the limbs without consuming them." A whale has snapped off one of Ahab's legs and his stump is made from whale ivory. "Ever since that almost fatal encounter, Ahab had cherished a wild vindictiveness against the whale . . . in his frantic morbidness he at last came to identify with him, not only all his bodily woes, but all his intellectual and spiritual exasperations." Ahab assembles his crew and nails a gold piece to the mainmast: "Who ever of ye raises me a white-headed whale with a wrinkled brow and a crooked jaw . . . shall have this gold ounce." Only one crew member, Starbuck, a quiet, serious, pious man, speaks out against the captain's purpose: "Vengeance on a dumb brute . . . that simply smote thee from blindest instinct! Madness! To be enraged with a dumb thing, Captain Ahab, seems blasphemous."

Ahab answers, "All visible objects, man, are but as pasteboard masks. But in each event—in the living act, the undoubted deed—there, some unknown but still reasoning thing puts forth the mouldings of its features from behind the unreasoning mask." Ishmael, the teller of the tale, pledges his commitment to the mad Ahab.

He is a heroic figure and his end is tragic: evil has taken hold of him and he battles against evil with the same physical force that all but destroyed him years earlier. And his overwhelming desire to satisfy his own violent feelings toward Moby-Dick leads to the death of the entire crew. There are parallels with Beatrice Cenci and her all-consuming desire to be rid of her father. Like the maniac captain she is overtaken and consumed by violence and her actions lead to other deaths including her own. Ahab's sense of purpose, his unrelenting quest for revenge, his fearless drive—all these catch the imagination of those around him. Nor would Ahab have come so close to achieving his goal without the physical support of his crew and, more crucially, their love.

Moby-Dick is an exhausting book and the story of Melville's collapse on completing it is equally dramatic. The physical, emotional and above all psychological effort of writing had been extreme. He may have been planning it for some time but the actual writing began only in the summer of 1850; a year later it was finished. When the reviews came out he had no reserves left. Melville knew that *Moby-Dick* was a great book. He may have expected that its reception would fall short of the acclaim which he privately thought it worth, but he was unprepared for the venom of some of his reviewers. *The Athenaeum* hoped that Melville's "horrors and his heroics are flung aside by the general reader as so much trash." Still more personal and cruel were the words of the *New Monthly Magazine* which described the language of the novel as "maniacal,—mad as a March hare— moving, gibbering, screaming, like an incurable Bedlamite, reckless of keeper or strait-waistcoat." Melville's father and brother had both died of mental illness and *Moby-Dick* was repeatedly described as the work of a madman. In his worn state he embarked on another story which explores the anguished depths of his own secret being, and tells of an author's self-destructive martyrdom and it is here that Beatrice Cenci makes her dramatic entry.

The hero of *Pierre* is a Melville blessed with good fortune, wealth and health. He lives with his widowed mother who at fifty remains good looking and attractive to men. Mother and son refer to each other as "brother" and "sister" and their intimacy goes beyond the expression of familial fondness. Pierre knows, just as Melville knew when his father died, that he must break free of the relationship. Pierre is about to announce his engagement to Lucy (who is reminiscent of Melville's Elizabeth), when a third woman, Isabel, further complicates his ties. She claims to be Pierre's half-sister and though Pierre had always assumed his father to have lived a wholly upright life, he believes her story. At different moments in the novel he expresses a vain hope that they might not, after all, be blood relations. Isabel's mother was a beautiful French woman and Isabel is dark and seductive. Now orphaned, she has come to throw herself on her half-brother's protection. Another relative of Pierre's, Delly Ulver, is on the point of expulsion from the family because of an illegitimate child, and he feels a duty to stand by her also. Pierre retreats to a boyhood haunt to contemplate the disaster which will inevitably result from his own moral instinct. His thoughts could be Shelley's: he sees the hypocrisy at work among his own kind and realizes that there is no possibility of explaining to his mother who Isabel really is. He finally lights on a heroic solution and resolves to run away with both Isabel and Delly and to live with the first under the fiction of marriage.

The situation is not unlike Shelley's when he decided to "save" Mary and Claire and absconded with them, leaving his wife Harriet behind. But Shelley consummated both relationships, sharing Claire with Byron who had in turn had an incestuous relationship with his own half-sister, Augusta. Even within the fiction Pierre resists all sexual closeness with each woman. He abandons Lucy in order to protect Isabel but the narrator dares to ask whether Pierre would have been so willing to act as he does if Isabel had been ugly and insensitive? Is his decision noble and self-denying or is he very much more attracted to Isabel and excited by the idea of running away with her—and Delly, who has herself dared to transgress? Unlike Shelley, Melville remained faithful to the letter of his commitment to his wife. He was cramped throughout his life by a rigid sense of what was sexually out of bounds. In *Pierre* these ideas are explored in relation to incest.

The three make their way to New York where Pierre has determined to carve out a career as a writer. He decides, in place of the anodyne poetry he has previously produced, to write an autobiographical novel wandering among the shadows of his new life. Lucy, who has now recovered from the shock of Pierre's abandonment, arrives in New York and moves in with them. Pierre is now living with three women. Most difficult of all, Pierre now acknowledges that his feelings for Isabel are not just the fraternal emotions which he had initially acknowledged. He has forfeited every chance of domestic happiness with Lucy, and can live only a charade with Isabel forbidden from sexual intimacy with her by ties of blood. The shadow of incest that darkened his relationship with his mother now obscures his life with Isabel.

And Pierre realizes, while writing his novel, that Isabel had given herself to him heedless of the taboos of society, and in the expectation that their growing intimacy will develop into a love affair.

In the final chapter of *Pierre*, "A Walk: A Foreign Portrait: A Sail: And the End," Pierre, Isabel and Lucy walk down to the wharf together. On their way Pierre sees a placard above a doorway inviting passers-by to a preview of paintings—"undoubted" or "testified" by Rubens, Raphael, Da Vinci etc.—imported from Europe, about to be sold by auction. They pass a sailor in the narrow alleyway. Seeing the women accompanying Pierre, the sailor mocks Pierre's prowess. The irony—Pierre lives celibately with three women—can only be comical. Once in the gallery Pierre is drawn to a painting cryptically described in the catalogue in the line: "No. 99. A stranger's head, by an unknown hand":

> Pierre and Isabel came to that painting of which Pierre was capriciously in search—No. 99. 'My God! see! see!' cried Isabel, under strong excitement, 'only my mirror has ever shown me that look before! See! see!'

The portrait is of a young man who resembles her strongly and Pierre recognizes the face of his father, confirming their shared paternity. His despair will lead to the violent burning of the portrait he has of his father, a symbolic act of patricide. Lucy, on the other hand, has been drawn to:

> a very tolerable copy (the only other good thing in the collection) of that sweetest, most touching, but most awful of all feminine heads—The Cenci of Guido. . . . The Cenci's hair is

golden—physically, therefore, all is in strict, natural keeping; which, nevertheless, still the more intensifies the suggested fanciful anomaly of so sweetly and seraphically *blonde* a being, being double-hooded, as it were, by the black crape of the two most horrible crimes (of one of which she is the object, and of the other the agent) possible to civilized humanity—incest and parricide.

The two portraits to which Isabel and Lucy are drawn hang opposite one another above the heads of the viewers, "so that in secret they seemed pantomimically talking over and across the heads of the living spectators below." The viewers are caught between a father and a patricide. A heady atmosphere of symbolism and inference surrounds them, but the real meaning of the two paintings is suggested rather than explained. The portrait of Beatrice adds to the weighty presence of incest and suppressed or displaced sexual violence, but its true meaning remains cryptic. The black atmosphere of the Cenci tale merges with the shadows of Pierre's (and Melville's) own secret self.

Within the fiction, when Pierre's novel is submitted to his publisher, its author is denounced as depraved, even mad. Lucy's brother and cousin arrive to defend her honor and when her cousin attacks Pierre, Pierre shoots him and is later arrested. Meanwhile, Pierre's mother has died of insanity or grief. Lucy dies similarly when she is told of the consanguinity between Pierre and Isabel. The only denouement available is suicide and Pierre dispatches himself first. Isabel then follows and the novel ends theatrically, if not tragicomically: "Isabel dropped an empty vial—as it had been a run-out sand-glass—and shivered upon the floor; and her whole form sloped sideways, and she fell upon Pierre's heart, and her long hair ran over him, and arbored him in ebon[y] vines."

Beneath its Gothic improbabilities and almost aggressive candor, there is a grandeur in *Pierre*. What its author-hero discovers has less to do with the messy complexities of understanding our true motives for action, and more to do with Melville's insights into what writing has to be. Pierre lights on a method of composition which requires that the river of thought be followed at all costs: "He did not build himself in with plans; he wrote right on; and so doing, got deeper and deeper into himself; and like a resolute traveller, plunging through baffling woods, at last was rewarded for his toils." Yet these rewards amount not to enlightenment, but to a recognition of the ever-receding nature of revelation: "For the more and the more that he wrote, and the deeper and the deeper that he dived, Pierre saw the everlasting elusiveness of Truth."

Melville's *Pierre* is a desperate appeal that serious writers be listened to. He railed against the shallowness of well-made books and admired those that reflected the "unravelable inscrutableness" of life even if this meant that the end results were mere "mutilated stumps." *Pierre* may be such a stump but it is also, in Melville's own words, "a magnificent failure." Critics, however, saw the deformities and none of its daring. The least condemning referred to it as an "unhealthy, mystic romance" or "an eccentricity of the imagination." Others spoke of Melville in much the same language that they had used when describing *Moby-Dick*'s creator: "thought staggers through each page like one poisoned. Language is drunken and reeling. . . . Let Mr. Melville stay his step in time. He totters on the edge of a precipice."

For several years after finishing *Pierre* Melville was silent, broken and utterly turned in on himself. He lost contact with his friends and even the Hawthornes shrank from him. There were no more great works. The failure of *Pierre* broke Melville's spirit and he gave up hope of achieving the kind of recognition from his contemporaries for which he had longed. *Pierre*'s candid exploration of social hypocrisy and sexual taboo had exposed him in ways which his bigoted public would never forgive. Alongside his failure as a writer, Melville had to contend with the failure of his marriage, which had never been happy. His health, in particular his mental instability, was a constant source of anxiety for Elizabeth Melville. She struggled on for years, always short of money, raising their three children, but in 1867, encouraged by her family, many of whom considered Melville insane, she discussed the possibility of a legal separation with her minister. On September 11 that same year, their eldest son Malcolm, at the age of eighteen, put his pistol to his head and committed suicide.

When Melville died over twenty years later, in 1891, no one outside his immediate circle was quite sure who he was. The major literary journal of the day, *The Critic*, resorted to copying out an entry from a reference work on American literature. There was some correspondence in the New York newspapers about the man who had sailed in the South Seas on a whaler. Today—along with Walt Whitman perhaps—the author of the epic *Moby-Dick* is often proclaimed America's greatest imaginative writer.

Melville's contemporaries recognized too little of themselves, of their values and beliefs, to take on board a great deal of what he was saying. He remained a stranger to them, and the countries he traveled remained strange and disconcerting too. He reminded people uncomfortably that beneath the petty triumphs of that period of American history lay the reality of life, one dominated by shadows and darkness. This is what Melville identified as Hawthorne's greatness too. He described Hawthorne's "blackness which so fixes and fascinates me." Melville knew the blackness well: "it derives its force from its appeals to that Calvinistic sense of Innate Depravity and original Sin, from whose visitations, in some shape or other, no deeply thinking mind is always and wholly free." Melville dived too deep, to regions where daylight scarcely penetrates. In *Moby-Dick* he had confronted the darkness of those depths in "that Leviathan," the monster of the deep, but his readership drew back in horror. In *Pierre* the portrait of Beatrice embodies the enigmatic, silent tragedy of Melville's private life: despite estrangement from his wife he felt constrained to abstain from loving other women. He may have identified with Beatrice's unjust fate at the same time as understanding men's capacity to terrorize women. He certainly persecuted the most vulnerable female presence in his life—his daughter Frances. Melville expected his children to be dutiful and submissive but also to show no signs of having been influenced by the bourgeois attitudes of those around them. When Frances picked up the word "property" and used it within the family Melville was appalled and punished her by giving her the nickname "Miss Property." He tormented her with the name for years, visiting on her all kinds of bitterness that had nothing whatsoever to do with her.

The areas of taboo that Melville explored in his fiction were places which he had hoped to explore with Hawthorne, in much the same way as Shelley had longed for imaginative, emotional and intellectual intimacy with Byron. But Hawthorne withdrew from Melville, just as Byron distanced himself from Shelley. Yet they "shared a good deal of the same"; at the heart of Nathaniel Hawthorne's last novel, *The Marble Faun*, Beatrice stages a chilling entry, fresh from the sheets of Melville's *Pierre*.

CHAPTER 5

Hawthorne: "The Sins of the Fathers"

It is very singular, the sad embrace with which
Rome takes possession of the soul.

NATHANIEL HAWTHORNE

Three decades after Shelley's death Beatrice Cenci became a focus of intense interest for a different set of expatriates living in Italy—American and British. One of Beatrice's "safest" resurrections was by the English writer Walter Savage Landor. He was one of an extraordinary Anglo-American colony in florence which included Robert and Elizabeth Browning, who provided a calm center for this remarkably diverse group: Robert Bulwer-Lytton, Frederick Tennyson, brother of the poet, the Trollopes, Nathaniel Hawthorne, the Irish feminist Frances Power Hobbes, Harriet Hosmer and Seymour Kirkup, an elderly painter. They had all seen the portrait of Beatrice in Rome and many of them had their own reproductions of it. The group became afflicted by a kind of Cenci fever and Landor and Hawthorne wrote about her and Hosmer sculpted her.

The painter Kirkup's passions for very young girls may have made Francesco's obsession all the more vivid. Earlier in life Kirkup had been a great friend of William Blake, and he attended both Shelley and Keats's funeral services. He always looked wild and unkempt, but at the age of eighty-seven he married an Italian girl of twenty-two. Hawthorne called him the "necromancer." Like so many of the group Kirkup was fascinated with the occult and regularly "talked" to Dante. The spectacle of the lecherous Kirkup in their midst, combined with discussion of feminist issues, and debates about the dangerous questions which preoccupy artists, provided fertile ground for the growth of new Beatrices. The first and by far the tamest version of Beatrice was Landor's and yet his own life had been far from conformist. Rebellion marked his childhood and as a young man he had no patience with institutional justice and was sent down from both Rugby school, a place of considerable privilege, and from Oxford. In his eighties he embarked on *Five Scenes* (1851), a series of tableaux based on the Beatrice Cenci story. It is remarkable for its omissions, its silences, and its collusion with the "unspeakable": incest is not written into his account. The dark depths that so intrigued and bewitched many of his contemporaries like Melville and Hawthorne are simply circumnavigated.

Nathaniel Hawthorne was born on July 4, 1804, in Salem, Massachusetts, and the date and the place proved to be curious burdens. Both are landmarks in American history: Hawthorne's birthday would forever coincide with his country's Independence Day and the family celebrated the two anniversaries as one. Not surprisingly he grew up with a strong sense of national loyalty and as a boy he wondered what glorious contribution he might make to a rapidly changing America. All this gave him an exaggerated and daunting sense of destiny. His place of birth, on the other hand, was haunted by the ghosts of the past; as a boy he was deeply disturbed, and at the same time intrigued, to learn that his own family had been intimately bound up with the Salem witch trials. Because of this he was peculiarly aware of the ever-present shadows of events that had taken place generations earlier and he also felt that these happenings were somehow part of who he was. Women's capacity for evil, if the stories were true, and their motivations for acts of violence, terrified and fascinated him. Yet, even as a boy he identified questions of crime and punishment as litmus tests for the decency of the societies in which they took place. Later, the weighty significance of the date and place of his birth became intimately bound up with his life as a writer. He was determined to make some contribution to a national American literature independent of the English tradition, one that was situated in a real American landscape and which plumbed the depths of the American psyche. He explored again and again the treatment of women like the Salem witches who allegedly stray from the Path of Righteousness. Hawthorne's life as a writer, which began very early, is then the story of a man wrestling with the sins of the past, sins which continue to linger beneath the superficial puritanical tidiness of contemporary American life.

Hawthorne's direct engagement with the story of Beatrice Cenci came late in his writing career, yet his whole life, and even much of the history of his forbears, can be read as preparation for that encounter. Beatrice's appearance is a moment of crystallization when disparate aspects of his experience and his sense of identity come together. The novel into which this is written,

1. The disputed *Portrait of Beatrice Cenci,* attributed to the Baroque Painter Guido Reni (1575–1642), which is still displayed as "Beatrice Cenci" in the Palazzo Barberini in Rome. It may be one of a series of Sibyls or prophetesses painted by Reni.

2. Drawing by A. Sandoz, after Paul Delaroche, *Beatrice Cenci marchant au supplice,* (Beatrice Cenci walking to the scaffold), 1855.

3. *Percy Bysshe Shelley,* 1819,
by Amelia Curran

4. *Mary Shelley,* around 1814,
by an unknown artist

5. *Claire Clairmont,* 1819,
by Amelia Curran

6. *Byron,* 1818, by James Holmes

7. Shelley's sketches from his Italian notebook.

8. "Boats attacking whales," from *The Natural History of the Sperm Whale*, by Thomas Beale, 1839.

9. "An Inhabitant of the Island of Nukahiwa," engraving of a fully-tattooed man by J. Storer in *Voyages and Travels,* by G. H. von Langsdorff, 1813. Melville feared he would be forcibly subjected to similar decoration while living with the Typee on Nukahiwa, in the Marquesas Islands.

10. "Punishment," watercolor by William H. Meyers, from his "Journal of a Cruise on the *U.S.S. Cyane,* 1842–3." Thomas Melville abhorred the regular floggings meted out on crew members.

11. *Herman Melville*, c. 1847, by Asa W. Twitchell

12. *Nathaniel Hawthorne*, 1840, by Charles Osgood

13. Harriet Hosmer and
her workmen, 1867.

14. Hosmer working on the
clay model of *Thomas Hart
Benton* in Rome, 1862. The
finished bronze is is Lafayette
Park, St. Louis, Missouri.

15. "The Prince of Wales in Miss Hosmer's
studio," *Harper's Weekly,* May 1859.

16. *Beatrice Cenci*, by Harriet Hosmer, 1856

17. *A Study of the Cenci*,
by Julia Margaret
Cameron, May 1868

18. Antonin Artaud in his early thirties, playing Frère Massieu in Carl Dreyer's film, *La Passion de Jeanne d'Arc*, 1927.

20. Artaud in his production of *Les Cenci*, 1935.

19. Artaud in 1946, aged fifty, two years before his death.

21. Sketches by Artaud, including one of his many self-portraits.

The Marble Faun of 1860, was also his last, his farewell to authorship, to art and to life.

Nathaniel was the second of the three children of Elizabeth (née Manning) and Nathaniel Hathorne. The "w" he added later, rendering the name more mellifluous, and a little grander, and distancing him perhaps from the vagaries of his heredity. But the dramas of ancestral history and the continuing instabilities of his family's social position had already shaped the man. William Hathorne, the first American settler of the family, arrived as part of the historic Massachusetts Bay Colony, headed by John Winthrop. They settled in Dorchester in the early 1630s, and in 1636 William Hathorne moved to Salem where he rose to the position of Speaker and then Deputy of the House of Delegates, positions of considerable influence. He was highly respected for his severe orthodox Puritanism and his uncompromising approach. He was responsible for ordering that the Quaker and "heretic" Anne Coleman be whipped out of town. Her injuries were so severe that she almost died. Two further brutal happenings occurred a year later. The Pequot War of 1637 was one of the starkest exercises of Puritan power. Large numbers of the Pequot tribe were murdered by white settlers who were convinced that they were carrying out God's purpose, ridding the land of the heathen. The massacre at the Pequot fort, now the site of Mystic, Connecticut, involved the deaths of some one hundred and fifty old men, women and children. Particularly disturbing was the intention of murdering women of child-bearing age. Significantly, the massacre occurred in the same year as another act of Puritan purging in which the victim was again a woman.

Ann Hutchinson's life overlaps with Beatrice Cenci's. Ann was eight when Beatrice was executed and she too was brought to trial and condemned, and like Beatrice she is remembered as a martyr. Their "crimes," on the other hand, could scarcely be more different. Ann was born in England in 1591 and immigrated to New England in 1634, following the Reverend John Cotton who had been silenced by Archbishop Laud. A dissenting group known as the "familists" who believed that women, as well as men, could preach had profoundly influenced her. In Boston, where she spoke about her religious convictions with great passion and persuasiveness, she became the central figure in what became known as the Antinomian controversy. The Antinomians did not consider themselves bound primarily to the law but rather to individual conscience. In their view there was an absolute difference between the laws of the state, which were man-made, and the spiritual rules which regulated the conscience, and were God-given. Governor Winthrop, however, who wrote a *Short Story of the Rise, Reign, and Ruin of the Antinomians*, mainly about Ann Hutchinson, considered her dangerous and "seditious." Winthrop acknowledged that among her followers there were many wise and pious members of the community, but took exception to the fact that there were people who considered her "a Prophetesse." If her doctrines were directly inspired by God she was a threat to the spiritual authority in Massachusetts where the mediation of the clergy and their interpretation of scripture were considered to be of fundamental importance. Ann held her own meetings where she openly discussed her views of the ministers' sermons and she gave her own advice and spiritual guidance to her followers. In November 1637 she was informed that the magistrates had been ordered to restrain her: she had broken the fifth commandment, the requirement to honor parental authority, which meant all in authority. Ann made her position very clear on leaving the Assembly: "The Lord judgeth not as man judgeth, better to be cast out of the church than to deny Christ." She was banished from Massachusetts in 1638. In 1643, in what is now Pelham Bay, New York, she and her whole family, except one daughter, were massacred by the Indians.

As a young man Nathaniel Hawthorne wrote a short sketch about her, entitled simply "Mrs. Hutchinson." He may have felt some troubling sense of hereditary guilt-by-association but his conclusion upholds his forbears' attitudes: religious individualism, he concludes, is incompatible with social stability. But the same conundrum which lies at the heart of the Beatrice Cenci story—the tension between individual conviction and the often unjust laws of the state—would return again and again in his fiction and his own beliefs gradually emerged as rather more complex and daring.

The Pequot massacre and the Antinomian controversy took place during the lifetime of Nathaniel's first American forbear— William Hathorne. William's son, Judge John Hathorne, achieved greater notoriety for his direct part in the Salem witchcraft trials. The darkest regions of the human mind, and the mysterious actions that make those hidden regions real, the processes of law and justice, these things fascinated Nathaniel Hawthorne early on and became the obsessive themes in his writing. The subject matter of his stories frequently includes witches and witches' Sabbaths, diabolical interventions, the guilt of hidden crimes, which are sometimes violent and often sexual, sometimes real, sometimes wholly imagined. Beatrice Cenci's story, he would discover much later, is one of psychosexual mysteries and extreme action, of passive suffering and resolve to act, to take charge of destiny. The stories of the Salem witches bear remarkable similarities. In 1692 nineteen women were hanged and another tortured to death. Hathorne family legend told of one woman, on her way to her execution on Gallow's Hill, placing a curse on Judge John and all his descendants.

Hawthorne's father Nathaniel, although a sea captain, never succeeded in buying his own boat. On August 2, 1801, he married Elizabeth Clarke Manning who was shy but striking on account of her large and unusually expressive eyes. Nathaniel was a great reader, somewhat inclined to melancholy, and a man of few words. But he was warm hearted and kindly, and very fond of children. Their first child, Elizabeth, was born on March 2, 1802, some seven months after their marriage. This anomaly led to a certain social ostracism and exaggerated Elizabeth's natural reclusiveness. Nathaniel arrived two years later. The children saw little of their seagoing father, and then late in 1807 he sailed for Surinam (then Dutch Guiana) on the *Nabby*. He contracted yellow fever and died. News of his death only reached Salem in April 1808. He died intestate with almost nothing to leave his family. Between the time of his death and news reaching his wife, a second daughter had been born, on January 9, 1808. The old witch curse, when young Nathaniel was first told of it, must have seemed very real.

After his father's death, Nathaniel became the only male heir. He was adored, particularly by his mother's family, the Mannings, and when his mother moved in, the household was large and busy, including his grandparents, three Manning aunts, and five uncles, all unmarried. Elizabeth Manning Hathorne, her two daughters and one son, rented the third floor. They lived for ten years in the large wooden building, known as a "mansion," on Salem's Herbert Street. Elizabeth was frail, mixed very little with people outside the family, and spent a good deal of her time alone in her room. Nathaniel was devoted to his mother and played mostly with his sisters. From an early age he read voraciously and in 1813, before his tenth birthday, he damaged his foot and this marked the beginning of a period of years in which ill health—real or psychosomatic—kept him home with his mother a good deal, which suited him very well. Later he described his own "delicate health which I made the most of for the purpose." The family fussed over him and at the time at least he welcomed their protectiveness, particularly his mother's doting care. But like the character at the center of one of his early stories, "The Gentle Boy," who is taunted by neighboring children because he is unlike them, Hawthorne was also angry at his partly chosen, partly imposed incarceration in the Herbert Street house. He and his mother dreaded separation; there was a mutual dependency that both found difficult to break but they spoke little about their feelings. Nathaniel's love for his mother was unusually passionate and incest would become a major area of fictional exploration later on. In a rare and cryptic comment about the nature of his intimacy with his mother he wrote, "there has been, ever since my boyhood, a sort of coldness of intercourse between us, such as is apt to come between persons of strong feelings." Much, it seems, was left unacknowledged and unspoken.

The summer of 1816, three years after Nathaniel's injury, was a summer of liberation. For all the cheerful bustle of life among the large family in Herbert Street, it exerted an introverting force, encouraging toleration of claustrophobia, rather than exploration. But Nathaniel's time at his Uncle Richard's house in Maine was bliss. He explored the shores of Sebago Lake, fished for salmon trout, shot, and was happy. In 1818 his mother moved to Maine permanently and he returned to live with his mother and sisters. But his Uncle Robert, who had assumed the position of paterfamilias, disapproved of Elizabeth's withdrawal from Salem. He had strong views about Nathaniel's upbringing and education, and was convinced that what he needed was not greater withdrawal from society, but greater involvement. In the winter of 1819, Nathaniel was sent to board in Stroudwater, near Portland, where he was miserable and threatened to run away. His mother and his Uncle Richard took him home. His favorite books at the time were Spenser's *The Faerie Queene* and Bunyan's *The Pilgrim's Progress* which he read and reread throughout his life. Stories within stories would become a dominant mode in his writing. Later Hawthorne argued the merits of self-education. What mattered was for a child to be "left much to such wild modes of culture as he chooses for himself while yet ignorant what culture means." Not only was he free to read what he chose, he read without being told what to make of this book or that.

In Maine Nathaniel wandered free, fished in the lake in summer, and skated on it in winter, often completely alone on the great expanse of ice. The scale and emptiness of the natural setting was what he remembered in later life: "Those were delightful days, for that part of the country was wild then, with only scattered clearings, and nine tenths of it primeval woods." Elsewhere he wrote, "I lived in Maine like a bird of the air, so perfect was the freedom I enjoyed." For all his nostalgia for the expansiveness and beauty of the place, he recognized that intimately bound up with his experience of freedom in nature was a growing sense of isolation from people. In the same letter to a friend he added: "It was there I first got my cursed habits of solitude."

In the summer of 1819 he was back in Salem; his letters to his mother make reference to continued homesickness. What he yearned for was a return to the Edenic years of life in Maine: "Oh, how I wish I was again with you, with nothing to do but go a-gunning. But the happiest days of my life are gone. Why was I not a girl that I might have been pinned all my life to my Mother's apron?"

By 1821 Nathaniel was preparing to enter Bowdoin College, a relatively new establishment in Brunswick, Maine, not too far from his mother. The prospect of spending vacations at home greatly lifted his spirits, and he longed to move permanently away from Herbert Street. He was seventeen, and still sharing a bed with Uncle Robert: "I dreamed the other night that I was walking by the Sebago; and when I woke was so angry that I gave Uncle Robert (who sleeps with me) a most horrible kick." Frustrations were mounting.

During that summer the apparent orderliness of Salem society was disrupted. In May, a young man, Stephen Clark, had committed arson. He had set fire to a barn and, under an old law, barn burning was a capital offense. The clergy preached clemency but the youth was sentenced to death. He was to be publicly hanged. A large crowd assembled to witness the execution, but Nathaniel chose not to attend: "I did not go to see Stephen Clark executed," he told his mother. He added, somewhat cryptically, "It is said that he could have been restored to life some time after his execution. I do not know why it was not done." It may be that he felt that the witnessing of the sentence would in some way represent collusion with forces from which he wanted to remain distant and detached, or it could be that he suspected he would find the sight too ghastly to bear. Still more mysterious is his reference to resuscitation. Was the job not properly done and the boy only half-dead when he was taken down from the scaffold? Or is Hawthorne referring to some extraordinary medical or magical feat? In Hawthorne's last and uncompleted tale, *The Dolliver Romance*, one of the characters is a hanged man who has been restored to life by

Dr. Dolliver, an immortal, although fully human, who possesses a secret elixir.

Before leaving for college, Nathaniel was already considering life beyond his studies. He was keen to be financially independent of the family, and free of the constraints that dependency might impose. He glibly ruled out the obvious professions in a letter to his mother: the life of a minister too dull, lawyers were too plentiful and thus many would starve. More revealingly he wrote of practicing medicine: "I should not like to live by the diseases and infirmities of my fellow Creatures. And it would weigh very heavily on my conscience if, in the course of my practice, I should chance to send an unlucky patient 'ad infernum,' which being interpreted is 'to the realms below.'" Self-mockingly he asks, "What do you think of my becoming an author, and relying for support upon my pen? Indeed, I think the illegibility of my handwriting is very author-like. . . . But authors are always poor devils, and therefore Satan may take them."

For all the offhandedness of Nathaniel's tone, he adds "Do not show this letter," conscious no doubt that if Uncle Robert knew his ambitions, he would do his level best to thwart them. But there is also a sense of guilty shame about the practice of writing that surfaces again and again in his descriptions of the role of the writer, and in his stories. He associates the writer's insight into the hidden realms of human experience as a kind of diabolical knowledge. The writer has to know and understand sin and guilt. He could therefore be described, in a sense, as in league with the devil. Among his early writing is a collection of tales entitled *The Story Teller*. The wandering storyteller is accompanied by a guardian and the teller of tales must evade the moral guidance of his minder in order fully to explore life and thereby glean material for his tales. Throughout these stories the storyteller is cast as a subversive, a rebel, whose art disrupts, disturbs, even corrupts. The stories threaten to condemn their author.

Hawthorne's time at Bowdoin overlapped with that of Henry Wadsworth Longfellow, who went on to be the most popular poet of his day. Although they did not spend much time together at college they later developed a long and untroubled friendship. Hawthorne's closest friend, to whom he would remain loyal at some cost in terms of other friendships and acquaintances, was Franklin Pierce, fourteenth President of the United States. Academically Hawthorne's years at college were undistinguished. Looking back he plainly stated "I was an idle student, negligent of college rules and the Procrustean details of academic life, rather choosing to nurse my own fancies than to dig into Greek roots and be numbered among the learned Thebans."

He left college at twenty-one, and as his mother had moved back from Maine he returned to Herbert Street to live with her and other members of the Manning tribe. He received a small income from his grandmother's estate and lived at Herbert Street for twelve years quietly determined to be a writer but ill at ease with his identity locally. Salem was not a place for the apparently idle and he felt himself "ranked with the tavern-hunters and town paupers,—with the drunken poet, who hawked his own fourth of July odes,—and the drunken soldier, who has been good for nothing since [the] last war." Around this time he changed his name from "Hathorne" to "Hawthorne."

For more than a decade Hawthorne read "all sorts of good and good-for-nothing books" and wrote, burning a good deal of his production. He read histories of New England, including Felt's *Annals of Salem*, and was particularly fascinated by Howell's *State Trials*. He read the great classical tragedies of

Racine and Corneille, and the essays of Montaigne, Voltaire and
Rousseau. He loved Cervantes' *Don Quixote* and he read the
momentous writings of Jefferson and Franklin. He read Samuel
Johnson but was disappointed. Johnson, he maintained,
scratched at the surface of things, unable or unwilling to delve
deep. Johnson, he maintained, "never cared to penetrate farther
than to plough-share depth." But he was much struck by a detail of Johnson's biography: as a grown man he had stood bare
headed in Uttoxeter, in the market place, doing penance for a
tormenting sin he had committed against his father when he was
a boy. The authors whom Hawthorne revered were Scott (whom
he started reading as a child), Dickens and Trollope. He read the
Romantic poets too, Wordsworth, Keats and Byron. Shelley was
a great favorite. He read Ann Radcliffe's Gothic tales, Horace
Walpole and a good deal of travel writing. He had little opportunity to discuss much of his reading although his sister Elizabeth provided some intellectual company. Indeed, she selected
most of his books, since one of Hawthorne's "peculiarities" during these years, according to his sister, was that he would never
visit the Salem Athenaeum himself, "nor look over the catalogue
to select a book, nor indeed do anything but find fault with it;
so that it was left entirely to me to provide him with reading."
The reclusive and extraordinarily passive features of Hawthorne's
"hiatus," these years of apparent non-productivity, as in Melville's
"quietus," suggest that some unspecified form of depression may
have been a contributory factor.

The unremarkable reception of Hawthorne's first novel,
Fanshawe (1828), might have served to break what little spirit
he had. It was published at the author's expense and anonymously. Although there was mention in magazines of "parts . . .
powerful and pathetic" and one reviewer prophesied: "The mind

that produced this little, interesting volume, is capable of making great and rich additions to our native literature," other commentators were less charitable: "*Fanshawe* ... It has, like ten thousand others, a mystery, an elopement; a villain, a father, a tavern, almost a duel, a horrible death, and—heaven save the mark! . . . an end." The vitriolic reviews of Melville's *Moby-Dick* had provoked a desperate and incautious response—the writing of *Pierre*, his novel of the Cenci tradition which served to ostracize him forever from his contemporaries. But Melville knew that *Moby-Dick* was a great work. Hawthorne, on the contrary, quickly recognized the adolescent weaknesses of his quasi-Gothic and overromantic novel. Within a couple of years of its publication Hawthorne reclaimed copies of the book that he had given to family and friends. These he burned. There is, at first sight, little remarkable about an aspiring author recognizing his own juvenilia and seeking to erase all trace of it. But in an early story, tellingly entitled "The Devil in the Manuscript," Hawthorne gives much darker significance to his own seemingly mundane act of petty vandalism.

The story tells of Oberon, an aspiring author, unable to find a publisher. "The Devil in the Manuscript" is in part a historically accurate account of the fragile American publishing industry of the day, when backing new American authors involved considerable financial risk. Piracy of European works was rampant, and reprinting English editions was relatively cheap and the return guaranteed. Oberon is bluntly advised: "no American publisher will meddle with an American work, seldom if by a known writer, and never if by a new one, unless at the writer's risk." The young man rages against circumstance, and against his own writerly being. To his friend's horror, Oberon throws his manuscripts into the grate declaring, "What is more potent than fire!" While watching the chasing flames consuming his work, Oberon thinks he can make out the face of the devil: "I tell you there is a demon in them!" But the action of the story only really begins here. Such is the scale of the fire that it escapes the grate and sets the chimney, and then the roof, ablaze. The sky is lit up, and the streets fill with people and fire bells. Oberon's stories have, after all, had power in the world. It is a twisted sense of irony that Oberon expresses when he declares, "My tales! . . . The fiend has gone forth by night, and startled thousands in fear and wonder from their beds! Here I stand—a triumphant author! . . . My brain has set the town on fire!"

Hawthorne was much encouraged by a letter from a Boston publisher, Samuel G. Goodridge, inviting him to contribute to his well-respected annual "gift album," *The Token*. Goodridge also offered to help him find a publisher for *Provincial Tales* on which he was working. In the event the project never came to anything but some of the material appeared in *The Token*. These were stories of crime and punishment, of sins exposed, including incest, of cruelty, violence, revenge, of blighted heredity, and the lingering presence of ghosts. Mothers are punished for unexpiated wrongs, fathers are murdered by their sons. Most striking is the veiled suggestion of guilt not yet recognized and transformed into remorse, and thus beyond redemption.

Apart from his short travels in the summer months, Hawthorne did not leave Salem until 1836, when he was thirty-two. He then moved to Boston and edited the *American Magazine of Useful and Entertaining Knowledge* and then a work for children, *Peter Parley's Universal History on the Basis of Geography*. His sister Elizabeth regularly sent him material. After months of unrewarded toil he resigned and returned to Salem. He had lasted only eight months away.

He had, however, seen a little more of the world. His *Twice-Told Tales* (1837) had received good reviews, one of them solicited from Longfellow, his former classmate. When he returned home he was ready to enter what little society Salem offered, and his introduction to the Peabody sisters was to have a dramatic effect on both his professional and private life. He was first drawn to Elizabeth, the most extroverted and energetic of the sisters (she was to become Miss Birdseye in Henry James's *The Bostonians*) who helped secure him the post of weigher and gauger at the Boston Custom House, the first of a series of public appointments which were to support him. But before leaving to take up his new post, his affection shifted from Elizabeth to her younger, semi-invalid sister, Sophia. For three years they exchanged love letters. Hawthorne resigned from his job in Boston in 1839 and became a member of the Brook Farm community. His intention was to live out his socialist ideals, but the physical exhaustion of laboring on a farm proved still less compatible with writing than the tedium of his work as a weigher and measurer. His stay lasted only two months. Sophia was pressing for their marriage to take place. It was now three years since they had made their secret pledge and Hawthorne had seemed compelled to delay and delay. The wedding finally took place on July 9, 1842. Some three months later Hawthorne wrote a peculiar short story, "The Birthmark," in which a newly wedded man becomes fixated by a dark stain on his wife's left cheek which symbolizes his powerful sense of sexual guilt. He insists that his wife undergo surgery to remove the birthmark and during the course of the surgical operation she dies. Hawthorne was preoccupied throughout his life by a desire to understand the mind of the perpetrator—and victim—of sexual violence.

To outsiders at least, the Hawthornes seemed happy enough. Sophia had suggested that they settle in Concord, a pastoral

community some twenty miles west of Boston. It was also the
locale of Ralph Waldo Emerson and Henry Thoreau, two of
America's most important nineteenth-century writers. Hawthorne, however, preferred to spend most of his time alone, or
with his wife. The tales he wrote during the early years of his
marriage, like "The Birthmark," explore the complexities of
sexual relations. "The Artist of the Beautiful" suggests a father's
fear that the birth of his first child will weaken his other creative power—to write. The Hawthornes' first child, Una, was
born on March 3, 1844 and not long afterwards the Hawthornes
were driven out of the Old Manse, seriously in arrears with the
rent. Through friends he secured the position of surveyor in the
Salem Custom House but three years later, when the Whigs un-
seated the Democrats, he was removed from his position, describing himself as "decapitated." The Hawthornes moved to
Lenox, Massachusetts.

Hawthorne's sense of injustice and rage, which became confused with his horror at his mother's death that July, fueled his
writing. Now that he was unemployed he had plenty of time
and he felt a hitherto unknown sense of purpose. With the encouragement of a poet-publisher friend, James T. fields, he
wrote his novel *The Scarlet Letter* in the space of a few months,
and it was published the following year. In Lenox he and Sophia
were renting the appropriately named "Red Cottage." "My
house is an old red farm house, (as red as the Scarlet Letter),"
he wrote. In Lenox they became friends with the notorious
actress Fanny Kemble who was to have a major influence on
Harriet Hosmer, now a pupil at the Sedgwick Academy nearby
and one of their circle some years later in Rome. It was at this
stage that the Hawthornes also became close friends with
Herman Melville, at that time a respected travel writer, not yet

having spoiled his reputation by writing *Moby-Dick*, and still more damagingly, by publishing *Pierre*.

At the heart of Hawthorne's *The Scarlet Letter* is the experience of private guilt and public shame. The structure of the work centers on three scenes at the scaffold of the pillory. Hester Prynne, an adulteress, is exposed to public shame. Arthur Dimmesdale, the minister with whom, unbeknownst to the community, the act has been committed, keeps silent vigil as an act of repentance. It is also here that he dies, following an ambiguous confession. What Hawthorne set out to write was "a story of the effects of revenge in diabolizing him who indulges in it." The story is a simple one, set in the Puritan Boston of the mid-seventeenth century. An English scholar, married to a much younger wife, sends her ahead from England, to set up home in advance of his emigration two years later. When he finally arrives he discovers her in the pillory, a newborn baby in her arms. Hester refuses to name her lover and is condemned to wear a scarlet letter, an "A" embroidered on her bosom, a public sign of her status as adulteress. Driven by a desire for revenge her husband changes his name and in the guise of a doctor sets out on a merciless and ultimately self-destructive quest to discover the father of Hester's illegitimate child.

Hawthorne obviously drew on historical material in conceiving *The Scarlet Letter*. Ann Hutchinson, although she committed no crime, is condemned for the same "freedom of speculation" which provokes Hester's judges more than her act of adultery. Hester is clearly an Antinomian too: "The world's law was no law for her mind." Her vision of a new world, "a whole system of society," quite unlike that which is in place, is quite as radical as Ann Hutchinson's. Both Ann and Hester are driven to question "the very nature of the opposite sex, or its long hereditary

habit, which has become like nature." Gender difference, or
society's claims for what it means to be a woman or a man, and
the laws which then regulate conduct, are areas which both Ann
and Hester dare to explore. Ann was motivated by spiritual passion. Hester is driven by physical passion.

Hawthorne wrote *The Scarlet Letter* in a creative flurry.
Sophia worried at the intensity of his mood: "He writes immensely. I am almost frightened about it." He was buoyed up
for a period by its very considerable critical success but by 1851
his restlessness prompted another move, this time back to Massachusetts, to West Newton. America was entering a volatile
political period and debates about slavery raged. Hawthorne
engaged very little with contemporary controversies and instead
worked on *The Blithedale Romance*, which is based on his experiences at Brook Farm. It is one of Hawthorne's less widely
read novels, a satire on philanthropic socialism, and it blends
incisive observation of utopian idealism with a marvelous bou-
quet of subjects including mesmerism, and writing women who
are as erotically energetic as they are prolific in their authorship.
The novel's heroine is Zenobia, whose classical namesake
Hosmer was to sculpt on a more than Amazonian scale. She is
the articulate, daring, contemporary version of Hester Prynne.
Both are at once a homage to, and rebellion against, strong sexual
women.

The narrator, like Hawthorne, finds her overwhelming, yet
Zenobia is in part a fictionalized version of Hawthorne himself:
a writer, a scribbler, an outsider, a nonconformist who nevertheless fails to free herself sufficiently from the conforming powers of society. In many ways she is delightful and admirable and
by no means embodies Hawthorne's espoused prejudices against
writing women. His propensity for self-satirizing leads one to read

any categorical statement he makes with a degree of discrimination as to his real views: "*All* women, as authors, are feeble and tiresome. I wish that they were all forbidden to write on pain of having their faces deeply scarified with an oyster-shell." But his injunction to his youngest daughter, when he discovered her writing tales, was straightforward and direct: "Never let me hear of your writing stories!" In order to bring *The Blithedale Romance* to a satisfactory conclusion Hawthorne drowns Zenobia. He then abandoned writing women (and men), conscious of the advantages to be won from the old-boy network, and embarked on a campaign biography of his old friend from college days, Franklin Pierce.

There is no doubt that Hawthorne aimed to write a piece of political puffery likely to assist Pierce in his ambition of becoming President. For all his revolutionary ideals Hawthorne was, like his subject, a conservative, a reactionary. The success of *The Scarlet Letter* had not dispelled his anxieties about his own image of himself as a member of an essentially female set of scribblers. Politics was men's business and his escape into the biography was something he felt at ease with. But however much politics might suit his self-image, his temperament could hardly have been less attuned to the very real questions which had to be addressed. The controversy surrounding slavery was one of the thorniest. On the one hand Hawthorne expressed, quite unequivocally, his detestation of it. It was a repugnant system; but far from siding with the abolitionists Hawthorne preferred to judge them quite as harshly. They were fanatics, driven by an unseemly and wholly inappropriate sense of urgency. In his biography of Pierce he counseled an extraordinarily *laissez-faire* approach. Slavery was merely "one of those evils which divine Providence does not leave to be remedied by human contrivances, but which, in its own good time, by some means impossible to be anticipated, but of the simplest and easiest operation, when all its uses have been fulfilled, it causes to vanish like a dream." Most of Hawthorne's friends were astonished by his incapacity to take the nightmare of the slave condition seriously, and by his unwillingness to give the matter any creative thought. The most charitable of his friends excused his fatalism, explaining it as a symptom of his not altogether earthed engagement with contemporary realities. But he lost many friends too.

Hawthorne's loyalty to Pierce needs some exploration. On the face of it there is little to explain their friendship. It is true that they had first met as young men and Hawthorne undoubtedly knew that Pierce would reward him with a well-paid job if he were able. But Hawthorne's commitment to Pierce went deeper. History has judged Pierce as decidedly mediocre. Even Hawthorne conceded that Pierce "was not far-seeing, nor possessed of vast stores of political wisdom." What he most respected, which was precisely what Hawthorne the writer and semi-recluse proved to be spectacularly short on, was the capacity to take immediate action. Hawthorne was bad at making decisions, all too aware of the complexities of the consequences of action. As a novelist he could walk around a problem and become increasingly interested not in solutions but in the very intractable nature of so many human predicaments. Pierce was unintellectual, lacked vision, spoke rather badly, but had the military man's ability to respond quickly and tactically to events. Hawthorne recognized that Pierce was "endowed with a miraculous intuition of what ought to be done, just at the time for action." Hawthorne's insights into the human condition concerned the dark recesses of human conscience and consciousness, but what he admired were men and women of action, resolve, determination, energy. He was in awe of those who dared to imprint on the world—through action—particular visions. The newly-wed husband in "The Birthmark" is not willing to tolerate the mark which has become horrible to him. Something must be done. The despairing author in "The Devil in the Manuscript" takes extreme action, ultimately committing arson. Hester Prynne lives out her passionate feelings and suffers the consequences with composure. Among the many reasons that he was attracted to Beatrice Cenci was a profound admiration for heroic action, however complicated and morally tortured the action may be.

Hawthorne was duly rewarded for his loyalty to Pierce. On July 6, 1853, the Hawthornes sailed for England where Nathaniel would take up the position of Consul in Liverpool. He held the post until 1857. On leaving America, he had just turned forty-nine. It was the first time he had left the country and Hawthorne proved predictably bad at settling. He worried constantly about money and felt unable to write. Yet his post was the most lucrative consulship of all. Sophia found the weather and the grayness of the city hard to bear and took Una and Rose to Lisbon from October 1855 until June 1856. Continued unrest back home preoccupied him far more than the goings-on in Liverpool, or his country of exile, or for that matter in continental Europe where political and social unrest engaged the minds of a good many writers and thinkers. For all his obsessive and generally unfounded financial worries, Hawthorne nevertheless resigned his consulship.

The Hawthornes headed south. Sophia was no doubt the moving force behind the decision to travel to Italy and she may well have supposed that the splendor of the Eternal City, the climate and the company of a sympathetic group of expatriate Americans might encourage Hawthorne to return to his writing.

In Paris Hawthorne's Puritan cast of mind denied him the pleasures that the change of diet might otherwise have offered: "All the dishes were very delicate and a vast change." Yet, he continued, "I doubt whether English cookery, for the very reason that it is so gross, is not better for a man's moral and spiritual nature, than French." When they finally arrived in Rome he was no more disposed to enjoy himself, remaining reluctant to meet people, and boasting "a horror of sight-seeing." He came down with flu. But for all his glib comments, the city was making a deep impression on him and he believed that his vision of the place exposed "modern Rome in an aspect in which it has never before been depicted." He was keeping two journals. And when his health and spirits improved he started to socialize.

Among the Hawthornes' closest friends was William Wetmore Story, the young Hatty Hosmer's self-appointed guardian. Story, a highly successful lawyer turned artist, was living in great style in the Palazzo Barberini, home to the portrait of Beatrice Cenci, and his apartments became one of the major meeting grounds for Americans in Rome. Among Story's many talents Hawthorne was struck by his ability as a sculptor. Kenyon, the sculptor in Hawthorne's *The Marble Faun*, who carves the faun of the title, was based on Story. Kenyon's gift was to give his static monumental pieces extraordinary inner life, and his sculpture of *Cleopatra* was "fierce, voluptuous, passionate, tender, wicked, terrible, and full of poisonous and rapturous enchantment." Trapped in the marble were terrible tales immortalized in stone, mute, yet crying out.

The Hawthornes regularly attended Story's extravagant parties and spent time in the Barberini's many picture galleries. One painting struck him particularly, the Beatrice portrait. It was, he wrote, "the most profoundly wrought picture in the world; no artist did it, or could do it again. Guido may have held the brush, but he painted better than he knew." Hawthorne's own resurrection of Beatrice would come, but his approach to the task would not be head-on, but oblique, even surreptitious.

Copious entries in his notebooks reveal Hawthorne's growing fascination for Rome's works of art, particularly those that connect with Italy's mythical past. Local history, folklore, and tales still told in taverns and at market places back home, had nourished Hawthorne's early writing. Now still more ancient stories came alive for him in the paintings, frescoes, statues and architecture of the city. But it was not until the spring when the Hawthornes withdrew to the hills, like so many others, to avoid the sweltering summer heat, that Nathaniel's idea for another novel finally took root. In a secluded hilltop villa overlooking florence, Hawthorne felt ready to write. The atmosphere was, he declared, "a very good air to dream in."

A copy of the *Faun* of Praxiteles, and what was exhibited in the galleries of the Capitol as the original sculpture (fourth century BC and probably a copy), inspired him to embark on his last novel: "This race of fauns was the most delightful of all that antiquity imagined. It seems to me that a story, with all sorts of fun and pathos in it, might be contrived on the idea of their species having become intermingled with the human race, a family with faun blood in them, having prolonged itself from the classic era till our own days." His faun would combine an honesty born of simplicity combined with a sensual, mirthful nature. Donatello would represent man before the Fall. But the stage on which Hawthorne requires him to act is one occupied by modern men and women, people who know evil. The romance takes place in Rome, against a backdrop of an ancient pagan past which develops into and overlaps with a Christian present.

Among the numerous expatriates the Hawthornes sought out, or who called to visit them, were the Brownings. Hawthorne was characteristically tentative: "He must be an amiable man," he noted having witnessed Browning playing with a small dog, and continued, "I should like him much (and should make him like me) if opportunities were favorable." But social life distracted him from his writing. "I feel an impulse to work, but am kept idle by the sense of being unsettled, with removals to be gone through over and over again, before I can shut myself up into a quiet room of my own, and turn the key. I need monotony too—before I can live in the world within." The months passed and conditions conducive to proper work seemed nowhere to be found. In October 1858 they were back in Rome but, despite finding "such a comfortable, cosy little house, as I did not think existed in Rome," progress on the novel was slow: "Began to write a Romance," he noted on October 25. Subsequent entries reflect his frustrations, "I scribbled Romance," "Scribbled romance poorly," "Scribbled romance ineffectually."

Una's sudden descent into serious illness further hindered Hawthorne's progress. In Rome Una contracted malaria and her little body seemed ill equipped to fight back. The doctors were certain that she would die, so certain that, bizarrely, they specified the day on which she would die: November 17. The Hawthornes accepted this prognosis and Sophia stayed at her bedside day and night, increasingly exhausted and counting down the days. Nathaniel struggled on with his writing: "Amid so much domestic trouble, I take some credit to myself for having sternly shut myself up for an hour or two, almost every day, and come to close grips with a Romance which I have been trying to tear out of my mind."

Miraculously, Una survived. The family then returned to England where Sophia had time to regain her own strength in a gentler climate. The plan was that they would then return to America. During these quiet months Nathaniel finished *The Marble Faun*. The novel took much longer to complete than any previous work in part because of Una's long illness, but also because of the complexities that lie only half-visible beneath its surface: questioning of gender roles, passionate murderous sexuality, and questions of sin, remorse and redemption. It had been seven years since Hawthorne published a book. This would be his last.

The *Beatrice Cenci* painting to which Story had introduced him in the Palazzo Barberini is central to the story. Of the portrait Hawthorne wrote, "her spell is indefinable. She is a fallen angel, fallen without sin." *The Marble Faun* has two heroines, the artists Hilda and Miriam (based on Harriet Hosmer). Their contrasting responses to Beatrice serve as opposing moral perspectives on the conundrum of the human condition that Hawthorne had long wrestled with: the clash between individual conscience and the mores of society. Miriam is a woman with a shadowy past, who has been involved in some "mysterious and terrible event." She is based on Henriette Deluzy-Desportes, governess of the Duc de Choiseul-Praslin. The Duke died of arsenic poisoning and the Duchess also died in questionable circumstances; Henriette was implicated in their deaths and fled to New York where she changed her name and eventually married an American clergyman. It was the kind of story that Hawthorne would have liked, but he refused to be drawn when asked about Miriam's origins: "It only concerns the present narrative inasmuch as the suspicion of being at least an accomplice in a crime fell darkly and directly upon Miriam herself." She is haunted by "a Model," a mysterious bearded being who follows her. He represents, and in some way shares, her sense of guilt. Donatello, the faun, motivated by "pure" love, attempts to rid Miriam of this menacing presence.

In his struggle with Donatello, the Model falls from a great height—to his death. As in Milton's *Paradise Lost* Donatello's spontaneous, but murderous act, transforms him. Donatello is now capable of a new kind of love, one that raises him above his animal self, while at the same time conscious that Miriam's sexual charms have been at the origin of his terrible act. He withdraws into self-absorption and experiences a misogynistic loathing for Miriam. Just as Hilda and Miriam are two very different kinds of women, and close friends, so Donatello is close to Kenyon, the sculptor. The latter seeks to sculpt Donatello (the "marble faun"), hoping that his creation will allow Donatello to begin to understand himself and thus to make sense of the crime he has committed. Kenyon has no transcendent faith, but seeks to win Donatello back from his state of utter self-loathing in order that Donatello may live again. Hilda is profoundly shocked by Kenyon, who believes that it is as a result of his crime that Donatello has been transformed into something more than an innocent, intuitive being. She reasons with Kenyon who argues: "Sin has educated Donatello, and elevated him. Is Sin, then— which we deem such a dreadful blackness in the Universe,—is it, like Sorrow, merely an element of human education, through which we struggle to a higher and purer state than we would otherwise have attained?"

Hilda and Miriam are both painters. Hilda is a copyist, Miriam an explorer, an experimenter, a subversive artist. For Hilda the paradoxical and darker sides of the human condition must be ignored, denied. For Miriam ideal humanity is sacred not in its suppressions of aspects of the self, but in its full embodiment of the part played by erotic passions. What Hilda sees as Virtue is viewed by Miriam as mere fastidiousness; what Hilda conceptualizes as Fallen Woman, Miriam recognizes as female humanity.

Hilda has finished a copy of *Beatrice Cenci*, which Miriam considers her greatest achievement:

> The picture represented simply a female head; a very youthful, girlish, perfectly beautiful face, enveloped in white drapery, from beneath which strayed a lock or two of what seemed a rich, though hidden luxuriance of auburn hair. The eyes were large and brown, and met those of the spectator, but evidently with a strange ineffectual effort to escape. There was a little redness about the eyelids, very slightly indicated, so that you would question whether or no the girl had been weeping. The whole face was quiet; there was no distortion or disturbance of any single feature; nor was it easy to see why the expression was not cheerful, or why a single touch of the artist's pencil should not brighten it to joyousness. But in fact it was the very saddest picture ever painted or conceived; it involved an unfathomable depth of sorrow, the sense of which came to the observer by a sort of intuition. It was a sorrow that removed this girl out of the sphere of humanity, and set her in a far-off region, the remoteness of which—while yet her face is so close before us— makes us shiver as at a spectre.

Miriam's sad self-knowledge permeates everything she produces, while Hilda's powers as copyist are wholly self-abnegating. But it is precisely Hilda's spiritual purity that limits what she sees, even in her own near-perfect copies. Miriam experiences such "painful sympathy" with Hilda's Beatrice that she implores her to cover it up. When Miriam questions Hilda about Beatrice's guilt, Hilda replies that she had "quite forgotten Beatrice's history." When reminded she is categorical in her judgment: "Yes, yes; it was terrible guilt, an inexpiable crime, and she feels it to be so. Therefore it is that the forlorn creature so longs to elude our eyes, and forever vanish away into nothingness! Her doom is just!" Miriam, however, is shocked at her friend's "innocence"; she describes it as a "sharp, steel, sword," and declares "If I could but clasp Beatrice Cenci's ghost and draw it into myself! I would give my life to know whether she thought herself innocent, or the one great criminal since time began!" Such strength of sympathy is physically transforming: "As Miriam gave utterance to these words, Hilda looked from the picture into her face, and was startled to observe that her friend's expression had become almost exactly that of the portrait; as if her passionate wish and struggle to penetrate poor Beatrice's mystery had been successful." Hilda is startled by the similarities between their expressions: "Oh, for Heaven's sake, Miriam, do not look so!"

In the Postscript to *The Marble Faun* Hawthorne supplied some detail to answer his frustrated readers but he gave little more away than to inform them that Donatello was imprisoned for his crime and Miriam was "at large." Kenyon explains: "Call it cruelty, if you like—not mercy!" Like Beatrice's youngest brother, Bernardo, Miriam has been left behind to live forever in the remembrance of evil. Miriam's part in the crime remains mysterious: "But, after all," Kenyon adds, "her crime lay merely in a glance; she did no murder." On the dreadful day when the Model is hurled from the high terrace to his death below, Donatello's act is committed on the heels of a conversation with

Miriam. "Who were they," Donatello asks, "who have been flung over here, in days gone by?" Miriam replies, "Men that cumbered the world. . . . Men who poisoned the air, which is the common breath of all, for their own selfish purposes. There was short work with such men, in old Roman times. Just in the moment of their triumph, a hand as of an avenging giant clutched them, and dashed the wretches down this precipice!" Miriam could equally, of course, be referring to Francesco Cenci's fate. Donatello asks, "Was it well done?" Miriam replies, "It was well done. . . . Innocent persons were saved by the destruction of a guilty one, who deserved his doom."

Kenyon and Hilda have withdrawn from the scene, but Miriam and Donatello are not alone. A figure appears and Miriam "must have had cause to dread some unspeakable evil from this strange persecutor." What she experiences is too frightful ever to be remembered: "in her whole recollection of that wild moment, she beheld herself as in a dim show, and could not well distinguish what was done and suffered." But Donatello acts. Miriam looks "wildly at the young man, whose form seemed to have dilated, and whose eyes blazed with the fierce energy that had suddenly inspired him. It had kindled him into a man; it had developed within him an intelligence which was no native characteristic of the Donatello whom we had heretofore known. But that simple joyous creature was gone forever." In a "horror-stricken whisper" Miriam asks, "What have you done!" He replies simply, "I did what your eyes bade me do, when I asked them with mine, as I held the wretch over the precipice."

Hawthorne's *The Marble Faun* ends tragically. Donatello and Miriam are punished and the happiness of Hilda and Kenyon's lives is forever blighted by their knowledge of their friends' encounter with sin. Yet Hawthorne's position is far from unambiguous, despite this ending. Early in the novel, when Miriam and Hilda discuss Hilda's copy of *Beatrice Cenci*, Miriam dismisses her friend's judgment of Beatrice as "terribly severe," arguing, "Poor sister Beatrice! For she was still a woman, Hilda, still a dear sister, be her sin or sorrow what they might." And Miriam adds, "If a woman had painted the original picture, there might have been something in it which we miss now." Hawthorne is still more daring in his description of Donatello and Miriam after the murder:

> She turned to him—the guilty, blood-stained, lonely woman— she turned to her fellow-criminal, the youth, so lately innocent, whom she had drawn into her doom. She pressed him close, close to her bosom, with a clinging embrace that brought their two hearts together, till the horror and agony of each was combined into one emotion, and that, a kind of rapture.

Once Donatello has committed the murder, no life is possible either for him or Miriam. And Hilda, who appears a moment later, is burdened forever by her knowledge of Donatello's crime and Miriam's mysterious involvement in it. The weight of their guilt transforms her; from this point on she sees as Miriam sees, aware of the range and depth of human experience and suffering. She now sees beneath surface realities:

> So the melancholy girl wandered through those long galleries, and over the mosaic pavements of vast, solitary saloons, wondering what had become of the splendour that used to beam upon her from the walls. She grew sadly critical, and condemned almost everything that she was wont to admire. Heretofore her sympathy went deeply into a picture, yet seemed to leave a depth

which it was inadequate to sound; now, on the contrary, her perceptive faculty penetrated the canvas like a steel probe, and found but a crust of paint over an emptiness.

It was with this same terrible sense of "emptiness" that Hawthorne had left Rome in May 1859. The narrator of *The Marble Faun* muses on the longevity of sculpture in contrast to human mortality: "But it is an awful thing, indeed, this endless endurance, this almost indestructibility, of a marble bust! Whether in our own case, or that of other men, it bids us sadly measure the little, little time, during which our lineaments are likely to be of interest to any human being."

Soon the Hawthornes left Europe forever. Nathaniel had little desire to arrive—anywhere: "I should like to sail on and on forever, and never touch the shore again." Not long after Shelley's resurrection of Beatrice in his *Cenci* play, Shelley too had set sail, and when his body again touched the shore it was already eaten away. And when Hawthorne docked safely in Boston on June 28, 1860, he was emotionally dead, weary of life.

Hawthorne's mood was exacerbated by Una's continuing ill health, now mental rather than physical. Her behavior was so uncontrollable that her parents, on at least one occasion, strapped her to the bed. Doctors were called and Una was forced to submit to what Hawthorne described as "an electrical witch," an early form of electric shock treatment. Hawthorne's own mood was such that he decided to receive similar treatment. Una gradually recovered, but Hawthorne never fully regained his spirits. He traveled, in an attempt to escape from himself, or to spare the family his gloomy presence. He saw one or two old friends. He tried to write. *The Dolliver Romance* was quickly abandoned: in it he had returned to his fascination with resurrection, but preoccupations with failure—physical, mental and literary—took over and it remained unfinished. He also sketched various political commentaries on the Civil War, now under full sway, and his racism and cynicism shocked even his closest friends.

Shelley had finished his *Cenci* drama at the top of the high tower of the Villa Valsovano, in a kind of glazed room. Hawthorne's last act—on any scale—was to build an extravagant extension to the house at Concord, felling four hundred and fifty Norway spruces in order to add an ill-conceived third-story tower. He wanted to rise above his sense of the pettiness of life, above the futility of it all, above his own sense of failure. Yet he was, by now, a famous writer. The tower was never used because Hawthorne deemed it too cold in winter and too hot in summer. He became ever more reclusive. Neighbors would spy him only when "dodging about amongst the trees in his hilltop as if he feared his neighbors' eyes would catch him as he walked." Disingenuously, or because he had lost all self-perspective, he told Ralph Emerson, one of his neighbors, that the well-worn track amid the trees would be his only memorial.

In April 1864 he set out on a final trip, to visit Pierce. It may be that he wanted to spare his family from dealing with his death. He had already told them to burn all his letters. Pierce recalled that Hawthorne had told him that his great hope was that he would die without a struggle. On the night of May 18–19, he died in his sleep. Emerson was one of many who confessed to never having felt he knew him. And in a letter to Annie fields, Sophia wrote: "The sacred veil of his eyelids he scarcely lifted to himself—such an unviolated sanctuary as was his nature, I, his wife, never conceived nor knew."

The obituaries and eulogies recognized him as one of the founding fathers of the new American tradition. That he was much admired in England further bolstered his position among his compatriots. Reservations were, needless to say, expressed about his political responses: "The character of his genius isolated him, and he stood aloof from the common interests. Intent upon studying men in certain aspects, he cared little for man; and the high tides of collective emotion among his fellows left him dry." And his admirers also tended to describe his genius as rarefied, remote. Richard Holt Hutton, an English critic particularly astute in this, wrote, "He has been called a mystic, which he was not and a psychological dreamer, which he was in very slight degree. He was really the ghost of New England—we do not mean the 'spirit,' nor the 'phantom'; but the ghost in the older sense in which the term is used as a thin rarefied essence which is to be found somewhere behind the physical organization."

Hawthorne's strange essence lives on in his writings, and nowhere more cryptically than in *The Marble Faun*, inspired by the presence of Beatrice Cenci which struck him so forcibly. Like the presence of the Salem witches and Ann Hutchinson and other women spirits of his New England past, Hawthorne's life was animated by a strong sense of ghostly presences. These phantom figures dominated his thoughts and imagination, obscuring the immediate realities so obviously visible to his contemporaries. When Julian Hawthorne was researching his biography of his parents he visited the aged Melville, "melancholy and pale." In Melville's *Pierre* the portrait of Beatrice Cenci plays a prominent role not unlike the one it plays in *The Marble Faun*, in its capacity to make real the mysterious forces of sexual guilt, whether real or imagined. Melville understood Hawthorne, and Julian reported of his interview with him: "He said several interesting things, among which the most remarkable was that he was

convinced Hawthorne had all his life concealed some great secret, which would, were it known, explain all the mysteries of
his career."

Melville had recognized Hawthorne's insight into those
areas of human experience that he had also dared to explore:
immorality and perversion and the repressions and frustrations
of the American family. Both writers had lost their fathers early
and in Hawthorne's case this cast a distinct psychological shadow
over his work. Surrogate fathers recur in his fiction and they are
frequently ominous figures like less exaggerated versions of
Francesco Cenci. There is often some ambiguity about the hero's
true paternity and a sense that the hero suffers from a kind of
sexual guilt that belongs more properly with his progenitors, not
unlike Beatrice's. Both Melville and Hawthorne fell for her and
wrote her intractable story into their most controversial works.
It is no wonder that Melville suspected Hawthorne of some dark
mysteries: Melville may well have been burdened by similar secrets. His instinct had been to exchange confidences with
Hawthorne that might have been a therapeutic balm for both,
but Hawthorne pushed him away.

—ᴕᴕ—

Harriet Hosmer:
Rebellious Innocence

*The first hole made through a piece of stone is a
revelation.*

HENRY MOORE

In December 1858, the year Hawthorne embarked on *The
Marble Faun*, Harriet Hosmer, the pioneering American sculptor, wrote to her patron and compatriot Wayman Crow in St.
Louis, Missouri. Hosmer was in Rome where she had settled and
would spend the most productive and important years of her life.
She was replying to a letter from Crow reassuring her that her
sculpture of *Beatrice Cenci* had finally arrived, at the end of a
long journey. From Rome *Beatrice* had traveled to exhibitions
in London, Boston, New York, Philadelphia and then finally to
St. Louis: "So the Cenci is finally at rest. I hope the light is good
and that the critics will deal leniently with her. As mothers say,
Beatrice has her good points and she has her faults. Nobody

knows it better than the parent who brought her forth, but I will leave it to others, to find out what they are."

On its travels the sculpture had generally prompted favorable reports, but reviews and notices were more taken up by comment and admiration for the young lady who had created it than by the work itself. In America there was a brief period of patriotic rallying for a new national heroine. Hosmer was to follow *Beatrice* home and in the meantime Cornelia Crow, Wayman Crow's daughter, kept her up to date with some of the reviews. Hosmer commented on these to Wayman Crow that the work had had "divers good notices and some that cut it up."

Those who admired the sculpture were particularly struck by the emotional power of the cold stone: "Beatrice, overcome by weariness, as on the night before her execution; but even in her sleep the bitterness of despair and her utter sense of abandonment never loose their hold upon the helpless girl." Hosmer described her not as asleep, but dreaming. And it was her own capacity to dream, to imagine a life for herself far removed from her birthplace and from the exclusive company of her father at home, that explains her remarkable life. The first signs of rebellion came early and in many ways her father responded appropriately, but in the end he wanted her for himself and when Hosmer refused, he betrayed her. Women who are victims of men's desires and who refuse to submit, like Beatrice, would become frequent subjects of her work.

"Hatty" Hosmer's fascination with sculpture began as a child and even in her early years her passion had the effect of molding her self-image: she cast herself as a sculptor. A childhood friend recalled her secret studio hidden beneath a natural overhang of bank, beside the Charles River near her home. She had found a clay pit in the garden and she took bucketsful to her studio where

she spent long hours modeling frogs, rats and snakes. She surrounded herself with specimens both dead and alive. The family
cat served as a model for savage tigers. She worked in a smock,
in the pocket of which she kept a small handgun decorated with
silver and ivory. She used it to shoot many of her subjects so as
to be able to inspect a motionless body, "just to get it right."
She was allowed free run of her father's office and Dr. Hosmer's
resident skeleton was a favorite plaything which she would dress
in different clothes as if it were just another doll. Death shaped
her childhood in more ways than one.

Hiram Hosmer, Hatty's father, had studied medicine at
Harvard. He took up his practice in Watertown, Massachusetts,
where he lived with his wife Sarah. It was a culturally vibrant
town founded in the seventeenth century by John Whitney, an
eccentric English statesman and cleric, and there were close links
with Boston and Cambridge. Harriet's parents had married in
1827 and the following year their first child, Sarah Helen, was
born. Two years later they had a second daughter, Harriet
Goodhue. Two sons followed, the first dying of consumption
after a few months; the second, George, was born in 1833. Neither parent believed in coddling their children: "I got them some
india rubbers in town yesterday," her mother told a cousin,
"that they might spat through the mud and snow at all times."
But not many months later George died, also of consumption.
And less than a year and a half on, in May, with the spring
flowers at their most beautiful, their mother Sarah died too. She
was thirty-three.

Years later Hatty wrote to her lifelong friend, Cornelia Crow,
sending her condolences on the death of a sister. Her reasoning
may have been lacking in tact, but it was well meant. The death of
a sister "however dear" was, she said, "but small in comparison

to the loss of a parent—a mother—the extent of which none can know but by experience. . . . Nothing can supply her place . . . no love can be so strong, no one with influence so great." But as a child Hatty seems to have expressed very little of the anguish she suffered as a result of her mother's early death.

Hiram's response to these multiple deaths was the response of convinced medic. He became utterly obsessed with his daughters' health and encouraged physical exercise to the virtual exclusion of all else. "There is a lifetime for the cultivation of the mind," he argued, "but the body develops in a few years, and during that period nothing should be permitted to interfere with its free and healthy growth." Yet at the age of thirteen Sarah Helen succumbed to the same consumption that had struck down her two brothers and her mother. Hatty was eleven and from now on she and her father lived alone.

Hiram's faith in his program for Hatty remained unchanged. She continued to enjoy the physical freedoms which her father considered paramount. In winter she skated on the frozen Charles River, in summer she swam and boated. Hiram had a magnificent gondola built for her, complete with velvet cushions, and she took her friends for unstable rides. She climbed trees and became a crack shot with a gun, or bow and arrows. She was competitive and fearless, outdoing boys of her age in all manner of physical challenges. She became an excellent horsewoman and practiced all kinds of stunts. At various points she was enrolled at school—and expelled on at least three occasions. In between times there were governesses and tutors but no one succeeded in taming her. She attended singing classes for a period and delighted in contributing strange guttural sounds. At church she was reputed to have contributed a forged banknote to the collection. However unruly Hatty's behavior, Hiram insisted that it was only a natural response to inappropriately stifling institutions. As she approached adolescence her capers became increasingly dangerous. She rode to Boston and back—at night—to win a bet. On one of her reckless sailing adventures on Fresh Pond she all but drowned. More bizarrely she dared herself to crawl in loose rubble, under a series of precariously positioned classical columns which were later to be raised up to form the structure of the new town hall. Then the police became involved when she was apprehended attempting to uncouple railway carriages to leave cars and their occupants behind as the engine pulled out of the station. Hiram had to bail her out.

As Hatty approached adolescence her pranks turned peculiarly morbid and Hiram's attitude to her changed. Hatty's latest plan may have been an unconscious protest against the randomness, the injustice of longevity as opposed to early death. It involved Dr. Eliakim Morse, a well-known local figure, something of a recluse, who lived in a palatial residence in the Watertown area. He lived on into great old age, his long white hair never cut, seemingly immortal, a living legend, the revered father figure of the community. Hatty wrote a brief note to a Boston newspaper informing them of Dr. Morse's death, an act of patricide at the stroke of the pen. She then hid nearby and watched the steady procession of friends and neighbors calling to leave their cards and other expressions of condolence, only to be informed that Dr. Morse was still in the land of the living. It was obvious that a hoax had been played and it was equally obvious that there was only one suspect. Hiram decided that the only option was to send her away to boarding school and he arranged for her to enroll at Mrs. Sedgwick's school at Lenox, Massachusetts. To be incarcerated in a boarding school, after years of freedom, was going to be a shock.

Mrs. Sedgwick's family, the Dwights, like her husband's family, were descendants of the Puritans and had been strict Calvinists, but they had been gradually won over to the Unitarians, along with other liberals. They practiced what they preached. Mrs. Charles Sedgwick's school for girls was founded in 1828, but before moving to Lenox she and her husband were living in New York. There they were drawn into a strange tragedy.

A young woman had been involved in a stabbing. She was arrested and charged with the offense. During the trial the defense argued that the young woman had acted in self-defense. The man had raped her. The young woman was acquitted. But her ordeal—both the crimes and the ignominy of the court proceedings—tipped her over the edge. She began to display symptoms of mental derangement. Elizabeth Sedgwick took her in and nursed her through her long illness and premature death. This experience strengthened Elizabeth's sense of vocation: she described her Lenox school as a "character factory." Elizabeth's horror at the destruction of a young woman's life shaped her educational approach to all the girls in her charge.

At the school Hatty was immensely popular. She was great fun, while at the same time displaying a serious side which made her attractive to the older girls. She also appealed to a frequent visitor to the school, Frances Anne Kemble, known simply as "Fanny," whom Elizabeth had known in New York. The daughter of the actor Charles Kemble, who at one time owned and managed Covent Garden in London, Fanny had been quickly drawn into the theater. When she and her father came to America she was universally adored. She married a wealthy American, Pierce Butler of Philadelphia, but the marriage quickly foundered. Her brief stay on her husband's plantation at St. Simons Island, in Georgia, played a part in exposing their differences: her letters reveal her abhorrence for slavery and the conditions in which the slaves lived on the plantation.

When the marriage came to an end, Fanny moved to Lenox and was regularly welcomed at the school. Other neighbors were more reserved. She fished in local streams wearing pantaloons and derided the contemporary American use of euphemisms: women, she insisted, had "legs," not "limbs." She also served. On Saturday afternoons she gave dramatic readings at the school which were completed in the evening in the more intimate surroundings of her cottage. The day would end with contributions by the girls—improvizations, stories, songs. Fanny was independent and she developed a highly successful career. Mrs. Sedgwick considered her a fine example of womanhood for whom male protection, in the form of a father or husband, was not necessary. She was determined that her girls would be equipped for life in its fullest sense, for decisive action. Hatty's years at Lenox passed happily but not altogether smoothly. Later Elizabeth described her as "the most difficult pupil to manage that I ever saw but I think I never saw one in whom I took so deep an interest and whom I learned to love so well."

When Hatty left Mrs. Sedgwick's she was clear that she wanted a career and she was equally clear that she wanted to be a sculptor. Her father fell in with this idea, recognizing that if this was to be more than a hobby she would need to work with someone good. She embarked on her studies of drawing and sculpting with Peter Stephenson, an Englishman living in Boston. Her first work was a bust of Byron. Impressed by Hatty's determination, Hiram Hosmer set about arranging lessons in anatomy, an aspect of a sculptor's training which he naturally considered of prime importance. Dr. Hosmer asked the Boston Medical Society if Hatty could attend the lectures in anatomy. But as one of the Hosmer friends recalled, "it seemed to them a gross impropriety for women to be thus inquiring into the structure of the human frame." The Society flatly refused.

Hatty was not to be easily beaten and a visit to St. Louis was arranged, to see Cornelia Crow, a close friend from her years at Mrs. Sedgwick's, whose father was a wealthy local businessman and philanthropist with a keen interest in local education and culture. Wayman Crow intervened on Hatty's behalf, persuading the Missouri Medical College to accept her. Hatty matriculated on November 6, 1850. The school's Director was Joseph Nash McDowell, brilliant and eccentric: he was given to rages and violence with those he considered his enemies, but with Hatty he was protective and fatherly.

McDowell's attitudes to death were many and varied. Cadavers were, of course, always in demand and their procurement was an unprofessional and unregulated business. Mostly they had to be "snatched" and students and teachers worked alongside one another, raiding local graveyards. McDowell himself also participated. Not surprisingly, local people regarded the students and professors of the anatomy school with fearful suspicion. McDowell's involvement with the "resurrectionists" was complicated by his ardent belief in spiritualism: he was regularly tormented by ghoulish visions. Departed members of his own family, however, were to be safely preserved in the family mausoleum that he had built. While he awaited completion of the elaborate octagonal building the bodies were preserved in large copper containers filled with alcohol and tightly sealed. A sober procession, mostly made up of his students, carried the bodies to a temporary resting place. When the mausoleum was finally ready, a second torch-lit procession led by McDowell playing his beloved violin accompanied the bodies.

When Hatty graduated in 1851, McDowell was sad to see her go. She returned home to Watertown where her cousin Alfred, two years her junior, was staying while studying medicine at Harvard. He and Hatty shared a passion for anatomy; in a letter to a friend written that summer she confessed she thought her interest "unnatural" and added, "Alf and I panted for something to dissect." A pet cat was sacrificed to the scalpel.

In the autumn Hatty was hard at work, seven days a week, in the studio that Hiram had built for her in the garden. At that time she was giving priority to her medallion of McDowell's profile, soon shipped to St. Louis. Its journey via the Great Lakes worried Hatty. She "fancied the Dr. resting quietly in a watery grave." McDowell wrote to thank her, and told her how much he missed her: "Dear Hat, I like, not love you, for my poor old heart, that has so often been chilled by the winters of adversity, cannot now love, but could I love any one, it would be the child who has so remembered me as to send me an undeserved monument of esteem, as you have done." He described the care with which he was treating it: "Hattie, I have covered the marble you sent me with crêpe, not to mourn for the loss of a friend, but for the absence of the one who wrought it and to preserve it as pure as the one who gave it to me. Long may you live, my child, long may you be comforted in this cold world by friends; and believe me ever yours, J. N. McDowell."

A few years later when Hatty's work was beginning to attract national acclaim, McDowell wrote excitedly to the editor of a St. Louis paper pointing out how proud the city should be to have provided Hatty with a crucial aspect of her formation as a sculptor. His praise for her was heartfelt:

> To see a man mount step by step through difficulties, and at last
> stand on the first round of fame's proud ladder, commands
> admiration. But to see a woman dare to scale the mountain height
> of fame, when she has the heroic courage to plant her ladder on
> a precipice and lean it on a storm cloud, and dare the lightning's
> angry passion of jealousy, makes the generous bosom heave with
> love for the sex, and glory that we were born of woman.

Hatty was much cheered by the letter at a time when jealousy
was shaking her ladder.

Back in Watertown Hiram may have hoped that Hatty's energies would be contained in her little studio. But she was already
dreaming of Italy. She knew that there could be no better place
in terms of her training. She yearned for the ready availability of
antique marbles to learn from, and the use of live models which
was unheard of in America at the time. And of course there would
be a ready supply of the right materials. Hiram was uneasy about
losing her: "Father went so long without visiting my shop [stu-
dio] and now comes first thing in the morning and the last thing
at night," she informed a friend. He was already planning a
larger, better studio to welcome her back from Rome when her
studies were completed. Hiram was to accompany her to Rome
to ensure that she was satisfactorily settled. He could not have
known how passionately she would fall in love with the city and
how reluctant she would be ever to return to him.

They arrived on November 12, 1852. She wrote excitedly
to a friend, "Can you believe that this is indeed Rome, and more
than all that I am in it?" Less than six months later she knew
that she would stay: "I have not the least idea that I shall see
America for five years at the inside. I have determined that,
unless recalled by accident, I will stay until I have accomplished

certain things, be that time, three, five, or ten years." She was euphoric:

> Don't ask me if I was ever happy before, don't ask me if I am happy now, but ask me if my constant state of mind is felicitous, beatific, and I will reply 'Yes.' It never entered into my head that anybody could be so content on earth, as I am here. I wouldn't live anywhere else but in Rome, if you would give me the Gates of Paradise and all the Apostles thrown in.

What mattered, above all, was what Rome could offer her as a sculptor: "I can learn and do more here, in one year, than I could in America in ten. America is a grand and glorious country in some respects, but this is a better place for an artist."

Before leaving his only child to return to the empty house at Watertown, Hiram had to find for Hatty a sculptor prepared to take her on as a pupil and there was, needless to say, a good deal of staunch prejudice to overcome. Women were considered unfit for sculpture on account of the heaviness and dirtiness of the work and the discipline was also considered too great: whatever their initial enthusiasm women would soon give up. John Gibson, the celebrated neoclassicist, was the sculptor the Hosmers soon had in mind. They were aiming high: Gibson had recently completed a commission of a full-length statue of none other than Queen Victoria herself. He had lived in Rome since 1817 and had studied under Antonio Canova, the most respected sculptor as far as Americans were concerned.

Gibson was shown two daguerreotypes of Hatty's work, her drawings and her certificate in anatomy, and was surprised by the quality of her draughtsmanship. He invited the Hosmers to his studio at number 4, Via Fontanella. Behind a shabby entrance lay a courtyard filled with the scent of orange and lemon trees, and the soothing sounds of a fountain. Hatty and John Gibson exchanged few words, Hatty simply announcing "I wish to become your pupil" and Gibson answering "I will teach you all I know." He suggested that she take a few days to see something of Rome before coming to work, but Hatty arrived the next morning and was taken up an outside staircase in the little courtyard to a small room. This, Canova's own studio, was to be her workroom.

Gibson worked hard and expected the same of Hatty and this was precisely the way she wanted things. Her admiration for him was enormous. He was, she said, "a god in his own studio; God help him out of it": she knew his incompetence in everything but his art: he was absent-minded and regularly got lost. Hatty's life outside the studio was a good deal fuller than Gibson's; the little colony of Americans and British expatriates in Rome was an interesting one. The English poets Robert and Elizabeth Browning, and Nathaniel Hawthorne and his wife Sophia, would soon become Hatty's close friends and supporters. Meanwhile, she copied the works of the great masters, rendering something either significantly larger or smaller than the original, the training process of the time. By February 1853, some two months after her arrival, she had made considerable progress. The sculptor William Story wrote of his fellow countrywoman: "Miss H[osmer] is also, to say the word, very wilful & too independent by half—& is mixed up with a set whom I do not like & can do little for her."

But Hatty had the devoted support of her master and needed nothing more. Gibson teased her about her diminutive size and happily reversed the power relationship of master and disciple—in his little notes to her he would sign off "your slave."

Hatty had quickly found a horse in Rome and continued to enjoy the freedom of the outdoors. But there were constraints. Story, who became a kind of self-elected guardian, overseeing Hatty's activities, wrote of her scoldingly: "The Hosmer takes a high hand here with Rome—& would have the Romans know that a Yankee girl can do anything she pleases, walk alone, ride on horseback alone & laugh at their rules." Apparently in response to local complaints, "The Police interfered and countermanded the riding alone on account of the row it made in the streets—& I believe *that* is over—but I cannot affirm." When it came to her work he was clear that it showed considerable potential, but he hesitated to conjecture as to her innate gifts in terms of originality:

> She is doing very well & shows a capital spirit—& I have no doubt will succeed. But it is one thing to copy & another to create. She may or may not have inventive powers as an artist. If she have, will she not be the first woman who ever had?

At the very moment when Hatty was about to throw herself into making that crucial transition from copyist to artist she received a letter from her father. She had been in Rome for well over a year by now and Hiram considered that her period of training was over. He found it difficult to live without her and had left the house at Watertown unchanged since her departure with her childhood possessions still brightening the quiet house. The new, enlarged studio was finished and Hiram longed to see it occupied. He told Hatty that he could no longer support her in Rome. Given that Hiram was "a man of competent property,"

Hatty recognized betrayal in his resorting to paternal pressure. She was adamant that she was not going to fall in with her father's scheme. She had no desire to return to the provincial dullness of Watertown and the stifling experience of living alone with him. She had old friends to turn to, and quickly wrote to Wayman Crow, who had already offered financial support:

> My father has made known to you his ill fortune, and had he made it known to me at an earlier period, I certainly should have sooner adopted the course I need to pursue, viz: that of support-ing myself. It now becomes my duty, as it is my pleasure, to re-lieve him of all expenses incurred by myself.

Whatever his intentions, the effect of Hiram's announcement alienated her. Buoyed up by her newly discovered independence from him, she accepted Crow's patronage without complication:

> On your goodness, then, my more than friend, I am forced to rely, and to accept the offer you have so generously made me. With such a start in the world, I think, nay, I am sure, I can make my own way, and perhaps the time may come when I can prove more sensibly than by words, that I am not unmindful of the obligations which I owe you. I am getting to know a little more of the world than I did once, and if I have gained this knowl-edge by costly experience, there is one comfort in thinking that it will never have to be paid for again.

Wayman's support came with no strings attached—and Hatty had cut herself free, forever, from her father.

Gibson's standards were high but he was confident that the time was right for Hatty to attempt her first original work. Her choice was Daphne. In this she was in part following contemporary fashion. The Victorians were fascinated by Greek myth and resurrections of mythological figures took place in all the arts. Daphne's story begins with her repudiation of love and marriage. Hatty herself was adamant that she too would never make such a commitment. "An artist," she insisted, "has no business to marry. For a man it may be well enough, but for a woman, on whom matrimonial duties and cares weigh more heavily, it is a moral wrong, I think, for she must either neglect her profession or her family, becoming neither a good wife and mother nor a good artist. My ambition is to become the latter." But as an attractive and vivacious woman, maintaining her independence required tenacity: "I wage eternal feud with the consolidating knot."

The Daphne of Ovid's *Metamorphoses* has first to rebel against the desires of her father, Peneus, that she marry. She resists paternal pressure, intent on a life of freedom, dancing alone in the forests, driven by her own secret passions. Cupid then shoots an arrow at her. Contrary to his usual mischievous intentions, his arrow kills all desire in her dead. At the same time he shoots an arrow at Apollo, filling him with a strength of passion that drives him to pursue Daphne with a fervor that terrifies her. Greek mythology is, of course, full of stories of women impregnated by gods against their wills, and forced to kill either the baby that results—or themselves. Daphne's prayers for protection are answered but she pays a terrible price for her escape: she is turned into a tree. She remains trapped beneath the bark and Apollo can still feel the vibrations of her heart from within the tree trunk.

There is great compassion in Hatty's *Daphne*—her expression is one of calm resignation rather than terror, and her shoulders and breasts are exquisitely rendered—John Gibson was much struck. He considered "the roundness of the flesh" to have been brilliantly executed.

Hatty described *Daphne* as "my first child." And she would quickly be followed by "another daughter." Her second child would be *Medusa*. Daphne's "sister," Medusa, is not the hideous woman of some renderings of the story, but of such astonishing beauty that Poseidon pursues her and seduces her in the temple of Athena herself. Athena punishes Poseidon for his sacrilege by turning Medusa's flowing hair into snakes. Her beauty remains, thrown into terrible contrast by the ghastliness of the writhing serpents about her face.

Transformations brought about by fate, the idea of metamorphosis, the co-existence of beauty and evil, the stuff of Beatrice Cenci's life—these subjects fascinated the Victorians. Gothic writers like "Monk" Lewis, one of the authors who intrigued Shelley as a child, and influenced Mary Shelley's own writings, are intimately concerned to make sense of either agonizing and inescapable processes of transformation or unexpected and terrible sudden metamorphoses. The monster that Mary has Frankenstein create has displayed remarkable longevity. In the writings of Hawthorne and Melville the progress from one state to another maps a moral journey toward a heightened awareness of responsibility and the ever-receding, and thus tragic, goal of human perfectibility. But Hatty's fascination with the agonies of Daphne and Medusa is at once simpler and more complicated. The very process of sculpture is one of metamorphosis as the dull mass with which the sculptor begins is slowly and painfully wrought into something quite different. Resurrection, Hatty explained, has then to be achieved: "the sculptor himself . . . must breathe into it that vitality which . . . only the artist can inspire." The artist animates dead material and the subject achieves immortality.

Many of Hatty's admirers became close friends. The Brownings, who arrived from Florence to spend the winter in Rome in 1853, quickly drew her in. Elizabeth was particularly struck by Hatty's openness and lack of pretension which contrasted sharply, she said, with the "crawling social falsities" of the city. She was as much struck by John Gibson as Hatty: "By the way I think I too may be falling in love with Gibson. I feel myself going."

Hatty and the Brownings shared many preoccupations including a fascination with spiritualism and the complex relationships between the living and the dead, and in stories whose core involves extreme emotion and sexual tragedy. Hatty hoped that one or the other would compose a poem based on a story that had long haunted her. One evening, returning home, she and the Brownings passed the ruined shapes along the Appian Way. One looked remarkably like a human head. She told them the story about a brutal and ruthless official named Apuleius who tried to force his daughter Apulia to give herself to the Emperor Domitian, to become his courtesan. But Apulia was much in love with a young captain, Belisarius, and refused to comply with her father's scheme. To punish her for her resistance, Apuleius had Belisarius brutally murdered. Apulia had no idea what had become of him but was distraught at his disappearance and withdrew to a tower, waiting vainly for his return. She died of a broken heart. Apuleius, filled with shame for his actions, had a monument erected to her memory. As time passed the monument eroded and gradually came to resemble Apulia and, in local legend, the head became known as the "weird watcher of the Roman Campagna." Elizabeth was much struck: "Did stone ever imprison so much wistful earnestness, so much weary longing, as does that poor, shattered form, old and gray and mutilated by centuries?" Neither of the Brownings took up Hatty's challenge to resurrect Apulia in verse, but Hatty would release from their stony prison two subjects intimately bound up with Apulia's story: *Oenone* and *Beatrice Cenci*.

Alongside *Oenone*, *Puck* was conceived and Hatty described them as a "marble son and daughter." The mischievous figure from Shakespeare's *A Midsummer Night's Dream* is perhaps Hatty's most famous piece. It was bought by the Prince of Wales, later Edward VII, on a visit to Rome in 1859, to decorate his rooms at Oxford. He was still in his teens and *Harper's Weekly* printed a cartoon depicting the young man with Gibson at his side, admiring Hatty's work. She stands by, erect and neat, clutching a riding crop.

Hatty was keen to sculpt *Oenone* and Crow gave her the commission although for some time Hatty kept her subject secret. Tennyson, whom Hatty had much loved as a schoolgirl, had published two Oenone poems which treat her tragic plight. The story is part of Troy's: forced to flee the city because the oracle has named him as the one who will be responsible for the city's downfall, Paris is banished to the country where he lives as a shepherd. He is unaware of his real identity. He falls passionately in love with Oenone and she with him. They become lovers and live in pastoral bliss. Later, Paris is chosen to judge the beauty of the goddesses. He picks Aphrodite, presenting her with the golden apple, and is then rewarded himself. He is given Helen, wife of Menelaus, and eagerly accepts his prize, abandoning the heart-broken Oenone.

The delay between investing in materials and receiving commissions or sales continued to make Hatty's life a precarious financial balancing act. In 1855 she canceled her trip with Gibson to Britain, afraid that it would prove too costly. Instead she worked on through the Roman summer and then out of the blue received an important commission for a full-length statue. It was to be the focal point of the Mercantile Library in St. Louis. The letter she received was from a "Mr. Vinton" and Hatty immediately suspected that Crow had invented him: "Come now, dear Mr. Crow, confess Mr. Vinton is a myth and yourself the liberal donor. . . . I have an inward feeling that you will chuckle a little at the idea of my corresponding with *him* on the subject," she wrote to her patron.

But Alfred Vinton was real, the chairman of the Board of Directors of the Mercantile Library, and Crow insisted that he had not played a decisive role. Hatty remained skeptical. If she received a request for a sculpture "from the Poles," she told him, "I should be persuaded that somehow or other you had a hand in it." At the time she was earnestly exploring the character and story of Beatrice Cenci which she felt might be a promising subject. Hatty knew Shelley's poetry, as her playful parodies of him testify, but she never recorded a debt to him in terms of her own conception of Beatrice Cenci. Nor does she refer to three more contemporary works: Jean-Charles Sismondi's *Histoire des républiques italiennes du moyen âge*, published by the Genevan historian in 1840, Giovanni Battista Niccolini's *Beatrice Cenci* (1844) or Guerrazzi's *Beatrice Cenci: Storia del Secolo XVI* of 1851. The frontispiece of the last shows Francesco lustily pursuing his daughter, an image very similar to Apollo and Daphne. In 1851 Walter Savage Landor wrote his *Five Scenes* in which Beatrice appears. Although Hatty

certainly knew Landor and presumably his work, again she
mentions nothing in relation to her *Beatrice*. But she certainly
knew the Guido Reni portrait in the Palazzo Barberini and later
acknowledged the painting's central role in her conception of
the sculpture.

The work was exhausting. She wrote to Cornelia Crow who
was struggling with her role as wife and mother: "I doubt if your
little body could be in an upright posture eight hours of the day,
and I'm sure those soft hands couldn't be dabbling in mud so
long." Although Crow had lent her an advance of £200 and she
had sold everything in her studio, she was still struggling. Re-
cession in Europe had hit all but the most famous artists hard:
"Nine-tenths of the artists will open glove shops or tobacco stalls
or something else, not for bread and butter, but for bread alone
without the butter," she wrote to Crow. And she allowed herself to confess: "In your ear in a very private way I grunt too . . .
somehow or other it still seems uphill work."

But an invitation from Sir Charles Eastlake, President of the
Royal Academy, who had visited her in Rome, to exhibit *Beatrice
Cenci* in London the following spring lifted her spirits. She
worked with tremendous concentration; in February 1857
Beatrice was finished. Hatty was twenty-six and her *Beatrice* is
slightly older than the young woman in Reni's famous painting,
closer in age to Hatty herself. She is lying on a marble block which
serves as a bed, but it is too short to support her whole body
and her left leg trails on the plinth beneath. Her hair is long and
flows freely over her shoulders, which are bare. Her left breast
is visible beneath a relaxed left arm. Most of her upper body and
legs are covered by a thin sculpted drapery, which reveals rather
than conceals the shape of her delicate figure beneath, quite a
feat in dense, hard, unyielding marble. Her right hand is tucked,

childlike, beneath her cheek and her head rests on a stone pillow. Her trailing arm finishes in a hand whose fingers have calmly opened, leaving a rosary across her palm. *Beatrice*'s face, like that of so many of Hatty's women, is strangely composed, even in sleep. Somehow the expression conveys a life within, thoughts, feelings and dreams, circulating within the smooth marble head. Hatty resurrected not a dead body, but a living one. Her *Beatrice* seems somehow to be free to travel beyond the cruelty and oppression of her life. Imagination—Hatty's and Beatrice's— triumphs.

The sculpture was carefully packed up and made ready to sail for England and Hatty would soon follow. The high point of her stay in London was the evening of festivities complete with illuminations at the RA. Her *Beatrice* was widely admired—by the Bishop of London and Lord and Lady Palmerston most notably. From London Hatty made her way home—to Watertown. Here she was greeted as a celebrity and numerous visitors called at Riverside Street, including the poet Longfellow and his wife. But while enjoying visits with many old friends, Hatty was keen to return to her adoptive home. John Gibson wrote to her regularly—and teasingly: "Be good; return soon; if you don't, I shall look out for another, but I do not expect to find such another clever fellow as you are." On October 24, 1857, Hatty sailed for Europe. To pass the time she wrote parodies of Shelley, including one dedicated to the hen aboard ship which had provided her with her breakfast egg:

> *Hail, laying bird, and thrice all hail!*
> *Thou'st raised an egg; my voice I'll raise.*
> *For will shall not, if flesh shall fail,*
> *To greet thy lays with other lays.*

Beatrice had been much admired, but Hatty's career remained as uncertain as ever. Although she was returning to Rome triumphant, her finances remained precarious and her successes had aroused fierce jealousy.

The Hawthornes were among many who now came to visit her studio in Rome. Sophia had met her more recently, but Nathaniel had not seen her since her schooldays at Lenox: "We found Miss Hosmer in a little up-stairs room. She is a small, brisk, wide-awake figure, of queer and funny aspect, yet not ungraceful, nor to be rejected from one's good graces without further trial." He was not, however, complimentary about her *Beatrice*. He found Gibson's sculptures "disturbing"—the marble, he claimed, was too palpable, too sensual. No doubt the latent eroticism in the work of a woman disturbed him all the more.

Many of Hatty's contemporaries were quick to judge her lifestyle, as well as her work. Around the time of the Hawthornes' visit, Hatty's reputation was almost literally on trial but nothing could reach the courts until slander turned to libel. For some years Hatty had soldiered on well aware of the malicious rumors that surrounded her production, and by extension her personal life. Her mentor, the English sculptor John Gibson, was also part of the gossip.

Hawthorne was struck by her outer appearance and was astute about the woman within:

> She had on a male shirt, collar and cravat, with a brooch of Etruscan gold, and on her curly head was a picturesque little cap of black velvet; and her face was as bright and funny, and as small of feature, as a child's. It looked, in one aspect, youthful and yet there was something worn in it, too, as if it had faced a good deal of wind and weather, either morally or physically.

There was never anything so jaunty as her movement and action; she was indeed very queer, but she seemed to be her actual self, and nothing affected or made-up; so that, for my part, I give her full leave to wear what may suit her best, and to behave as her inner woman prompts.

He said nothing about her appearance below the waist, no doubt knowing that the height of her hem had to allow her to mount a scaffold without encumbrance. Had he mentioned that it was unusually high this could easily have been misconstrued. There were plenty of people out to topple her from her pedestal.

Hatty could not be sure who had started the rumors which had circulated for years. On November 21, 1863 she wrote excitedly to a friend: "I hope and trust I may soon be involved in a law suit. For seven years it has been whispered about that I do not do my own work but employ a man to do it for me. This scandal has now reached the point when I am accused of being a hypocrite and a humbug." Her girlfriends egged her on. Charlotte Cushman, the celebrated American actress who was close to Hatty, wrote to a friend pointing out how important it was "to take the matter up and set the question now and forever at rest. You have no idea how the report has been propagated abroad." The gossip originated in Italy. Unlike her massive sculptures, it traveled effortlessly across the English Channel and the Atlantic and Hatty's career as a sculptor depended on American and British commissions. Muddled up in the whole affair were suggestions that Gibson's relationship with Hatty went beyond that of master and apprentice, but he was quite clear that he had to stand by her. She wrote to a friend: "He is ready to go into any Court of Law for me, and many others have I got to fight for me. So you see it will be no joke." She had engaged a London lawyer and as one of the foremost woman sculptors of the mid-nineteenth century it was no exaggeration for Hatty to call the lawsuit "the Battle of the Amazons." It was not going to be easily won.

One of Hatty's most astonishing sculptures, in part because of its mammoth size, *Queen Zenobia*, had been shown at London International Exhibition in 1862 at the Crystal Palace. There she was prominently displayed and her enemies were further stirred to hostility; *Zenobia* had been poorly received:

> Her heavy English limbs, stained, as was currently reported,— whether in jest or not, we cannot say,—with tobacco juice, to suggest the rosy-tinted Aphrodite; her hair, a pale straw-colour; the pupils of her eyes a light blue; golden earrings in her ears, and a golden collar around her neck; with a face of the common place, house-keeping type, and an attitude devoid of character or intention—it was, to us, a work of unmitigated vulgarity.

The comments on color represent a hostile response to Hatty's subtle polychroming—a common neoclassical practice which she had toned down. The effect was to make the marble look uncannily like real flesh. But the reviewer seems covertly to be criticizing the sculptor rather than her work. The Amazonian *Zenobia* became the symbolic focus of the battle that was to follow.

Open warfare began in the *Queen*, and continued in an obituary of the English sculptor Alfred Gatley in the *Art Journal*. The writer regretted that Gatley's work had received too little attention and, as an aside, contrasted Gatley's position with Hatty's: "The Zenobia, said to be by Miss Hosmer—but really executed by an Italian workman in Rome." Hatty thought it "Capital" that she was now in a position to retaliate publicly. She wrote to the journal describing the sculptural process—as practiced by the neoclassicists including Canova and Gibson—lucidly and succinctly. *Zenobia* had started life as a small clay piece some four feet high and this she worked herself, without assistance. Workmen then constructed an iron skeleton, a framework to support the massive amounts of clay necessary to create such a substantial sculpture. The clay had been worked on to the frame by her men. For a period of eight months she herself then sculpted the clay to bring the piece to a satisfactory conclusion. The clay model was then cast in plaster and given into the hands of marble workers. This was the common practice, she wrote, acknowledging that "this disclosure, I am aware, will shock the many, who often ingeniously discover traces of the sculptor's hand where they do not exist."

Gibson entered the fray. The "long study and finishing is by herself, like any other sculptor." He stood shoulder to shoulder: "If Miss Hosmer's works were the productions of other artists and not her own, there would be in my studio two imposters—Miss Hosmer and myself." The *Queen* offered its apologies but the letter that Hatty received was flippant, belittling the significance of the accusations. Irritated by such an off-hand response Hatty threatened to sue for damages to the tune of £1,000, a considerable sum at the time. In addition they would publish apologies that Hatty would dictate. The tone of the letter she received by return was more to her liking. She considered taking the matter to court nevertheless, as she was curious to see what kind of defense could possibly be mounted, but in the end she realized that she would do her own reputation no good. She had no real intention of pressing for damages and the matter was settled. Apologies were to be printed in *The Times*, *the Galignani* and the *Queen* itself.

The experience molded Hatty into an altogether harder woman. Jealousy of success was a fact of life, but for women matters were different: "a *woman* artist who has been honored by frequent commissions, is an object of peculiar *odium*." Hatty's libeler was named: Joseph Mozier was a hypocritical, shrewd little man with a studio in Florence. His work was not much liked and he was repeatedly accused of plagiarism. Hatty's friends were delighted at her success but there were other sudden difficulties to be confronted.

She had made her commitment to neoclassicism at the outset of her career as a pupil of Gibson's who had himself received Canova's mantle. Then, in 1866, Gibson fell ill. She visited him just before his death, leaving a "kiss on his forehead." The next time she called her "beloved master" was still, "grand and calm and beautiful"—the very image of what neoclassical sculpture strove to be. Her much-loved friend and mentor was gone and Hatty left Rome for a time to recover. His death strengthened her determination to maintain a particular sculptural tradition. An anonymous critic caught up in the *Zenobia* affair commented that Hatty's failure had nothing to do with being a woman; it was inextricably bound up with her blind allegiance to a group of male artists whose classical themes were dead. He may have been right about her aesthetic conviction, but Hatty had struggled against flagrant prejudice from the beginning. To be a woman sculptor in the mid-nineteenth century challenged all sense of propriety and the artistic establishment had often been quick to judge.

In the years after the Civil War in America a growing number of women artists, particularly sculptors, looked to Hatty as an emblematic inspiration. Romanticism was gaining ground and Paris had become the new center of the arts, while political and economic difficulties in Italy had changed life in Rome. She left the city and traveled a good deal, continuing to produce massive commissions from time to time, mainly of a civic and nationalistic kind. Among the most impressive is her statue of Thomas Hart Benton in Lafayette Park, St. Louis, where it was dedicated in 1868.

But Hatty had no home and few resources. For a period Lady Ashburton protected her and gave her a studio at Kent House in London. Here, and at her other residences, Hatty's work was exhibited alongside Raphael, Rubens and Titian. But while she never stopped sculpting altogether, her energy and optimism were directed in new directions too. Her support for feminist causes took up some of her time. Addressing the Women's Club of Chicago she pointed out that in Rome "the evidence of three women was necessary to balance that of one man." How much had changed since Beatrice Cenci's time? The law might have moved on in numerous ways since the Renaissance, but there was still much to reform. "The political disabilities of women," were, she argued, "the stigma of civilization of the nineteenth century."

Hatty also developed a keen interest in new inventions. She followed Edison's work with electricity with great excitement and for some years she worked on the design of a perpetual motion machine, driven by magnets. It may have come to nothing, but it provoked a controversy much like the *Zenobia* scandal. Hatty was accused of having stolen the invention from a man. A court case followed and she was able to defend her claims.

In the last years of her life Hatty looked back very little and instead continued to dream of the future. The idea of a world made smaller by technological developments appealed greatly and she wrote excitedly of the day when it would be possible to breakfast in America one day and lunch in London the next—thanks to airships. The past had never seemed very distant to Hatty and the stories of her subjects, whether classical, like *Oenone*, or Renaissance, like *Beatrice Cenci*, had never been remote but bound up with permanent human struggles. She hoped that things would nevertheless get better: "What fun it would be to come back to this earth after having been a wandering ghost for a hundred years or so and see what has been going on in the flesh while we have been going on in the spirit." Perhaps she imagined that years after her death some brave "resurrectionist" student of anatomy would dig her up, and, like the plastic artist she described at the end of the sculptural process, "breathe life" back into her, aided by some extraordinary scientific breakthrough.

Harriet Hosmer stands apart from the other artists of the dangerous tradition. If society treated her in hostile fashion, which was often the case, it was not only because of the quietly controversial nature of her pieces but also because of the controversial nature of her sense of vocation: sculpture was men's business, not women's. She was not afraid of sculpting subjects about which she had tremendously strong feelings. Again and again she treated women who were victims of sexually predatory male figures, whether gods or men, lovers or fathers. Her sculptures breathed life into the lives of both mythical and real women and her techniques, particularly her use of polychromy, gave her sculptures uncanny fleshiness. Most of her work is, of course, still in existence today and what is particularly striking about these pieces, however outdated their neoclassical conventions may be, is the tension between passivity and strength. Hatty's *Beatrice* looks quite incapable of having meted out revenge on her violent father. Instead she lies quietly and innocently atop her marble bed. Yet her face is full of character, like Hatty's. Beatrice, like her sculptor, is dreaming of a better future: Daphne will be safe dancing alone in the forest and the woman sculptor will no longer be looked on with suspicion. Hatty identified closely with the subjects of her sculptures: they were "daughters" or "children." More curious is her idea of them as her forebears: "I begin to think myself a lineal descendant of the Queen of the Cannibals [Zenobia], whose husband was forced to devour her to make her keep silence."

Nineteenth-century women writers were deemed subversive just for taking up the pen, and many hid behind male pseudonyms: this throws the act of taking up the chisel into its proper perspective. Not only did Harriet Hosmer have the audacity to become a sculptor, at the same time she sculpted subjects, like Beatrice, who were still more subversive—and shocking. And when, as she wrote in a letter to Cornelia Crow, people "laughed at the idea of a woman becoming an artist at all," her desire was to have the opportunity to take matters into her own hands, to do what her much-loved mentor Gibson had counseled and "give some of those fellows a twist."

CHAPTER 7

—•◦•—

The Voyeurs

By the glow of the lamplight . . . poor Lucrezia
could see what he was doing with Beatrice.

STENDHAL, "LES CENCI," 1837

The Cenci fever that took hold of the Florence set affected Robert Browning too, but somewhat indirectly. *The Ring and the Book* (1868–9), which he was writing at the end of his life, and which is generally considered his masterpiece, has often been compared to Shelley's play, *The Cenci*, the first work of the dangerous tradition. The parallels are both textual and biographical. Like Shelley, Browning was working with historical records fortuitously discovered. "The Book" of the title refers to a collection of documents relating to another Italian murder trial of the late seventeenth century, which Browning found on a market stall in Florence. Like Shelley's source, it involves a monstrous aristocrat whose victim is a beautiful girl. In Browning's story

Pompilia Comparini marries Count Guido Franceschini, an impoverished nobleman. Pompilia is deeply unhappy in her marriage and eventually runs away with the help of a young priest, Giuseppe Caponsacchi, and she falls pregnant. Guido first has them arrested and later, with the help of four accomplices, murders them. Guido is brought to trial and claims justification for the murders because of Pompilia's adultery but his appeal is rejected and the five are executed.

Browning's poem, in blank verse, runs to twelve books and more than 21,000 lines. The story is told by a variety of speakers—citizens of Rome, the accused, lawyers, the Pope—which allows Browning to explore an area that greatly interested him: individual perceptions of truth vary and it is only by making sense of myriad points of view that a "Ring" of truth can be constructed. Browning's use of authentic documents also allowed him to explore questions of historical truth, and its ultimate elusiveness. He was concerned to make use of any and every available document and in 1862 rumors reached him of a further possible source. Reference to accounts of the executions of some of his "characters" particularly interested him. In a letter he asked for confirmation that this new manuscript "really related" to "*my* Count Francesco Guidi." The odd thing is that he got the name of his character wrong. Browning's monster of evil is Count Guido Franceschini. He seems to have conflated the alleged painter of the portrait of Beatrice Cenci (*Guido* Reni) with the Machiavellian monster of Shelley's play (*Francesco* Cenci). Browning had read Shelley as a child, and remained in awe of him throughout his life, and Shelley's *Cenci* would seem to have been very much in mind while he worked on *The Ring and the Book*.

Browning's relationship with Beatrice was a tangential one and he never engaged directly with the Cenci story. Charles Dickens can also be placed in the safe tradition. He wrote a good deal about women as victims, and spent much of his adult life abroad. In his *Pictures from Italy*, written in 1846, he describes the portrait of Beatrice in Rome. He mentions the private palaces with their "portraits innumerable, by Titian, and Rembrandt, and Vendyke," "subjects by Correggio, and Murillo, and Raphael," but he never bothers to describe them, yet he devotes an entire page to Beatrice, "a picture almost impossible to be forgotten":

> Through the transcendent sweetness and beauty of her face, there is a something shining out, that haunts me. I see it now, as I see this paper, and my pen. The head is loosely draped in white; the light hair falling down below the linen folds. She has turned suddenly toward you; and there is an expression in the eyes— although they are very tender and gentle—as if the wildness of a momentary terror, or distraction, had been struggled with and overcome, that instant; and nothing but a celestial hope, and a beautiful sorrow, and a desolate earthly helplessness remained. Some stories say that Guido painted it, the night before her execution; some other stories that he painted it from memory, after having seen her, on her way to the scaffold. I am willing to believe that, as you see her on his canvas, so she turned to him, in the crowd, from the first sight of the axe, and stamped upon his mind a look which he stamped on mine as though I had stood beside him on the concourse.

Like many others, Dickens was moved to explore the most tangible remaining link with Beatrice's suffering:

> The guilty palace of the Cenci: blighting a whole quarter of the town, as it stands withering away by grains: had that face, to

my fancy, in its dismal porch, and at its black blind windows, and flitting up and down its dreary stairs, and growing out of the darkness of its gloomy galleries. The History is written in the Painting; written in the dying girl's face, by Nature's own hand.

Dickens was preoccupied by the present. The past only mattered to him insofar as it offered insights into the present and the future. He didn't develop Beatrice as a subject, but during his international lecture tours he returned again and again to the institution of prostitution and the physical and psychological abuses of women. This was a subject that he spoke about with his customary passion and charisma. And he was wonderfully optimistic about the world gradually getting better. At the end of *Pictures from Italy*, he refers to the country's "miseries and wrongs," its "years of neglect, oppression and misrule." But the past, Dickens fervently believed, threw the present into perspective, and offered hope: "In the fragment of her fallen Temples, and every stone of her deserted palaces and prisons, she [Italy] helps to inculcate the lesson that the wheel of Time is rolling for an end, and that the world is, in all great essentials, better, gentler, more forbearing, and more helpful, as it rolls!" Most of his contemporaries would not have agreed. The writers and artists of the dangerous Cenci tradition were all too aware of their own capacity for violence and evil, and afraid that revolutionary energies would continue to wreak havoc throughout the so-called "civilized" world. They were drawn to the Beatrice story because it allowed for the exploration of something very private and intimate, while at the same time allowing for the treatment, in symbolic form, of essentially political questions about power, authority and justice.

Shelley's brooding among the ruins of the Cenci Palace and Byron's contemplation of the fallen Colosseum framed the vision of Italy seen by the expatriate communities of Florence and Rome. Byron's description of the Colosseum in his drama *Manfred* became a talisman for tourists:

> *When I was wandering,—upon such a night*
> *I stood within the Colosseum's wall,*
> *Midst the chief relics of almighty Rome!*
> *The trees which grew along the broken arches*
> *Waved dark in the blue midnight, and the stars*
> *Shone through the rents of ruin . . .*

The glory and might of empires that crushed and broke individual lives lay in magnificent ruins and monumental tragedy. In the Romantic imagination such tragedy was breaking like a great wave over the powers and principalities of their own day, as had happened to ancient Rome, to the Cenci in the late Renaissance, and recently to the absolute French monarchy and then to the Napoleonic French Empire. Writers and artists of the Cenci tradition recognized in her tragedy the incipient tragedy of their own lives, and in the moonlit contemplation of monuments of contemporary powers, the ruins of future contemplation. Goethe's reflection on the Colosseum in his *Italian Journey* (1816) makes this explicit:

> Presently the smoke made its way up the sides, and through every
> chink and opening, while the moon lit it up like a cloud. The
> sight was exceeding glorious. In such a light one ought also to
> see the Pantheon, the Capitol, the Portico of St Peter's, and the
> grand streets and squares.

The early nineteenth-century French novelist Henri Marie Beyle, better known as Stendhal, was torn, in his writings and his life, between an almost childishly romantic vision of things and a harsh and cynical realism. Stendhal considered that there was only one place in the world where these two coexisted spectacularly: he fell in love with Italy—and with Beatrice. Of the artist and his painting he wrote:

> He has cast about Beatrice's neck an insignificant piece of drapery; he has placed a turban on her head; he has evidently exactly reproduced the costume which she had made for her execution, and the dishevelled hair of a poor girl of sixteen who has just surrendered to despair. The face is sweet and beautiful, the expression very gentle, the eyes extremely large; they have the astonished air of a person who has just been surprised at the very moment of shedding scalding tears.

Stendhal is a slippery character. For one thing he wrote about himself with an irony that comes and goes imperceptibly so that you never feel you know him and you are constantly aware of the pleasure he derives from slipping through his readers' fingers or from shocking them. He claimed that for as long as he knew his mother he was in love with her and that in her presence he was intent only on covering her with kisses and, he adds, "that there should be no clothes. She loved me passionately, kissed me often, and I returned her embraces with such ardour that she was often obliged to leave the room. . . . I was as criminal as possible, frenzied in my adoration of her." His father, on the other hand "was an excessively dislikable man." Stendhal was only seven years old when his mother died in childbirth, and for this reason he blamed his father for her death. He went on to

love a great many other women but in his twenties he complained
to a friend, "I need a woman with an exalted soul but they're all
like novels—interesting up to the denouement and two days later
you're astonished at having been interested in anything so common." His somewhat frantic quest for an exceptional woman
resulted in his contracting syphilis in his twenties. He continued
to be attracted to much younger women, some barely in their
teens, but when he fell in love with Giulia Rinieri de' Rocchi,
who was in her early twenties while Stendhal was forty-seven,
he was prevented from marrying her by her aged uncle and pro-
tector. Stendhal railed against paternal authority, believing that
his proposal had been turned down because Giulia's wicked uncle
wanted her for himself. Stendhal's conquests continued until only
months before his death from apoplexy, at the age of fifty-nine.

When Stendhal came to publish his story "Les Cenci," in *La
Revue des Deux Mondes* in 1837 (later part of his *Italian
Chronicles*), he did so anonymously. It is true that he had copied the manuscripts on which he based his *Chronicles* from a private collection while he was French Consul in Civitavecchia and
there were thus questions of professional discretion involved in
his exposure of the machinations of the courts of Rome, cruelty,
eroticism and other excesses displayed by the Italian nobility
and senior dignitaries in the Church during the late Renaissance
period. Several hundred years had passed, but too little had
changed. On the other hand Stendhal was not noted for his cau-
tion or tact. What he did with his Italian source was to make it
all the more disturbing and then publish it without his own
name.

The manuscript on which Stendhal based his story, dated
September 14, 1599, "An account of the Cenci Executions," is
in the Italian Manuscript Collection in the Bibliothèque Nationale

in Paris and his marginal jottings provide insights into his intentions. He was interested in the satanic pleasure derived from transgressions—in the margin of the Italian manuscript he cites "de Sade." Stendhal's compatriot, the Marquis de Sade (1740–1814), was condemned to death for his cruelty and sexual perversion at the age of thirty-two. He escaped, was later imprisoned and died insane, his name living on, of course, in the term "sadism." Stendhal was fascinated by de Sade and yet, strangely, he chooses to ignore those crimes of Francesco Cenci's which were also those of de Sade, despite references in the Italian text to sodomy and the entertainment of boys and young women in his wife's bed. Stendhal makes the text into something altogether darker, a tale in which the psychological matters far more than the physical. In "Les Cenci," he dramatizes the conflict that goes on in the mind, between Francesco and Beatrice: he dwells on Francesco's attempts to corrupt not only her body but also her soul. Stendhal sensationalizes the manuscript sources, inventing various details and writing in a good deal of nudity—a subject that delighted him. He also uses a number of artful storytelling tricks, claiming, for example, "here it becomes quite impossible to follow the Roman narrator in his extraordinarily obscure account of the strange ways that François Cenci sought to astound his contemporaries," leaving the reader's imagination to consider all manner of extravagant possibilities. And he adds, "his wife and benighted daughter were, it seems, victims of his abominable ideas." Adding pace to his story he continues:

> But all this was not enough to satisfy him; using threats and force he attempted to rape his own daughter Beatrice, who was already grown-up and beautiful; he was not ashamed to wait in her bed, he being wholly naked; then he would take her to his

wife's bed, so that by the glow of the lamplight the poor Lucrezia could see what he was doing with Beatrice.

The description is a good deal more vivid and explicit than the manuscript source, but Stendhal is not yet ready to introduce details of Beatrice's attempts to escape her fate. He wholly invents a peculiarly Sadian twist, while feigning prudery in the telling:

> He led the poor girl to believe a terrible heresy, that I scarcely dare relate, that is that if a father knows his own daughter, the children that are born are necessarily saints, and that all the great Saints venerated by the Church are born in this way, that is to say that their maternal grandfather was their father.

Stendhal's fascination with sadism and transgression, his hatred of paternal authority, his yearnings for very young women, his admiration for women of noble birth, all these drew him to the Cenci story. But the hasty jottings in the Italian manuscript and his wholesale plagiarism of it suggest that he was drawn to the story in much the same way he was to women. The passionate attraction that he felt on first encounter seems to have been dealt with in summary fashion, like those women he likened to novels. He fell for Beatrice and was seduced by her spell, but he was soon able to abandon her and move on.

Stendhal was not the only nineteenth-century French writer to see the sensational potential of the Cenci story. Alexandre Dumas, the amazingly prolific writer famous above all for *The Count of Monte Cristo* (1844–5) and *The Three Musketeers* (1845), wrote a collection of tales, *Celebrated Crimes*, in 1839, two years after Stendhal's story of Beatrice had appeared. One of Dumas' stories tells the same tale but further develops Francesco's scheme to seduce his daughter, not by force, nor simply by trickery. "Les Cenci" is about a father's attempts to arouse latent eroticism, to excite sexual desire for the first time, for his own indulgence. The description of his tragic heroine is based, of course, on the Beatrice portrait:

> Her long fair hair, a beauty seen so rarely in Italy, that Raffaelle, believing it divine, has appropriated it to all his Madonnas, curtained a lovely forehead, and fell in flowing locks over her shoulders. Her azure eyes bore a heavenly expression; she was of middle height, exquisitely proportioned; and during the rare moments when a gleam of happiness allowed her natural character to display itself, she was lively, joyous, and sympathetic, but at the same time evinced a firm and decided disposition.

Up until she is thirteen Francesco has treated Beatrice with ruthless severity, but to the young woman's astonishment his behavior suddenly changes: "He all at once became gentle and even tender. Beatrice was a child no longer; her beauty expanded like a flower; and Francesco, a stranger to no crime, however heinous, had marked her for his own."

On account of her long incarceration, Beatrice "knew not good from evil," and Francesco sets about initiating her into his own erotic world. He arranges for her to be awakened at night by strains of beautiful music, which she assumes float in from Paradise. Her father promises to reward her obedience and gentleness by heavenly sights, as well as sounds. One night she wakes to see the door of her apartment ajar, and beyond "a suite of apartments brilliantly illuminated, and sensuous with perfumes; beautiful youths and girls, half clad . . . moved to and fro . . .

seemingly full of happiness. These were the ministers to the pleasures of Francesco, who, rich as a king, every night revelled in
the orgies of Alexander." After an hour, Beatrice's door is closed,
leaving her "full of trouble and amazement."

The following night the scenes are repeated, but this time
Francesco arrives naked in Beatrice's bedchamber and invites
her to join the company. Beatrice refuses, aware that there is
some "impropriety" about her father's desires. She adds, by way
of an excuse, that she is uneasy about joining in when her stepmother Lucrezia is not there. The next night Francesco com-
pels Lucrezia to take part and then leads Beatrice, "covered with
blushes and confusion, into the middle of this orgy. Beatrice
there saw incredible and infamous things," but she continues
to refuse to submit to her father's ultimate wish. With the "slow
persistence of a demon," Francesco gradually works on her.
Telling Beatrice what Stendhal's Francesco told his daughter,
Dumas' Francesco "added heresies to warp her mind," in particular "that the greatest saints venerated by the Church were
the issue of fathers and daughters." He then forces Lucrezia and
Beatrice to share his bed. "So matters went on," Dumas writes,
"for about three years."

All this is invention, based on scant evidence. So too is Dumas'
description of Beatrice's execution, to which he adds macabre
detail: "the axe fell. A gruesome sight was then afforded: whilst
the head bounced away on the side of the block, on the other
the body rose erect, as if about to step backward; the executioner exhibited the head." As one of the brotherhood of Mercy
is attempting to lift Beatrice's body on to the bier, "it slipped
from him and fell from the scaffold to the ground below; the
dress being partially torn from the body, which was so be-
smeared with dust and blood that much time was occupied in

washing it." There is no documentary evidence to support Dumas' elaboration.

The story as a whole is a good deal more polished than Stendhal's—Dumas knew how to appeal to a wide public. His interest in the Cenci tale was partly its commercial appeal but it also had a politically symbolic meaning for him. He was a committed socialist and republican keen to expose corruption, and the abuses of power prevalent not only in the Renaissance but also in Italy's contemporary political set-up. When Giuseppe Garibaldi, the great Italian patriot, returned to action in 1859 with the outbreak of the country's war of liberation, Dumas soon joined him and remained in Italy until 1864: his resurrection of Beatrice was bound up in part in his political commitment to new democratic European orders.

At the end of the nineteenth century the photographer Julia Margaret Cameron became intrigued by Beatrice for quite different reasons. If there was a political corollary in the story it was a feminist one. Cameron separated Beatrice from Francesco and treated her in isolation: her relationship with her was both sustained and intimate. Her father was a larger-than-life figure, brilliantly described by his great-niece, Virginia Woolf:

> A gentleman of marked, but doubtful, reputation, who after living a riotous life and earning the title of "the biggest liar in India," finally drank himself to death and was consigned to a cask of rum to await shipment to England. The cask was stood outside the widow's bedroom door. In the middle of the night she heard a violent explosion, rushed out, and found her husband, having burst the lid off the coffin, bolt upright, menacing her in death as he had menaced her in life.

A family friend recorded the effect of this remarkable encounter on his wife: "The shock sent her off her head then and there, poor thing, and she died raving."

The daughter of this colorful couple became one of Britain's most celebrated woman photographers. But it was only after years of marriage, travel, socializing and domesticity that she first experimented with a camera. She was middle-aged and her daughter was worried that she would miss her family, now grown up, have too much time on her hands and would dwell too much on the past. Photography seemed an appropriate hobby which would allow her to surround herself with images of the people she loved. Not only did she repeatedly photograph members of her family, expecting them to pose for hours in stiff agony, she transformed them, dressing them up in costumes appropriate to biblical tales, classical subjects or figures from Arthurian romances. Boatmen, parlor maids and gardeners were called upon too and underwent similarly extravagant metamorphoses. A subject she returned to at least five times was Beatrice Cenci.

The Camerons were part of a network of Victorian writers and artists which included the Brownings, the Tennysons and their Florence set. Cameron would almost certainly have known of Hawthorne's *The Marble Faun*, and she must also have seen Hatty Hosmer's marble statue of *Beatrice*, exhibited at the Royal Academy, to which she went in 1857. She may well have known Shelley's play too. Cameron returned to Beatrice repeatedly, at two-yearly intervals, producing portraits in 1866, 1868 and 1870. Her subjects dressed up as Beatrice were always virgins, in the case of one on the eve of her marriage. Capturing virginity on celluloid, immortalizing a prenuptial innocence and purity, was clearly part of the project. These images are full of sorrow and combine innocent sensuousness with anticipation of dark experience.

Cameron's photographs explore the Victorian sensibility and suppressed sexuality in all its paradoxes and murkiness. Androgyny plays a part in her images of children: some of her Madonnas with the Christ child turn out to be women caressing baby girls and the constant moves between the sexual and asexual, between male and female, between earthly and heavenly, leave the viewer perplexed about what has been seen. Like the post-mortem photographs of children in their most precious clothes, which Cameron also took, these images are at once compelling and disturbing: sensuality, sexuality and death come into uneasy relationship. The viewer is on the verge of being implicated in something close to necrophilia, pedophilia, or at least voyeurism.

Cameron's Beatrices, like the bulk of her religious and mythical work, found few admirers. She sought to evoke an emotional, religious response—one of awe, reverence or adoration. The cross-dressing of her subjects, however, can be seen as a kind of feminist theological subversiveness that many of her contemporaries either misunderstood or took exception to. Could she be implying that Jesus might just as well have been a woman, or simply that what mattered was his humanity and not his gender? Today Cameron is remembered almost exclusively for her magnificent portraits of great Victorian men including Tennyson, Darwin, Carlyle, Newman, Dickens, Holman Hunt and Lewis Carroll. These are portraits of geniuses and we are invited to respond with that same sense of deference, astonishment, even adoration, that her religious images encourage. Her Beatrice portraits, on the other hand, encourage an altogether more anguished response: in the faces of her Beatrices nothing has been resolved, nothing can be resolved. Cameron's Beatrices have no captions; what she has to say remains unspeakable. But one of her other portraits, that of her beautiful young maid Mary Hillier of 1867, is accompanied by the quotation, "Call, I follow, I follow, let me die!," and her striking portrait of a young friend, Agnes Mangles, posing as Tennyson's "Marianna," carries the quotation, "I am aweary, aweary, I would that I was dead." This makes explicit what the Beatrice portraits only hint at: a fascination with the relationship between nascent female eroticism and death.

—◠◠◠—

CHAPTER 8

Antonin Artaud: "Unbearable Truths"

*Many suffer from the incurable disease of writing
And it becomes chronic in their sick minds.*

JUVENAL

*We must wash literature off ourselves. We want to
be men above all, to be human.*

ANTONIN ARTAUD

Antonin Artaud felt the pull of literature early on. As a boy he wrote poetry but it was the theater that became his obsession, a theater transformed into something quite different from what most of his contemporaries imagined. For years he struggled to be in a position to produce plays, and for years his plans foundered. He wrote plays and essays, and acted in films and the theater, but he longed for an opportunity to demonstrate, with all the control of a producer, his radically new convictions about the transforming power of drama.

In 1935, late in his relatively short and unconventional career, he wrote excitedly to the novelist André Gide, informing him, "I have just finished a tragedy," and he described the play's "ultimate violence" and cited the subjects of his attacks: society, order, justice, religion, family and patriotism—"nothing escapes." The play in question was *Les Cenci* and Artaud had based it closely on Shelley's *Cenci* (translated into French by F. Rabbe in 1887), although Artaud's text is very much shorter. Artaud soon found backers in the unlikely alliance of his publisher Robert Renoel and Iya Abdy, a wealthy aristocrat keen to establish herself as an actress. She was to play Beatrice and she enthusiastically set about helping to raise the necessary capital. Artaud had a talent for choosing collaborators: the artist Balthus agreed to design the scenery and costumes, Jean-Louis Barrault was to play the part of Bernardo, Beatrice's youngest brother, and Roger Blin one of the murderers. Barrault and Blin would later emerge as two of the great talents of French theater. Artaud himself would play Francesco. Things were set and it looked very much as though Artaud's "Theatre of Cruelty" as he had termed it, would finally be inaugurated.

The title, "The Theatre of Cruelty," is something of a misnomer. Artaud wanted to create a theatrical experience that would profoundly affect his audience. People would be there not so much to witness as to be part of the performance, and they would leave the theater emotionally, even physiologically, changed. What Artaud saw as the spurious realism of the Western tradition, its pretense of psychological and analytical insight into the human condition, was swept aside in favor of an exploration of the very deepest and darkest forces of the individual and collective psyche. Challenging the structures of so-called civilization and its moral codes, Artaud exploited gesture, movement, color, light, sounds and music. Words and the rational thought that they purport to convey are treated as an inferior, even suspicious, vehicle of meaning. There is no doubt that there is a madness in some of Artaud's thinking, or at least in its strange and difficult expression, but there is something visionary too. He has had a profound and lasting influence on the development of modern drama: both Barrault, as producer, and Peter Brook, have expressed their fundamental debts to Artaud. The closest he himself came to demonstrating his daring and dangerous vision was with his Cenci play.

Artaud's life and work are intimately bound up and they become inseparable at the moment of the *Cenci*. The performance constituted a final and terrible turning point in a life that had twisted in agonizing, only half-controlled movements, since childhood.

Artaud was born on September 4, 1896, in Marseilles. His family was relatively prosperous. His father was a shipping agent who chartered cargo vessels for trade with the eastern Mediterranean, from where part of the family had originated. His paternal grandfather, Marius-Pierre Artaud, had married a Greek woman from Asia Minor, Cathérine Schili (also spelled Schily, Schiley, Chili or Chilé); his mother was the daughter of Cathérine's sister, Mariette. His parents were therefore first cousins and he himself three-quarters Levantine Greek. Both his grandmothers—who were, of course, sisters—mattered a great deal to him throughout his life and he wrote about them with almost religious veneration. The great love of his life, Genica Athanasiou (1897–1966), came from the same Levantine background. Years later, in the hospital, he would draw up lists of the women he had loved and he always included his grandmothers. To confuse matters further, he referred to all these women as his "daughters."

On June 2, 1901, at the age of three days, Artaud's newborn brother died. Around this time Artaud, aged five, started to suffer from facial cramps and he was increasingly racked by headaches. A few months later he contracted a serious illness, possibly meningitis, and was expected to die. At this point he had only one younger sister, Marie-Ange, and although his mother bore nine children in all, only three survived their infancy. When he was eight a baby sister, Germaine, died. Of all the deaths he had suffered this was the worst. Later he would speak of her, mysteriously, as "Germaine Artaud, strangled at seven months," as though he believed that violence had been done to her by an individual rather than a disease. Antonin and Marie-Ange developed an extraordinarily close relationship similar to Shelley's with his sister Elizabeth. And incest would become the subject that most attracted him in theater. In an early playlet, *The Spurt of Blood*, there is a scene of incest between a brother and sister, followed by hauntingly disgusting erotic images of old women.

Artaud's obsessions with self-knowledge also began around the time of Germaine's illness and death, and as he watched the doctors coming and going during the days leading up to her death he may well have wondered what part they played in life. The guilt that so many children feel at the death of a sibling was no doubt an often intolerable burden to carry:

> From the age of eight and even earlier I remember constantly asking myself who I was, what I was and why live. . . . What it was to exist and to live, what it was to see myself breathe and

to have wanted to breathe to prove the reality of life and to see whether it was desirable and if so why. I asked myself why I was there and what existence was.

Artaud was sent to a Catholic school, the Collège du Sacré Cœur, where he and a friend published a school magazine in which poems by a certain "Louis des Attides" were published. The young man behind the arch-Romantic name was, of course, Artaud. A few years later, in 1914, at the age of eighteen he fell into a serious depression and destroyed everything he had written. Not many months later he was admitted to a sanatorium for nervous disorders at Rougières, outside Marseilles. In 1916, approaching his twentieth birthday, he returned home. The First World War was in its third year and Artaud soon received his call-up papers, but after nine months training he was released on unspecified medical grounds. Artaud claimed that it was because of his sleepwalking.

Artaud's family was desperate to find some cure for his nervous disease and for three years he was moved from sanatoria to clinics all over France; at the clinic at Divonne he met a young painter, Yvonne Gilles, and kept in touch with her, sending her letters and poems for a number of years. Finally, he was sent to Switzerland to a sanatorium at Le Chanet, near Neuchâtel, and here he at last received proper therapeutic psychiatric care. But it may well be that it was also here that he first took laudanum and began his lifelong enslavement to opiates.

At Le Chanet he was under a Dr. Dardel who succeeded in bringing him on to a point where, two years later, he could return to Paris to embark on the literary career that he was passionately keen to pursue. Dardel was anxious that Artaud remain under some medical supervision and explored the possibility of his lodging with a pioneering psychiatrist in Paris, Dr. Edouard Toulouse, head of the asylum of Villejuif, a man of wide-ranging interests both scientific and literary. Since 1912 he had been editing a review called *Demain* to which Artaud contributed poems, articles and reviews. Toulouse recognized, as his wife later reported, that Artaud was an "exceptional being," and after their first meeting in March 1920 considered him "of the race that produces a Baudelaire, a Nerval, a Nietzsche—a man teetering on a knife-edge between genius and madness."

Through Dr. Toulouse Artaud met a large number of *avant-garde* artists including, crucially, men of the theater. Lugné-Poe, an up-and-coming director, offered him a walk-on part in Henri de Régnier's *Les Scrupules de Sganarelle*. The director was deeply moved by Artaud. He described him as "sensitive in the highest degree, intelligent, tormented with beauty." He was equally struck by his performance: "This astonishing artist . . . His make-up, his poses were those of an artist among actors." By now Artaud had started thinking seriously about theater, and the direction in which it should move. Through his uncle, Louis Naplas, he was put in touch with Charles Dullin, the great French theatrical personality of the 1920s who was setting up a new enterprise, "l'Atelier" (the Studio), part theater school, part *avant-garde* troupe.

Dullin was much taken with Artaud and offered him a place, and Artaud was quickly struck by the similarities between their ideas about theater. Artaud had conceived of a theater "in which there are no props" and where gesture, mime, color, music and movement would matter as much as speech. He cited Japanese theater as an origin and inspiration. Dullin, similarly, aimed at performances that would "give the impression of *things never seen before*. Everything takes place in the mind. The sets are even more stylised. . . . The Gods of the school are not Tolstoy, Ibsen and Shakespeare but Hoffman and Edgar Allan Poe. Our first performance will display stern frenzy and demented sharpness . . . . It is, to say the least, curious that I with my tastes should have stumbled on an enterprise so closely linked with my own ideas." But there were tensions too. Dullin often thought Artaud overexaggerated, extravagant in his make-up and interpretations. Artaud always tended to stand out in a way that was not always appropriate to his part. But there were also successes, and major moments in the history of French theater.

On December 20, 1922 Cocteau's *Antigone* opened. Shelley had wondered at the story of Sophocles's original *Antigone*. Like the story of the Cenci it dramatizes the conflict between the individual's sense of what is just and the decree of the state. Antigone sets out to bury the body of her brother Polynices who has died a traitor and who has no right, therefore, to a decent burial according to Creon (the new ruler of Thebes). But Antigone defies Creon and is condemned to death. Tiresias, the prophet, successfully persuades Creon to relent but his messenger arrives too late: Antigone has hanged herself. In the Cocteau play, Genica Athanasiou, with whom Artaud had started what would be a tempestuous seven-year affair, had the title role and Artaud played Tiresias. Picasso designed the set, Coco Chanel conceived the costumes and the music was by Arthur Honegger. The production attracted huge attention—and typically Parisian controversy. Raymond Duncan, Isadora's brother, claimed that Cocteau had betrayed the mythical spirit of the play, and André Breton and the Surrealists argued that Cocteau was collaborating with the world of commercial fashion.

It was Artaud's interpretation of his part as Emperor Charlemagne in Alexandre Arnoux's *Huon de Bordeaux* that finally led to a break with Dullin. Artaud entered, and approached

his throne, on all fours: no doubt he believed that to crawl
animal-like on to the stage perfectly expressed the moral deg-
radation of his character but Dullin thought it too much. Artaud
left the Atelier. Toward the end of August 1923 he wrote to
Dr. Toulouse:

> If, in six months from now my health has not achieved an equi-
> librium, I will withdraw from life, retiring to a very remote spot
> in the mountains or by the sea. . . . Here I am again in Marseilles,
> where I am again having feelings of numbness and dizziness, of
> a sudden and MAD need for sleep, of INSTANTANEOUS *stu-
> pefaction*, of sudden loss of strength accompanied by an enor-
> mous grief.

But a year later he seems to have had little difficulty gaining
employment with the Comédie des Champs-Elysées. In 1924 he
also won parts in two films, including Luitz-Morat's *Surcouf*, in
which he played the evil traitor. Meanwhile, he continued his
literary career, publishing in *Demain, Mercure de France* and
Action. But the journal in which he most wanted his poems to
appear remained ill disposed toward his work. In arguing with
the editor of the *Nouvelle Revue Française* for the significance
of his writings, Artaud came to express, if not to see, that the
subject of his writing was the difficulty, the physical pain, of
artistic expression. Jacques Rivière, one of Albert Camus' greatest friends, rejected Artaud's poems but asked to meet him and
tried to describe what he felt to be the poems' weaknesses. Artaud
wrote to Rivière that evening, explaining that what mattered
was not the product of the creative process, but the traces it
necessarily displayed of the grueling process through which the
poems passed:

I am suffering from a terrible sickness of spirit. My thought abandons me in all possible measure, from the simple fact of thought itself to the external fact of its materialisation in words. Words, the shape of sentences, the internal direction of thoughts, simple reactions of the mind—I am in constant pursuit of my intellectual being. When, therefore, *I can hold a shape*, however imperfect, I set it down out of fear that I might lose the whole idea. I am below my own level, I know it, I suffer from it, but I submit to it rather than die altogether.

Rivière missed the point. He advised Artaud to persevere and suggested that in six months' time or so his poems might have improved and that the *NRF* might well be willing to publish them. But Artaud persisted: what mattered were not the polished but often lightweight poems that the *NRF* regularly published, but a whole experience of the creative life, the artist's wrestlings, successfully communicated, even within ragged and imperfect forms—these deserved publication. On January 29, 1924, six months after they had first met, Artaud wrote desperately, "I am a man who has suffered much in his mind, and because of this *I have the right* to speak." This sense of the importance of articulating experiences that non-artists may be unaware of, combined with a conviction that it is the integrity of the artistic process that matters most in art, and not some abstracted notion of perfection evident in the end product, is a belief shared by most of the artists of the "dangerous tradition."

In the end Rivière suggested that rather than publishing Artaud's poems what should be published was the correspondence generated by their rejection. The *Correspondence avec Jacques Rivière* was published in the *NRF* in September 1924 and later as a book. And in 1925 Artaud published two volumes of essays which reveal the degree to which he felt confirmed in his choice of artistic subject matter: his own consciousness. In *L'Ombilic des Limbes* (*The Navel of Limbo*), he wrote, "Where others want to produce works of art, I aspire to no more than to display my own spirit." But by December of the same year, in a piece entitled "Manifesto in Clear Language," he recognized that his control of his own thought sometimes slipped, suggesting spurious correspondences:

> My mind, weary with discursive reasoning, wants to be caught up in the works of a new, absolute force of gravity. For me it is like an overwhelming reorganisation determined only by the laws of unreason and the triumphant discovery of a new faculty. This sense is lost in the chaos of drugs, which gives contradictory dreams the semblance of profound intelligence. This faculty is a conquest of mind over itself, though it cannot be reduced to reason, it exists, but only on the inside of the mind. It is order, it is intelligence, it is the signification of chaos. But it does not accept this chaos as it is: it interprets it, and in doing so, loses it.

Not surprisingly, given the direction of his thinking, Artaud was soon drawn into the Surrealist group and came into close contact with André Breton, Robert Desnos, Louis Aragon, Paul Eluard, Max Ernst, Raymond Queneau, and many of the leading writers of the day. Artaud was nominated editor of the third issue of *La Révolution Surréaliste* (April 15, 1925) but continued to pursue his acting career alongside his literary—or anti-literary—activities. While acting in the cinema paid well and allowed Artaud largely to support himself, theater remained his obsession. Through his associations with the Surrealists he met Roger Vitrac and the two men set about realizing their shared idea of theater: a theater of dreams, the fantastic, the grotesque, the obsessive. It was to be called after Alfred Jarry, who at the age of fifteen had written the remarkable *Ubu-roi*. Jarry invented a "logic of the absurd" which he termed *pataphysique* and became a Surrealist saint after his death, following years of destitution and alcoholism.

The Théâtre Alfred Jarry became a reality largely thanks to the financial support of another enlightened psychiatrist and his wife: René and Yvonne Allendy. The *First Manifesto of the Théâtre Alfred Jarry* (published in the November 1926 issue of the *NRF*) insisted on the absolute seriousness of theater. It addressed not simply the audience's emotions, or senses, or intellect, but "their whole existence. Theirs and ours." One of the examples given was of a police raid on a brothel. The tactics of the forces of law would be done with ballet-like movement and precision. The prostitutes would file out like cattle to the slaughter. The experience would be much like that of a visit to "a surgeon or the dentist." Artaud's preoccupations with sex, violence, powerlessness and the forces of law and order were as evident as ever.

Funding the enterprise was not easy and alongside financial worries Artaud suffered a terrible personal blow. At the end of November 1926 the Surrealists announced the verdict of a secret trial: Artaud was to be expelled by the Surrealists and there was no mechanism for appeal. The only legitimate reason for his expulsion would perhaps have been Artaud's continuing links with the world of commercial cinema. But Artaud's father had died the previous year and his mother had moved to Paris and lived very modestly. Artaud had to make his own living, and do so in a way that left time for theater. The real break came, however, when Breton and his followers turned what had been an

abstracted literary commitment into a concrete political commitment: collective adherence to the Communist Party. For Artaud
organized politics was of no real consequence. The language of
the "official document" detailing the reasons for Artaud's expulsion is deeply disturbing, the work of "thought police";
Artaud's earlier commitment to Catholicism was cited, and there
were suggestions that he might commit a further transgression—
reconversion to the Christian faith.

Artaud fought back against the Surrealists and in the summer of 1927 he published *A la grande nuit ou le grand Bluff
surréaliste*: "Did not Surrealism die the day Breton and his ad-
epts thought they had to join Communism and to seek, in the
realm of what is factual and concrete, the fulfilment of an en-
deavour which could not normally develop anywhere but in the
inner recesses of the brain." What mattered to Artaud were the
inner realities, not the superficialities of the external world,
whether social or material. But he had not yet found a subject
that would allow these ideas to come alive.

In 1927 Artaud played two of his most successful roles in
film—Marat in Abel Gance's *Napoléon* and the friar in Carl
Theodor Dreyer's great *La Passion de Jeanne d'Arc*. In the first
he played the father figure murdered by the young woman martyr, and in the second he is the comforter of the female rebel and
martyr. As he accompanies Joan of Arc to the stake his expressions convey the intensity of his insights into her experience as
she approaches the moment of her violent death. Artaud lives
on most tangibly in these two remarkable films.

Meanwhile the Théâtre Alfred Jarry somehow survived.
Among the most notorious events were the two performances
of Strindberg's *Dream Play*. Yvonne Allendy was friends with

various Swedes in Paris and explored the possibility of a subsidy from the Swedish Embassy for the production of a play by
such a famous Swedish playwright. The first performance took
place on June 2, 1928. It was a dazzling society occasion but
the audience also included some thirty Surrealists intent on
disrupting the performance. Artaud's acceptance of foreign
capitalist subsidy and fraternizing with high society was unac-
ceptable. Insults were hurled at the actors as soon as the play
was underway and Artaud had to appear front stage to try to
calm things. Ever honest and naïve, Artaud insisted that it was
because Strindberg had been a victim of the Swedish establishment that he had taken the play on. At which point numerous
members of the Swedish establishment walked out of the theater. The second performance landed Artaud in deeper water
still. Afraid that it would suffer from equally disruptive interference by the Surrealists, Artaud announced that every necessary means of protecting the integrity of the performance would
be employed—meaning the presence of police. No other move
on Artaud's part could have been calculated to be more pro-
vocative. Their supporter, Robert Aron, had had enough and
abandoned Artaud and Vitrac.

They went on to produce by far the most important theatrical event in the theater's history. The play was by Vitrac himself: *Victor or Children in Power*. It is a play that vivifies the
mysteries of sex and adult anxieties about what children should
"know" of sex. The plot is essentially that of a classic French
bedroom farce but everything is seen through the eyes of a hyper-
sensitive and all-seeing child. Victor tries to make sense of the
absurdities of sex, and his interaction with the adults he has
watched leads them to behave more and more irrationally. The

role of Ida Mortemart proved difficult to fill. A woman of extraordinary beauty, she is afflicted with a strange compulsion—to fart. Tania Balachova, who was to play Ida, withdrew in horror when her character's unusual defining characteristic began to emerge. It was left to Domenica Blazy to represent the intrusion of the sordid into the beautiful.

For the next six years Artaud struggled desperately to find funds to produce another play on the Parisian stage and it was not until 1935 that he finally succeeded. This production proved catastrophic in terms of both his career in the theater and his life—he would stage his Cenci play.

The intervening years between 1929 and 1935 were spent largely working in film. He traveled abroad from time to time, sometimes to Germany to take part in German versions of French films and vice versa. Bertolt Brecht's plays made a deep impression and in the French version of Brecht's *The Threepenny Opera* Artaud was cast as the young man who asks Peachum to join his beggars' collective and demonstrates to Peachum the techniques for arousing human pity.

Artaud loved the theatricality of Berlin, "a city of astonishing luxury and frightening licentiousness. I am constantly amazed by what I see. They carry their obsession with eroticism everywhere, even into the shop-windows in which all the dummies thrust their middles forward." Gradually he was offered fewer and fewer jobs and he struggled to make any kind of a decent income. He tried to make money out of writing, even producing fake accounts "from overseas" for the magazine *Voilà*—on the Galapagos Islands and the brothels of Shanghai.

But his theoretical ideas were continuing to take shape and in July 1931, at the Colonial Exhibition in the Bois de Vincennes, he experienced a revelatory moment, when, on the steps of the

Indonesian Temple which housed the Dutch colonial exhibits, he saw Balinese dancing for the first time. He was deeply struck by the coming together of movement, light and color in myriad abstract patternings. His writing took off again and he delivered a prestigious series of lectures at the Sorbonne, in Paris. Some of this material was later incorporated in *The Theatre and its Double*, Artaud's most famous, and famously difficult, book. At the same time he continued his quest for the means to found another theater. There were talks with the *NRF* and suggestions that the journal might inaugurate a theater under the same banner. A number of well-known writers were supportive—Jean Paulhan (editor), André Gide, Paul Valéry and Gaston Gallimard (head of the *NRF* publishing enterprise), among others. Despite doubts raised by Paulhan and others, Artaud insisted that the proposed theater be known as "The Theatre of Cruelty." In 1932 he worked feverishly on an adaptation of Seneca's tragedy *Atreus and Thyestes* and by 1933 he was working on a scenario—*The Conquest of Mexico*.

This was also the year in which he met and fell passionately and utterly hopelessly in love with Anaïs Nin who was studying psychoanalysis with Dr. Allendy. Her descriptions of Artaud are lucid, and painfully vivid:

> Artaud. Lean, taut. A gaunt face with visionary eyes. A sardonic manner. Now weary, now fiery and malicious. The theatre is for him a place to shout pain, anger, hatred, to enact the violence in us. . . . He is the drugged, contracted being who walks always alone, who is seeking to produce plays which are like scenes of torture. His eyes are blue with languor, black with pain. He is all nerves. Yet he was beautiful acting the monk who was in love with Joan of Arc in the Carl Dreyer film. The deep-set eyes of

the mystic, as if shining from caverns. Deep-set, shadowy, mysterious. . . . He is poor. He is in conflict with a world he imag-
ines mocking and threatening.

Allendy had told her that he had tried unsuccessfully to free
Artaud from the drug habit that was destroying him.

On April 6, 1933 she took up Artaud's invitation to attend
his lecture at the Sorbonne entitled "The Theatre and the Plague":

> Is he trying to remind us that it was during the plague that so
> many marvellous works of art and theatre came to be, because,
> whipped by fear of death, man seeks immortality, or to escape,
> or to surpass himself? But then, imperceptibly almost, he let
> go of the thread we were following and began to act out dying
> by plague. No one quite knew when it began. . . . His face was
> contorted with anguish, one could see the perspiration damp-
> ening his hair. His eyes dilated, his muscles became cramped,
> his fingers struggled to retain their flexibility. He made one feel
> the parched and burning throat, the pains, the fever, the fire
> in the guts. He was in agony. He was screaming. He was de-
> lirious. He was enacting his own death, his own crucifixion.
> At first people gasped. And then they began to laugh. Every-
> one was laughing! They hissed. Then one by one, they began
> to leave, noisily, talking, protesting. They banged the door as
> they left . . . but Artaud went on, until the last gasp. And stayed
> on the floor.

She described the hall emptying and Artaud approaching her
graciously, but broken. He kissed her hand and asked her to go
with him to a café. He was bewildered by the reaction of the
crowd:

They always want to hear *about*; they want to hear an objective
lecture on "The Theatre and the Plague," and I want to give them
the experience itself, the plague itself, so they will be terrified,
and awaken. . . . They do not realise *they are dead.* Their death
is total, like deafness, blindness. This is the agony I portrayed.
Mine, yes, and everyone who is alive. . . . I feel sometimes that
I am not writing, but describing the struggles with writing, the
struggles of birth.

Artaud continued to send Nin long love letters. In May 1933 she
recorded in her diary her peculiar feelings for him: "Such an
immense pity I have for Artaud, because he is always suffering
. . . . Physically I could not touch him, but the fire and genius
within him, I love." In June, they met in a café and Artaud asked
her simply whether she thought him mad. Other people, he said,
considered him to be mad, but did she? Nin noted, "I knew at
that moment, by his eyes, that he was, and that I loved his madness. I looked at his mouth, with the edges darkened by
laudanum, a mouth I did not want to kiss. To be kissed by Artaud
was to be drawn toward death, toward insanity."

At the time Artaud was writing his book on the mad Roman
emperor Heliogabalus (*Héliogabale ou L'Anarchiste Couronné*).
Here he explored a number of the themes of the Cenci story.
Heliogabalus was only fourteen when he became Emperor in
218 AD. He was extremely cruel and irresponsible and let loose a
"plague" on Rome: "If Heliogabalus brings anarchy into Rome,
if he appears as the ferment that precipitates a latent state of anarchy, the original anarchy is in himself and it ravages his organism, throws his mind into a sort of precocious madness." Here
Artaud suggests that sin is a given, and that its manifestation in

destructive acts in the world is accompanied by an internal destruction. Both are outside the individual's control. Heliogabalus
is homosexual with transvestite desires. Yet he is also in charge of
a phallic cult. This concatenation of male and female fascinated
Artaud and represented a kind of symbolic hermaphrodite solution to the evils of heterosexual, reproductive engagement. There
is incest too. The young Emperor has a sexual relationship with
his mother—and there is patricide. Artaud was equally fascinated
by castration and justifies the Emperor's frequent orders that the
act be carried out as punishment by suggesting that Heliogabalus's
motive was to free the subject from internal sexual conflict. Above
all, Artaud was drawn instinctively to violent imperial rule as a
parallel to theater. In both cases what was manifest was the relationship between supreme ruler and society, between individual
mental imbalance and political chaos:

> I think there is . . . a human duty to take account of the evil forces
> that constitute the *Zeitgeist*. There is a disordering, somewhere,
> which we cannot control, whatever name we choose to give to
> it. All sorts of incomprehensible and gratuitous crimes, inside
> the self, are part of this chaos. . . . What we do not want to
> recognise is that theater can be a lightning-conductor, and that
> what is enacted on stage can later be acted out in life.

It was during this period of his life that the significance of
Artaud's background is most visible in his thinking. This emerged
in his extraordinary interest in, and sympathy for, the Hellenistic world, and in particular the Gnostics, groups which sought
to explore secret knowledge and mysterious belief, to construct
a kind of spiritual Grand Unification Theory. Artaud's religious

and cosmological fantasies, which dominated the last decade and a half of his life, bear striking parallels with the Hellenistic Gnostics of the third to seventh centuries. A sundry group of philosophers and mystics, the Gnostics were condemned by the Christian Church as heretics. They developed a wide variety of often perplexing syntheses between Christianity, Greek philosophy and Eastern religious thought and myth. Like Artaud they mixed Christian teachings with Neoplatonism and the Cabbala, to which he added Hindu beliefs about the transmigration of the soul, Egyptian cults, Manichean scriptures about the world as a duality of good and evil, Persian Zoroastrianism, Babylonian astrology that makes sense of the universe as a rigid hierarchy of ascending and descending spheres, and fragments of the classical Greek mystery religions like the cult of Dionysus and the mysteries of Orphism.

Some obvious parallels between Gnosticism and Artaud's thinking would be his conviction, shared by Marcion of Halicarnassus, that the God who created the world must be evil and incompetent, the only explanation for the wickedness and imperfection of His universe. Salvation could only come from a God outside our world, innocent of its creation. The Barbelo-Gnostics developed an elaborate ritual of spilling their sperm in order to break the terrible cycle of sexual procreation. Artaud came to believe early on that sexuality was an evil and the language of his most savage writings is injected with dense sexual and bestial images. The body, that collection of human organs, had to be reinvented, he believed: "I hate and despise as a coward everyone who refuses to recognise that life is given to us only for us to recreate and reconstitute the whole of our physical organism." Or again:

Man is sick because he is badly constructed. . . .
We must decide to strip him naked to scrape off this
   tiny animal
Whose itch is fatal,
         god
         and with god
         his organs
Contradict me if you want to
but there is nothing more useless than an organ.
When you have made a body without organs
you will have saved him from the compulsions and
   restored his
true liberty.

During 1934 Artaud continued to appear in films. His role as Savonarola in Abel Gance's *Lucrè Borgia* stands out in its sensitivity to the complexities of violence and the victim's instinct to collude in it. A year later, in 1935, he finished his play *Les Cenci.*

Artaud believed himself to be poised, finally, to enact ideas which he had so far only been able to write about. His visionary understanding of theater was, he imagined, about to live. He was drawn to the Cenci story because of its violent extremes and because the catalyst for all its violence is incest, a phenomenon that had long fascinated him. Incest was, he believed, symbolic of violence done to another but also to the self by dint of the closeness of the blood relationship. Beyond this symbolic significance, he also believed that incest precipitated a revelation of "cosmic cruelty." Francesco's monstrousness figures at the very beginning and animates much of the play. He stands for unredeemed evil and is without conscience. The play opens with a

colloquy between Francesco and Cardinal Camillo in which
we gather that Francesco has committed another murder. The
Pope, according to Camillo, will overlook the matter providing
Francesco hands over a third of his estate. But Francesco has no
desire to placate the Pope nor to "bury" his crimes: he is proud
of them and intends to continue to practice "exquisitely refined"
wrongdoing. He sees himself as bound up in an elemental order,
and subject to its forces: "I believe that, and I am, a force of nature. For me, there is no life, no death, no god, no incest, no
repentance, no crime." Francesco's motive in raping his daughter is to ensure that she is eternally condemned. And he expresses
a view, shared by the Marquis de Sade, that we act only in accordance with our God-given natures and the God-given circumstances in which we find ourselves. Artaud has Francesco declare:

> Repent? Why should I repent? Repentance is in God's hands. It
> is for him to regret what I did. Why did he make me father of
> such an utterly desirable creature? Let those who condemn my
> crime first condemn fate. Free? Who can speak of freedom when
> the heavens are about to fall on our heads? I open the flood-
> gates only so as not to be submerged. There is something like a
> devil inside me destined to avenge the world's transgressions.
> From now on there is no destiny to stand between me and my
> dreams.

Beatrice's corrupted innocence is the main antagonistic force and
it is with this that the play ends. She also argues that our acts are
as random as so-called "acts of God"—thunderstorms and vol-
canic eruptions, floods and hurricanes. This idea of the individual
inescapably bound up within a larger set of forces is represented
theatrically in various ways. When Beatrice is being tortured, for

example, it is the wheels and beams in her cell that scream, not
Beatrice. The speech is deliberately stilted and interspersed with
absurd "truisms," for example "Evil must be granted its share
of pleasure." Sometimes dialogue collapses into speech and echo,
again suggesting the powerlessness of individuals to reason with
one another, or maneuver into a position where they can take
control of their destinies.

Artaud's innovations were not simply to do with the text itself which is for the most part a shortened version of Shelley's.
One of the most striking differences between the two texts is that
in Shelley's play Beatrice never articulates what it is that her father has done to her; the crime remains unspeakable. In Artaud's
play Beatrice tells her stepmother, "He has polluted me." And
although Beatrice is the victim, as opposed to the perpetrator of
evil at this point, her involvement with sin brings an enlightenment similar to Donatello's in Hawthorne's *The Marble Faun.*
Beatrice tells Lucrezia, "I know now how the alienated suffer."
And madness, which is in the wings, if not center stage, throughout the tellings and retellings of the dangerous tradition from St.
Dympna onwards, is again proposed as part of the heady mixture associated with Francesco's incestuous act. Having articu-
lated her sense of solidarity with victims, she says, "Madness is
like death. I am dead, and my spirit, which tries desperately to
live, is unable to free itself." This is a more direct pronounce-
ment of what Shelley's Beatrice declares, "My God! I never knew
what the mad felt / Before; for I am mad beyond all doubt!"

What is really striking about Artaud's *Les Cenci* is the manner in which the play works as theater. The movements of the
actors, their paths crisscrossing and circling each other, were
significant in terms of relationships. And these Artaud literally
mapped out in sketches issued to the actors with all the totali-

tarian control of his character, Francesco. In the banquet scene when Francesco summons his family and friends to celebrate the deaths of his sons, the scene is populated by dummies as well as actors, suggesting the complete powerlessness of the assembled company in the face of Francesco's overwhelming sense of purpose and excitement in satisfying his desires.

Finding a suitable venue for the production was problematic. The only available theater was the Théâtre des Folies-Wagram, which was designed for music hall, an entertainment at the furthest remove from Artaud's. The auditorium was vast and surrounded by a promenade, the walls were highly decorated. Not only was all this quite inappropriate, but the place was shabby too. Rehearsals were exhausting for Artaud and perplexing for the actors: Artaud switching uneasily between his part as Francesco, and his role as director. André Frank, who managed the administrative side of things, described the rehearsal period: the actors often failed to understand Artaud's concerns and this in turn undermined Artaud's confidence. His anxieties would then communicate themselves to the actors who, increasingly, lost their nerve. The lines of demarcation between Artaud the visionary and Artaud the madman, and between theater and reality, became dangerously blurred. Iya Abdy's confidence in Artaud had all but drained away. "At one point in the play," wrote Frank:

> Artaud wanted to see her [Beatrice] hanging from the torturer's wheel by her magnificent head of hair. It could not have failed to be effective. A convenient footstool under her feet, camouflaged, would prevent her from hanging in reality. Rightly or wrongly Mme Abdy suspects Artaud of wanting to overturn the little stool on the night of the première to make her reaction more truthful, more striking. . . . Stool or no stool she does not want

to be hanged.... There will be no wheel and no hanging. Artaud's fury is terrible.

The play opened on May 6, 1936 and its reception was not altogether unenthusiastic but the reviews were decidedly mixed. One of the most understanding was Jean Jouve's in the *Nouvelle Revue Française* but it too had major criticisms to make: Jouve found Artaud's Francesco too self-conscious and psychologically self-aware for a Renaissance man and his speech, filled with blasphemies and atheistic declarations, all too reminiscent of de Sade. Artaud's production, on the other hand, was praised for its innovation which "continually and creatively brought the space to life. . . . The complex lighting effects, the movement of individuals and groups, the sounds, the music, demonstrate to the audience that space and time constitute an affective reality." But most of the reviews were mocking and uncomprehending and a number of critics referred specifically to the "paroxysms" of Artaud's performance. The supreme artificiality of his delivery removed the play from psychological realism and suggested, instead, that Cenci's lust for his daughter is part of his wider lust to commit crimes thereby uncovering himself to himself through criminality, a feature of the Cenci tradition which begins with Shelley. Like other works of the dangerous tradition Artaud's *Cenci* is not quite a warning: it allows glimpses of a certain envy for Francesco's superhumanity.

The effect of Artaud's intimate encounter with the Cencis was personally—and professionally—catastrophic. Frank describes one of the last nights of the play's run:

I remember a terrible evening in the theatre, when Antonin Artaud for the first time showed the cramped, "remote" face, cut off from the world, which has become the face by which we know him today. He no longer felt able to live within society.

Artaud's instinct was to leave Paris, France, Europe. Some months earlier, while working on a project to dramatize the Spanish colonial conquest of Mexico, he had learned of the existence of a mystical cult, one very much bound up with peyote, a powerful hallucinogenic. Although Artaud had made a number of attempts to free himself of drug addiction he had failed each time. Rather than suffering the agonies of withdrawal once again, Artaud decided to explore the possibility of living in a community in which addiction was the norm and drugs an integral part of the culture, the mystical cult.

Artaud traveled to Central America and found the tribes of the Sierra Tarahumara and experimented with peyote: "Then, at that moment [I felt] that I was living through the happiest days of my life. I had ceased to be bored, to seek a reason for my existence, and I ceased to have to carry my body. I understood that I invented life, and that *that* was my function and my *raison d'être* and that I was bored when I no longer had my imagination and that the peyote gave me imagination." Artaud was on a slippery slope. When he returned to France, arriving on November 12, he was ravaged by drugs and lived rough on the streets of Paris. But he rallied once again, in part because of his love for Cécile Schramme, a young Belgian woman whom he had first met before his trip to Central America. A small government subsidy from the *Caisse des Lettres* was spent on a detoxification program at the Center Français de Médecine et de Chirugie in Paris. But the treatment lasted only a week. Given the decades of drug dependency and the sense in which it had become very much a part of his life (soothing the physical pains he had always

claimed he suffered) and a stimulus to his thinking, it would have
been miraculous if it had freed him. He underwent a second
period of detoxification, this time lasting two weeks, at a clinic
in Sceaux, but again it brought no permanent solution. Artaud
nevertheless felt able to meet Cécile's parents in Brussels, and
became increasingly desperate to marry. Her parents were wholly
against the idea. Artaud's response was to deny his identity:
Antonin Artaud, he claimed, no longer existed: "Very soon I shall
be dead or else in a situation . . . in which I shall not need a name.
I am counting on you for the three asterisks." He was writing to
Paulhan at the beginning of June 1937, pleading with him to
publish his account of his Central American adventure. But he
wanted it to be published anonymously, hence the "three asterisks" as a signature.

The last nine years of Artaud's life were spent in mental institutions, but the support that he received, particularly at the
end of the Second World War, was remarkable. The playwright
Arthur Adamov descended on the mental hospital in Rodez intent on persuading Dr. Ferdière to allow Artaud's transfer to Paris.
This was duly organized. When Artaud's *Letters from Rodez*
were published, he was about to journey north. The *Letters* are
five which he sent to a young admirer, Henri Parisot, and they
describe his periods of confinement, explorations of the meaning of madness, the experience of drug-taking and addiction, language, poetry, art. One of the conditions of Artaud's release was
that he have reasonable financial security. His friends formed
a committee and set about raising capital. Early in 1946 an
auction of donated works of art, manuscripts and autographs
took place. The artists who had contributed included Picasso,
Giacometti, Duchamp, Arp, Masson, Léger, Braque, to name a
few. The writers who rallied included Jean-Paul Sartre, André

Gide, François Mauriac, Tristan Tzara, Jules Supervielle, René Char, Paul Eluard. His friends in the theater planned a gala matinée involving Barrault, Blin, Dullin, Jouvet, Cuny, Vilar. In short, almost all the significant artists among the Parisian *avant-garde*, and a good many others who are no longer as well remembered, participated in Artaud's return to the body within which he belonged—in his resurrection to new life. Shortly after his arrival in Paris he signed a contract with Gallimard for his *Complete Works*.

At the end of 1946 Artaud started to plan a public reading of some of his new work. Particularly because of the publication of his *Letters from Rodez*, Artaud had become relatively well known. The theater sold out early on. A short way into the performance Artaud dropped his papers, abandoning his prepared texts. Instead, he delivered an extraordinary spontaneous monologue which described his sufferings—particularly at the hands of psychiatrists. He railed against electric-shock treatment and conveyed the horrors of his own experience of it. His voice dried up. He ran from the stage. Among the accounts of this remarkable performance—although it mattered precisely because it was simply the spectacle of a life and not performance—is Gide's: "Nothing remained of his material being except what was expressive."

During the spring of 1947, Artaud was writing about Van Gogh:

And what is an authentic madman? Is it a man that has preferred to go mad, in the sense that society understands the term, rather than be false to a certain superior idea of human honour. That is why society has had all those of whom it wanted to rid itself, against whom it wanted to defend itself, because they had refused to become accomplices in certain acts of supreme filthiness, condemned to be strangled in asylums. For a madman is also a man to whom society did not want to listen and whom it wanted to prevent from uttering unbearable truths.

Artaud could equally be describing Beatrice—or Francesco. Artaud described the painter's "superior lucidity" which had allowed him "to see further, infinitely and dangerously further than the immediate and apparent reality of facts." His work should be seen as "morbid alchemical experiments" which "took nature as an object and the human body as a crucible." He had gone beyond "the inert act of imitating nature." Beneath his imitation "he raised an atmosphere; isolated a nerve, which do not exist in nature, but they are of a nature and an atmosphere that are truer than the atmosphere and the nerve of true nature." The title of Artaud's essay, "Van Gogh and the Suicide of Society," turns the story of Van Gogh's life and death on its head. The essay was also a passionate plea for his own cause.

Some months later, one final performance looked to be taking shape. The "drama" was not to be staged, but broadcast on the radio. The title—*To Be Done with God's Judgment*—points to the kind of material that was to be included. Other texts, like the first piece, are more unexpected. Here Artaud explained that the United States was stockpiling, in frozen form, the sperm of small boys to be used for artificial insemination to produce cannon-fodder for future wars. Then the idea would have seemed scientifically improbable. The broadcast's alleged blasphemy persuaded the Director General of Radio Diffusion Français to withdraw it. Fernand Pouey, who was in charge of literary and dramatic broadcasts, was dismayed and angry. The press was furious and stirred up a furor. It was decided that the broadcast should be heard by a jury including Cocteau and Vitrac. The verdict was unanimously in favor of a broadcast. But the Director General was not to be moved. Pouey resigned and controversy raged for a good while. This was Artaud's last performance failure. He felt betrayed once more and in a prophetic poem written at the end of February he intimated his current commitments:

> *I will never have to do with Radio again,*
> *and will from now on commit myself*
> *exclusively*
> *to the theatre*
> *as I conceive it, a theatre of blood,*
> *a theatre which at every performance will achieve*
> *something*
> corporeal
> *as much for the one who acts as the one who comes*
>   *to watch the acting.*

During the last days of Artaud's life, he was treated with a humanity that is at the furthest remove from what he suffered earlier on. At the end he was living in Dr. Delmas's clinic, the last of a series of institutions in which he had spent the greater part of his life. The clinic was in Ivry, on the outskirts of Paris, and it was at last possible for his family and friends to stay in better touch with him. He had been complaining of intestinal pain. His friends rallied and arranged for him to be seen by a gastro-enterologist who took extensive X-rays. Artaud was told not to worry and advised to get plenty of rest, and to eat a healthy diet. His friends, however, were told that he was dying of an inoperable rectal cancer and that he was to be given as much opium as he wanted. A few days after the prognosis, when his breakfast was taken in to him, Artaud was found dead. He was fifty-one. The walls of his room were covered with his drawings, mostly in the blackest charcoal, exuding ferocious energy and freneticism. The self-portraits that stared out from the wall opposite his bed are unforgettable, the furrowed, ravaged faces of a wasted and toothless old man. The contrast with the lean, ascetic face of the young monk, played by Artaud years earlier, is heartbreaking. Standing by St. Joan as she mounts the scaffold in Carl Theodor Dreyer's film *La Passion de Jeanne d'Arc*, his penetrating dark eyes, caught in the close-ups, understand injustice and suffering.

For three days, until his funeral, his friends guarded his body from the rats. These last days could have been a great deal worse. Unlike Van Gogh there was no delay before he was proclaimed a visionary and a martyr: he had been consumed in the fire of his own art. His life had become pure expression and it was during the performance of the *Cenci* play that he had left normal life. From that moment on people were afraid of his incapacity or total unwillingness to distinguish between life and art. But they remained intrigued and deeply admiring.

André Frank described *The Cenci* as "a financial failure, a chain of incomprehensions." The performance, Frank went on to argue, "had decided his fate. Artaud, the tragic genius, Artaud the prophet and magus, had come into existence." Artaud's *The Cenci*, like all the resurrections of the dangerous tradition, had ceased simply to be a play about the suffering and revenge of a Renaissance woman. Here was the most extreme example of the artist's projection of the self into the Cenci story since Shelley's play. Melville, however obliquely, had touched on questions of incest, infidelity and the vagaries of sexual passion in a novel which his contemporaries found uncomfortable in its ambiguities. Hawthorne, likewise, had alluded to a dark psychosexual experience that Americans did not want to associate with the Renaissance world, a world they were looking to understand, even to appropriate. At the time individuals and groups were buying sculptures and paintings to domesticate in their own galleries, museums and libraries, in a bid to create a cultural base for a modernizing America. Hosmer's use of Beatrice was more enigmatic, but by the standards of her day her life and work were heroic and controversial. But the pathology of Artaud's Cenci disease is the most extreme, the most profoundly disturbing, and the most intractable. His play left its problematic source behind, and became a play about the inner torment of Antonin Artaud and the agonies of trying to communicate his visionary ideas to others who could not, or would not, fully understand.

Afterword

———

Beatrice Cenci lived on into the twentieth century in other guises as well as Artaud's torment. The controversial Italian writer Alberto Moravia describes his *Beatrice Cenci* (1955) as a "genuine tragedy" and at the heart of the play lie his two lifelong preoccupations—sex and the family. Moravia's play, which, like Artaud's, is written with great economy, explores the nature of justice and the inadequacy of any society, whether a family or a much wider social group, to administer justice fairly. At the climax of the play, Beatrice says:

> According to *your* justice you will certainly be able to prove that I am guilty of my father's death. But you will never be able to prove that I am not at the same time innocent according to another justice—a justice which you can neither know nor, even less, administer.

Moravia's writings have been censored and banned and many people have taken exception to his relentless explorations of sex in all its shapes and forms, while others have had deep reservations about his political ideas, particularly those shaped by his fascination with revolutionary violence. As he himself made clear, describing himself as a very young man, the man he would always be: "I was fascinated by revolt in every form, from criminality to political conspiracy." His interest in his compatriot Beatrice Cenci chimes with this but his resurrection of her fails to communicate the horror of what she suffered; instead it is understated, remote, unfelt. Moravia played it safe in his engagement with the Cenci tale and the play made little impact. Later the playwright more or less disowned it and even went as far as to proclaim theater "dead."

Still more recently Beatrice has reappeared within a musical tradition which originates in the late eighteenth century but became increasingly vibrant through the nineteenth and twentieth centuries. Berthold Goldschmidt's opera *Beatrice Cenci* was written in 1949. Here too, the Cenci story proved a rich source of political analogy. Goldschmidt's career had been interrupted in 1932 by the Nazi takeover of power in Berlin. Performances of the opera on which he was working had been scheduled at the Mannheim Nationaltheater for the 1932–3 season but Goldschmidt was barred from all official duty. He trained Jewish musicians for the Palestine Orchestra (later the Israel PO) but was permitted to appear as composer, pianist or conductor only in concerts in aid of a Jewish charity. In 1935 Goldschmidt came to London and he became a British citizen in 1947. It was in England that he composed *Beatrice Cenci*, which is bel canto in manner and re-creates the atmosphere of Renaissance Italy by means of a somewhat retrospective musical style. But it is an immensely powerful work, evoking strong emotion in its explorations of cruelty, corruption and injustice, echoing the violent tragedy, totalitarianism and madness of twentieth-century history he had lived through.

Goldschmidt's late compositions (he died in 1996) mimic the problems of being out of step with contemporary realities, preoccupations and tastes. This mirrors his own life, and the dislocations of his career: his life, and much of his work, including his remarkable *Beatrice Cenci*, reflects on the process of expulsion and the problems of being reintegrated into a community, into society.

A more recent, highly acclaimed *Beatrix Cenci* was premiered at the Kennedy Center for the Performing Arts on September 10, 1971, the eve of the anniversary of Beatrice's execution. The opera, by the American Alberto Ginastera, with a libretto by William Shand and Alberto Girri, focuses on the themes of madness and evil, in a work of fourteen scenes. In the 1971 production, the use of films and projections vividly portrayed the work's lurid and nightmarish aspects in an amalgam of music, theater and film. The technique of cinematic slow motion, used at least in this its first staging, vividly dramatized the vagaries of time at moments of great suffering—and just prior to the moment of death. Another American composer who has been repeatedly drawn to Beatrice is Robert Anthony Di Domenica. He has produced no less than three operas in rapid succession: *Beatrice Cenci*, in three acts "after Alberto Moravia" (1993), *The Cenci*, in one act "after P. B. Shelley" (1995), *Francesco Cenci*, in two acts, "after A. Artaud" (1996). After finishing the first three-act work, Di Domenica felt that he was still very much caught in Beatrice's spell and felt compelled to come back to her again— and again. Di Domenica has been haunted by the intractable nature of her predicament and her attempt to escape a life of torture by taking the law into her own hands. He is not alone in his obsession: his wife, Ellen Bender, has co-authored a libretto (based on Hawthorne's *The Marble Faun*), which centers very much on Beatrice's plight.

Twentieth-century novelists, as well as composers, have turned to Beatrice's story. Three notable examples, among many, are Robert McLaughlin's novel, *The Axe Fell: The Story of the Cenci* (1938), Suzanne Kircher's *A Roman Scandal: The Story of Beatrice Cenci*, a work of biographical fiction (1976), and Christina Stead's deeply disturbing tale of a dysfunctional family based on the Cenci, *The Man Who Loved Children* (1940; revised 1965). This last, brilliantly introduced by Doris Lessing in an Everyman edition (1995), went unrecognized for twenty-five years. Stead examines the hatred at work within a disintegrating family and gradually exposes Sam Pollit, husband and father, revealing him to be a tyrannical madman, rather than the civilized and cultured individual he believes himself to be. As Lessing eloquently points out "the reader is made to feel part of something as grand and impersonal as Greek tragedy." A little later Lessing situates Stead's fiction hundreds of years later: "It is like being admitted into some frightful Victorian melodrama . . . but one made ordinary and even commonplace due to the intensity and inevitableness of it." Stead's remarkable novel testifies to the power of Beatrice's four-hundred-year-old story to continue to prompt stark and meaningful resurrections. *The Man Who Loved Children* is set in the 1930s, but it still speaks about the present, with compelling urgency. Like so many of those who have been drawn to Beatrice's story, Stead's novel was only taken seriously decades after it had first been published. After it came out, and aware of its failure to capture the public imagination, Stead's mental health deteriorated, she became alcoholic, stopped writing and died in miserable circumstances. *The Man Who Loved Children* is only very loosely based on the

Cenci story, but in all other respects it qualifies Stead for inclusion in the "dangerous tradition" alongside Shelley, Melville, Hawthorne, Hosmer and Artaud.

Something disposed these particular individuals to engage wholeheartedly with Beatrice's story. Investigating why they were so hopelessly drawn to her has often been grimly engrossing. They share various common traits and preoccupations: above all the conviction that certain taboos need to be exposed and explored, or even experimented with, if we are truly to know ourselves. Relationships with the father or father figure emerge as crucially important, frequently as an aggressive force that needs to be challenged. Violence if not sadism interested them all and some, like Shelley, practiced it. Many of them suffered from periods of severe depression, if not madness, and in each case their encounter with Beatrice Cenci exacerbated their imbalances. They were all preoccupied by death, and in some cases the relationship between death and sex, and they displayed extreme, if very different responses to guilt. Shelley was fantastically immune to it, abandoning his first wife for good in 1814, and when she committed suicide two years later, placing the blame squarely and exclusively with her father. Nathaniel Hawthorne, on the other hand, felt the oppressive weight not only of his own wrongdoings, but those of his ancestors during the Salem witch trials generations earlier. A profound and desperate desire to know themselves unites them all. Each one dared to recognize something of themselves in the Cenci story and this overwhelming feeling of sympathy prompted their various recreations of her, but what they produced also revealed a good deal of themselves and this brave confessional strain in their Cenci works was invariably something for which they were condemned by their contemporaries. They were already outsiders and some were even misguided enough to suppose that their Cenci work would bring them artistic recognition and social reintegration. Instead, they became martyrs to Beatrice's cause.

Beatrice Cenci has lived on across the centuries in myriad resurrections and in varied art forms, but unlike other famous and infamous women of the past she did not distinguish herself for her military bravery, or political astuteness, or artistic creativity, or any other contribution to the society of her age. She suffered, took action and died. The cynic might claim that the resilience of her reputation comes down to the sensationalism of her story, one that runs the full gamut of titillating experience. By now it should be evident that for a good many artists her story was somehow painfully familiar and echoed their own experience as outsiders of various kinds. Shelley railed against the hypocrisy of his contemporaries and staunchly believed in speaking the unspeakable. Beatrice's story, for all the ambiguities of his telling, emerges from his play with a clear moral: violence can never be an adequate response to violence. On the other hand a society which denies the individual basic freedoms, or supports a social system that allows one individual to rob another of freedom, invites tragedies like Beatrice's. If the action she takes in a bid to win her own freedom is in any sense heroic, then this too should be a warning to unjust societies. Natural justice, Shelley implies, is better than no justice at all, and natural justice will always prevail in the absence of something nobler. Shelley's moral and ideological convictions were very strong indeed and the tragedy of his own life is balanced by his own heroic strength. This proved ultimately self-destructive, but it was how he chose to live, and to die.

Melville and Hawthorne were also preoccupied by a need to explore areas of transgression, to speak out about the truths of

human errors and human suffering which a rapidly modernizing America in some ways wanted to ignore in its march onwards.
The adulteress of Hawthorne's *The Scarlet Letter* is, in a sense,
condemned and although there are moral and political gray
areas within the story, Hawthorne's readers were comfortable
with his ideological base. *The Marble Faun*, on the other hand,
is a peculiar work and here and there Hawthorne reveals areas
of human experience, the relationship between eroticism and violence for example, that his contemporaries were deeply uncomfortable with. The sexual excitement, the gasp of ecstasy, that
Donatello and Miriam briefly experience after the murder of the
Model, aroused an instinct to censor. Similarly, in *Pierre*, Melville
wrote about the temptations of incest in a way that few of his
contemporaries were prepared to consider. Beneath or beyond
the apparent innocence of Hosmer's restrained neoclassical sculptures lies the sculptor's obsession with women as victims, and
often as victims of sexual abuse. Combined with Hosmer's own
determination to compete in an almost exclusively male world,
her life and work were often taken as an affront and Hosmer
was made to suffer for her subversiveness. Like all the artists of
the dangerous tradition—except ironically Artaud—she died in
penury and virtually forgotten.

There is something heroic in these artists' and writers' commitment to Beatrice, and there is something tragic about their
contemporaries' treatment of them. But at the same time a certain shared misanthropy also accounts for the appeal of Beatrice's
story. Her fate justifies a bleak view of human nature, one indelibly marked by what, in one tradition, would be termed "Original Sin." For all the gloominess and pessimism in so many of the
retellings, the artists and writers of the dangerous tradition as-
sert something which balances with this, in the very act of their

struggle to create. Melville, I believe, articulates this for them all, in a poem written at the very end of his life when his novel writing is over, his marriage has failed and two of his three children have already died. "The Lake" is a dialogue between the spirit of the poet and the spirit of Lake Pontoosuce, a long-beloved haunt. The poet is preoccupied by death and the spirit of a woman, the spirit of the lake, a Beatrice-like figure, comes to reassure him that he can let go of the pain and suffering of this world, and that death will forever be bound up with life and the living:

> *"Since light and shade are equal set,*
> *And all revolves, no more ye know;*
> *Ah, why should tears the pale cheek fret*
> *For aught that waneth here below?*
> *Let go, let go!"*
> *With that, her warm lips thrilled me through,*
> *She kissed me, while her chaplet cold*
> *Its rootlets brushed against my brow,*
> *With all their humid clinging mould,*
> *She vanished, leaving fragrant breath*
> *And warmth and chill of wedded life and death.*

Source Notes

---〰〰〰---

The place of publication is London, unless otherwise stated.

Epigraph and Introduction

The quotation from Pindar which I use (along with one from Heaney)
is used by Marina Warner as an epigraph to her fascinating study of
"fairy tales and their tellers," *From the Beast to the Blonde* (1994). My
discussion of the incest theme and its relation to madness is based on
Warner's. The most direct way of tracing the myriad Cenci resurrections in literature, opera and the visual arts is by using the resources of
the worldwide web.

PART I. A TRUE STORY
1 Rome Mourns and 2 "No Other Remedy . . ."

The Italian art historian Corrado Ricci's *Beatrice Cenci* (first published
in Italian in 1923) was translated by Morris Bishop and Henry Longan
Stuart (2 vols, New York, 1925). Ricci's research was extremely thorough: he reviewed the large body of published material and unearthed
important manuscripts. My reservations about Ricci's suppositions in

areas where a lack of evidence encourages hypothesis and conjecture are written into Part I. For an extensive bibliography of the history of the Cenci see Ricci's (reproduced in full only in the Italian edition, Milan, 1923).

PART II. RESURRECTIONS
3 Shelley's "Secret Caverns of the Human Heart . . ."

There is a delightful wistfulness about Richard Holmes's evocation of Shelley's life and the biographer's sympathy for his subject provides penetrating insight in *Shelley: The Pursuit* (1974). Newman Ivy White's two-volume *Shelley* (1940) remains the standard biography and includes more detail; some corrections to this early study are made in the important *Shelley and his Circle: 1773–1822*, Cambridge, MA, vols. I–II, 1961, vols. III–IV, 1970, vols. V–VI, 1973. This is a catalogue edition, with commentaries, of the manuscripts of Shelley, Byron, Mary Wollstonecroft et al. Shelley's sympathy for Beatrice, and fascination with the Cenci family, reveal a more complex and tortured man than emerges in the biographies of Holmes, White or Walter E. Peck's lively *Shelley: His Life and Work*, 2 vols (New York, 1940) or, not surprisingly, the "official" biography sponsored by the Shelley family: Edward Dowden, *The Life of Percy Bysshe Shelley*, 2 vols (1886). *The Letters of Percy Bysshe Shelley*, edited by F. L. Jones (Oxford, 1964) make fascinating reading. For an interpretation of the political and historical themes in Shelley's *The Cenci* see Stephen C. Behrendt, "Beatrice Cenci and the Tragic Myth of History" in *History and Myth: Essays on English Romantic Literature*, edited by Behrendt (Ohio, 1990). For a thorough study of the composition and fortunes of Shelley's play see Stuart Curran's *Shelley's Cenci: Scorpions Ringed with Fire* (Princeton, 1970). Mention should also be made of *Shelley: The Critical Heritage* (1975), edited by J. E. Barens, which provides ample insight into the complexities of Shelley's literary critical reception, and a number of highly accessible

240 BEATRICE'S SPELL

studies: M. O'Neill, *Percy Bysshe Shelley: A Literary Life* (Basingstoke, 1989), Edmund Blunden, *Shelley: A Life Story* (1946), Patricia Hodgart, *A Preface to Shelley* (1985) and Claire Tomalin, *Shelley and His World* (1980). Two recent biographies of Mary Shelley include Miranda Seymour's lively *Mary Shelley* (2001) and Martin Garrett's *Mary Shelley* (2002). The two volumes of *The Letters of Mary Wollstonecroft Shelley* (Baltimore, 1980), edited by Betty Bennett, are indispensable for anyone interested in Mary or the Shelley relationship. The standard edition of Shelley's poetry (including *The Cenci*) is Neville Rogers' *The Complete Poetical Works of Percy Bysshe Shelley*, 4 vols (Oxford, 1974–).

4 Melville: Ambiguous Confession

Sympathy and compassion suffuse Lewis Mumford's highly readable *Herman Melville: A Study of His Life and Vision*, first published in America (New York, 1929; revised 1963). A much fuller biography was published by Hershel Parker (Baltimore, 1996) and, although its tone is flatter and the personality that emerges less sympathetic than in Mumford's account, the scholarly attention to detail is immensely useful in helping to form a fair view of Melville. A less full but equally engaging biography was published the same year: Laurie Robertson-Lorant, *Melville: A Biography* (1996). I have, I believe, been little influenced by Melville criticism but Harry Levin's *The Power of Blackness: Hawthorne, Poe, Melville* (1958) is excellent on these writers' preoccupation with the dark side of things. Two other useful studies are Merlin Bowen, *The Long Encounter: Self and Experience in the Writings of Herman Melville* (1963) and Rowland A. Sherrill, *The Prophetic Melville: Experience, Transcendence, and Tragedy* (1979). The standard edition is Melville's *Pierre or the Ambiguities* (New York, 1995), edited by Hershel Parker. My reading of Melville's *Pierre* is, I think, very much my own.

5 Hawthorne: "The Sins of the Fathers"

James R. Mellow's *Nathaniel Hawthorne in His Times* (Baltimore, 1998) is an excellent and very well researched recent biography. Edwin Miller's *Salem Is My Dwelling Place: A Life of Nathaniel Hawthorne* (1991) is more psychologically preoccupied. On *The Marble Faun* I should cite Judith Sutherland's *The Problematic Fictions of Poe, James, and Hawthorne* (Columbia, 1984) and Milton R. Stern, *Contexts for Hawthorne: The Marble Faun and the Politics of Openness and Closure in American Literature* (Illinois, 1991). Although *The Marble Faun* is not key to Gloria Erlich's *Family Themes and Hawthorne's Fiction: The Tenacious Web* (New Brunswick, 1984), it is an engaging, if not always wholly convincing, study of its subject. As for my readings of Shelley's *The Cenci* and Melville's *Pierre*, my reading of *The Marble Faun* is, to use Emily Dickinson's term, something I have come at "slant." That is to say that I see Beatrice's presence, and the author's awareness of the tradition of writers preoccupied by Beatrice, as of central importance in making sense of these writings. The motives of the literary critics that I have read have been other, and thus not wholly relevant to my endeavor. An up-to-date edition of Hawthorne's *The Marble Faun* is Richard H. Brodhead's (1990); this is based on the scholarly edition prepared by the Ohio State University Center for Textual Studies, *Centenary Edition of the Works of Nathaniel Hawthorne* (Ohio, 1968).

6 Harriet Hosmer: Rebellious Innocence

Far too little has been written about Hosmer and, indeed, other nineteenth-century women sculptors. Dolly Sherwood's *Harriet Hosmer: American Sculptor 1830–1908* (Missouri, 1991) is enormously useful; also *Harriet Hosmer: Letters and Memories*, edited by Cornelia Carr (New York, 1912). By way of background material a useful art historical study is William H. Gerdts, *American Neo-classical Sculpture: The*

Marble Resurrection (New York, 1973). Hosmer's *Beatrice Cenci* lies
in the St. Louis Mercantile Library.

7 The Voyeurs

There is, of course, a huge body of material on the writers and artists
discussed in this chapter. A sense of immediate insight into what women
photographers think about their medium is provided by *Illuminations:
Women Writing on Photography From the 1850s to the Present* (1996).
For a general introduction to Cameron see H. Gernsheim's *Julia Margaret Cameron: Her Life and Photographic Work* (1975) and Margaret Harker's *Cameron, Julia Margaret Pattle* (1983). Cameron's
photographs are beautifully reproduced in the expanded and revised
edition of Cameron's *Victorian Photographs of Famous Men and Fair
Women*, with introductions by Virginia Woolf and Roger Fry (1992),
Cameron's *An Album of Photographs Presented to Sir John Herschel*,
compiled by Colin Ford (Wokingham, 1975) and *Julia Margaret
Cameron's Women* by Sylvia Wolf (Yale, 1998). Good introductions
to Dumas include A. C. Bell's *Alexandre Dumas: A Biography and Study*
(1950), F. W. J. Hemmings, *Alexandre Dumas: The King of Romance*
(New York, 1979), Claude Schopp, *Alexandre Dumas* (Paris, 2002).
Stendhal's passion for Italy is fully explored in A. E. Greaves, *Stendhal's
Italy: Themes of Political and Religious Satire* (Exeter, 1995); other
interesting books on Stendhal include B. Didier's *Stendhal* (Paris, 2002)
and Charles Dedeyan, *Stendhal et les chroniques italiennes* (Paris, 1956).
Dickens's *Pictures from Italy* first appeared serially in the *Daily News*
and in the two-volume *American Notes* in 1842. The Oxford University Press edition (1987) is excellent. Christopher Woodward's *In Ruins*
(2001) is an atmospheric and enchanting study of the power of ruins
to inspire the imagination; there is a good deal on Italy, and Roman
ruins in particular. My own view of Shelley's response to ruins, for
example those of the Cenci Palace, is bleaker than Woodward's. I see
Shelley contemplating the grim remains of a violent past, considering

the inevitability of decay, and despairing. Stendhal's *Chroniques Italiennes* (Paris, 1973) is a good scholarly edition. Dumas' Cenci story is among his *Crimes célèbres*. There is a sound, if dated, English translation, *The Crimes of the Borgias and Others* (1907).

8 Antonin Artaud: "Unbearable Truths"

Martin Esslin's introduction *Artaud* (1976) is balanced and informative. F. Bonardel's *Antonin Artaud, ou la fidelité à l'infini* (Paris, 1987), although too uncritical, provides insight into Artaud's difficult theatrical theories. *Artaud and After* by Ronald Hayman also privileges Artaud's theories and their influence. The scholarly edition of Artaud's complete works is the *Oeuvres complètes*, 5 vols. (Paris, 1976).

Index

A la grande nuit ou le grand Bluff surréaliste (Artaud), 210
Adamov, Arthur, 224
Adby, Iya, 200, 221
Allendy, René, 209, 213–214
Allendy, Yvonne, 209, 210–211
Antigone (Cocteau), 205
Antinomian controversy, 124–125
Antiochus, King, 3
Apuleius, 171
Apulia, 171–172
Aragon, Louis, 208
Arias, Beatrice (later Cenci, later Recchia), 22, 28–29
Arnoux, Alexandre, 205
Aron, Robert, 211
Arp, Jean, 224
Artaud, Antonin 199–229; and BC, 234; childhood, 199, 201–203; and the cinema, 206, 208–210, 212, 218, 228; death, 6, 228; and Gnostics, 216–217; mental health and drug habits, 202–204, 206–207, 213–215 223–226; and Nin, 213–215; and poetry, 206–207;

and sexuality, 216, 217–218; studies and editions, 243; and Surrealism, 208–211; and the theater, 204–206, 208–213, 218–223, 228; and Théâtre Alfred Jarry, 209–212; Theatre of Cruelty, 200–201; and violence, 216
Artaud, Antonin, works: *A la grande nuit ou le grand Bluff surréaliste*, 210; *Les Cenci*, 200–201, 212, 218–223, 228, 234; *Correspondence avec Jacques Rivière*, 207–208; *Héliogobale*, 215–216; *Letters from Rodez*, 224, 225; 'Manifesto in Clear Language', 208; *L'Ombilic des Limbes*, 208; *The Spurt of Blood*, 202; *The Theatre and its Double*, 213; 'The Theatre and the Plague', 214–215; *To Be Done with God's Judgement*, 226–227; 'Van Gogh and the Suicide of Society', 225–226
Artaud, Germaine (AA's sister), 202

Artaud, Marie-Ange (AA's sister), 202
Artaud, Marius-Pierre (AA's
    grandfather), 201
'The Artist of the Beautiful'
    (Hawthorne), 136
Ashburton, Lady, 181
Assisi, Lorenzo d', 24
l'Atelier, 204, 206
Athanasiou, Genica, 201, 205
Atreus and Thyestes (Seneca), 213
The Axe Fell (McLaughlin), 233

Balachova, Tania, 212
Balthus, Count Balthasar, 200
Barrault, Jean-Louis, 200–201, 205
Bartoli, Marco Tullio, 44
Beatrice Cenci (Di Domenica), 232
Beatrice Cenci (Ginastera), 232
Beatrice Cenci (Goldschmidt), 231–232
Beatrice Cenci (Hosmer), 155–156,
    172–176, 234, 241
Beatrice Cenci (Moravia), 230–231
Beatrice Cenci (Ricci), 7–10, 238–239
Belisarius, 171
Belmonte, Father Andrea, 20
Bender, Ellen, 233
Benton, Thomas Hart, 181
Berlin, Artaud on, 212
Bertoletti, Antonio, 8
Bettellini, 6
Beyle, Henri Marie. *See* Stendhal
'The Birthmark' (Hawthorne), 135–
    136, 141
Blake, William, 121
Blazy, Domenica, 212
Blin, Roger, 200, 225
The Blithedale Romance
    (Hawthorne), 138–139
Braque, Georges, 224
Brecht, Bertolt, 212
Breton, André, 205, 208, 210
Brook, Peter, 201
Brook Farm, 135, 138
Brothers of the Sacred Stigmata, 20
Browning, Elizabeth Barrett, 120,
    144, 166, 171–172, 196

Browning, Robert: and Cameron,
    196; and Florence Anglo-
    American community, 120; and
    Hawthornes, 144; and Hosmer,
    166, 171–172; *The Ring and the
    Book*, 184–185
Bulwer-Lytton, Robert, 121
Butler, Pierce, 160
Byron, George Gordon, Lord: and
    Claire Clairmont, 76–78, 87; on
    the Colosseum, 188; and
    Hawthorne, 132; Hosmer's bust,
    161; literary representations, 52–
    53; and Melville, 99; and Shelley,
    52–53, 76–77, 88–89

Calvetti, Olympio, 3–34, 38–40,
    42
Cameron, Julia Margaret, 195–198;
    studies and editions, 242
Camus, Albert, 206
Canova, Antonio, 165–166
Celebrated Crimes (Dumas), 192–
    195; editions, 242
Les Cenci (Artaud), 200–201, 212,
    218–223, 228, 234; influence on
    Di Domenica, 232
'Les Cenci' (Dumas), 193–195
'Les Cenci' (Stendhal), 190–192
The Cenci (Di Domenica), 232
The Cenci (Shelley), 56–59, 67, 73,
    79–87, 235; influence on other
    writers, 185, 200, 220, 234
Cenci, Antonina (BC's sister), 29
Cenci, Beatrice: birth, 23; and
    Browning, 185; and Calvetti 33–
    34, 38–40, 42; and Dickens, 185–
    186; end of education, 29;
    execution, 16, 18–19; and father's
    death, 38–39; funeral, 19–20; and
    Hawthorne, 141, 142–143, 145,
    147–148, 153; at La Petrella, 32–
    41; lasting attraction of, 234–237;
    and madness, 4–6; relations with
    father, 9–10, 36–38; Ricci on, 7–
    10; and Stead, 233–234; and

Stendhal, 190–192; trial, tortures and imprisonment, 15, 37–38, 41–42, 45–46
Cenci, Beatrice, artistic and literary representations, 5–7; Artaud, 200, 219–222, 228–229; Cameron, 196–198; Di Domenica, 232–233; Dumas, 192–194; Ginastera, 232; Goldschmidt, 231–232; Guerazzi, 173; Hawthorne, 122–123, 145–150, 236; Hosmer, 155–156, 173–176, 182–183, 236; Kircher, 233; Landor, 120–121,173; McLaughlin, 233; Melville, 90–91, 112, 115–116, 119, 236–237; Moravia, 230–231; Shelley, 56, 83–85, 89, 235; Shelley, Mary, 79–80; Stendhal, 191–192. *See also* Reni, Guido, BC portrait
Cenci, Francesco (BC's father): background 22–23; death 39; death, investigation of, 41–45; description in BC's sentence, 15; at La Petrella, 32–33, 36–39; marriage, first, 23, 26; marriage, second, 29–30; outline history, 2; relations with BC, 9–10, 36–37; relations with family, 27, 29, 32; sexual practices, 23, 30–32, 37; and Sixtus V, 27–29; and violence, 18–26; will, 26–27
Cenci, Francesco, artistic and literary representations: Artaud, 157, 218–222; Di Domenica, 232; Dumas, 193–194; portraits, 173; Shelley, 56–57, 59, 64, 73, 84 Stendhal, 191–192
Cenci Palace, 29; Dickens on, 186; Shelley on, 50–51, 71–72
Chanel, Coco, 205
Char, René, 225
Clairmont, Allegra, 78, 81, 87
Clairmont, Claire (Jane): and Allegra, 78, 81, 87; background, 72; and Byron, 76–78, 87; and Shelley, 72–76

Clark, Stephen, 129
Clement VIII, Pope, 45–46
Cocteau, Jean, 205, 227
Coleman, Anne, 123
Colosseum, Rome, 188
Corday, Charlotte, 51–52
Correspondence avec Jacques Rivière (Artaud), 207
Crow, Cornelia, 156–158, 162, 174, 183
Crow, Wayman, 156, 162, 168, 172–173
Cuny, 225
Curran, Aemilia, 57
Cushman, Charlotte, 177

Dana, Richard Henry, Jr, 99
Dante Alighieri, 121
Daphne (Hosmer), 170
Dardel, Dr, 203
Day, Thomas, 69
Delmas, Dr, 227
Demain, 206
Desnos, Robert, 208
'The Devil in the Manuscript' (Hawthorne), 133–134
Di Domenica, Robert Anthony, 232
Dickens, Charles 185–187; editions, 242
The Dolliver Romance (Hawthorne), 129, 151
Dream Play (Strindberg), 210–211
Dreyer, Carl Theodor, 210, 213, 228
Duchamp, Marcel, 224
Dullin, Charles, 204–205, 225
Dumas, Alexandre, 192–195; studies and editions, 242
Duncan, Raymond, 205

Eastlake, Sir Charles, 174
Edward VII, king of Great Britain and Ireland, 172
Eluard, Paul, 208, 225
Emerson, Ralph Waldo, 136, 152
Ernst, Max, 208

Este, Cardinal d', 37
Eton College, Shelley at, 62

Familists, 124
Fanshawe (Hawthorne), 132–133
Farnese, Cardinal, 24
Ferdière, Dr, 224
Fields, Annie, 152
Fields, James T., 136
Five Scenes (Landor), 121, 173–174
Florence: artistic and literary
    community, 120–121, 144, 184,
    196; Hawthornes in, 143
Francesco Cenci (Di Domenica), 232
Frangipani, Muzio, 25
Frank, André, 221–223, 228
Frankenstein (Mary Shelley), 91, 170
Freud, Sigmund, 4–5, 54

Gallimard, Gaston, 213, 225
Gance, Abel, 210, 218
Gansevoort, Peter (Melville's
    grandfather), 94–96
Gansevoort, Peter (Melville's uncle),
    94–96
Garibaldi, Giuseppe, 195
Gatley, Alfred, 178
'The Gentle Boy' (Hawthorne), 127
Giacometti, Alberto, 224
Gibson, John: background, 165;
    cartoon of, 172; death, 180; and
    Elizabeth Browning, 171;
    Hawthorne on, 176; and Hosmer,
    apprenticeship, 165–167, 170,
    175, 179; and Hosmer, rumored
    affair, 177
Gide, André, 200, 213, 224–225
Gilles, Yvonne, 203
Girri, Alberto, 232
Gnostics, 216–217
Godwin, Mary. See Shelley, Mary
Godwin, William, 63, 72
Goethe, Johann Wolfgang von, 188
Goldschmidt, Berthold, 213–232
Goodridge, Samuel G., 134
Green, Toby, 101–102

Grove, Harriet, 65, 67
Guerra, Lucrezia, 22
Guerra, Monsignore Mario, 44–45
Guerrazzi, 173

Hathorne, Elizabeth (NH's sister),
    126, 132, 134
Hathorne, Elizabeth Manning (NH's
    mother): background, 123, 126;
    death, 136; relations with NH,
    126–129
Hathorne, Judge John (NH's
    ancestor), 125
Hathorne, Nathaniel (NH's father),
    123, 126
Hathorne, William (NH's ancestor),
    123
Hawthorne, Julian (NH's son), 153–
    154
Hawthorne, Nathaniel, 120–154; and
    BC, 122, 141, 142–143, 145, 152,
    234; background, 121–129; and
    the Brownings, 144; children, 136,
    141, 144–145,151, 153; death,
    152; education, 128, 129–130;
    and fathers, 154; and guilt and
    sin, effect of past, 122; and guilt
    and sin, in writings, 134–135; and
    Hosmer, 145, 166, 176–177; and
    incest, 127; influences, 132;
    marriage, 135; and Melville, 108–
    111, 117–119, 136–137, 153–154;
    and his mother, 126–129; and
    Pierce, 131, 139–141, 152; in
    Rome, 141–144, 166, 176–177;
    on slavery, 139–140; and women,
    122
Hawthorne, Nathaniel, works: 'The
    Artist of the Beautiful', 136; 'The
    Birthmark', 135, 141; The
    Blithedale Romance, 138–139;
    'The Devil in the Manuscript',
    133–134; The Dolliver Romance,
    129, 151; Fanshawe, 132–133;
    'The Gentle Boy', 127; Provincial
    Tales, 134; The Scarlet Letter,

108, 136–139, 236; *The Story
Teller*, 130–131; *Twice-Told
Tales*, 135. *See also The Marble
Faun*
Hawthorne, Rose (NH's daughter),
141
Hawthorne, Sophia Peabody (NH's
wife): and Hosmer, 166, 176;
marriage, 135; and Melville, 109–
110, 117; on NH, 138, 152; in
Rome, 141–144, 166, 176
Hawthorne, Una (NH's daughter),
110, 136, 144–145, 151
Hazlitt, William, 90
Heaney, Seamus, xi
Héliogobale (Artaud), 215–216
Hillier, Mary, 198
Hitchener, Elizabeth, 71
Hobbes, Frances Power, 120
Hogg, Thomas Jefferson, 62–65, 68,
72, 76
Honegger, Arthur, 205
Hosmer, Alfred (HH's cousin), 163
Hosmer, George (HH's brother), 157
Hosmer, Harriet, 155–183; and BC,
155–156, 234, 236; background
and education, 157–161; early
sculpting, 156–157; and feminism,
180–181; and Hawthornes, 145,
166, 176–177; and inventions,
181; and Kemble, 136, 160 –161;
libel against, 178–180; literary
representations, 145; in Rome
164–177; and Story, 142, 166;
studies, 241
Hosmer, Harriet, works: *Beatrice
Cenci*, 155–156, 172–176, 234,
241; *Byron*, 161; *Daphne*, 169–
170; McDowell medallion, 163;
Medusa, 170–171; *Oenone*, 172;
Puck, 172; *Queen Zenobia*, 138,
178–179; *Thomas Hart Benton*,
181
Hosmer, Hiram (HH's father):
background, 157; and HH, 156–
159, 161–165, 167–168

Hosmer, Sarah (HH's mother), 157–
158
Hosmer, Sarah Helen (HH's sister),
157–158
Hunt, Marianne, 82–83
Huon de Bordeaux (Arnoux), 205–
206
Hutchinson, Anne, 123–125, 137
Hutton, Richard Holt, 153

'In a Church in Padua' (Melville), 93
incest: in Artaud's work, 202, 218;
and Byron, 52; and Cencis, 9–10,
36–38; daughters' consent, 3–4;
and Freud, 4–5; in Hawthorne's
work, 127, 134; in Landor's work,
121; in Melville's work, 90–91,
98, 113–116, 236; as mythical
theme, 2–4; Ricci on, 9–10; and
Shelley, 78–80; Stendhal on, 191–
192
Italian Chronicles (Stendhal), 190;
editions, 242
Italian Journey (Goethe), 188

Jarry, Alfred, 209
Johnson, Samuel, 132
Jonson, Ben, 13
Jouve, Jean, 222
Jouvet, Louis, 225
'Julian and Maddalo: A
Conversation' (Shelley), 53–56, 79
Juvenal, 199

Keats, John, 88, 95, 132
Kemble, Charles, 160
Kemble, Fanny, 136, 160
Kircher, Suzanne, 233
Kirkup, Seymour, 120–121
Kohl, Clemente, 6
Kronich, Aurelia, 4–5

La Petrella: BC's imprisonment at,
32–37; cover-up at, 39–41;
Francesco's death at, 39–40
'The Lake' (Melville), 237

Landor, Walter Savage, 120–121, 173
Laon and Cythna (Shelley), 78
Lawrence, J.H., 71
Léger, Fernand, 224
Legoux, L., 6
Lessing, Doris, 233
Letters from Rodez (Artaud), 224–
    225
Lewis, 'Monk' G, 60, 170
Linder, 6
Liverpool, Melville on, 99
Longfellow, Henry Wadsworth, 131,
    135
Lot, 4
Lucrè Borgia (Gance), 218
Lugné-Poe, 204
Luitz-Morat, 206

McDowell, Joseph Nash, 162–164
McLaughlin, Robert, 233
madness: and Artaud, 201, 203–204,
    207, 214–215, 220–221, 223–229;
    and incest, 5, 6; and Shelley, 53–
    56, 67, 77
The Man Who Loved Children
    (Stead), 233–234
Manfred (Byron), 188
Mangles, Agnes, 198
'Manifesto in Clear Language'
    (Artaud), 208
Manning, Richard, 127–128
Manning, Robert, 127–130
The Marble Faun (Hawthorne), 122–
    123, 142–143, 145–151, 236;
    influence on Bender, 233; studies
    and editions, 241
Marat, Jean Paul, 51–52, 210
Mardi (Melville), 107
Masson, 224
Mauriac, François, 225
Medusa (Hosmer), 170–171
Melville, Allan (HM's father), 94–96
Melville, Elizabeth (HM's wife), 107,
    111, 118–119
Melville, Frances (HM's daughter),
    119

Melville, Gansevoort (HM's brother),
    96, 106–107
Melville, Herman, 90–119; and BC,
    234, 235–236; background, 93–
    96; children, 108, 118, 119; on
    civilization, 103–104; European
    trip, 97–99; and Hawthorne, 108–
    111, 117–119, 136–137, 153–154;
    influences, 99, 104–105; marriage,
    107, 111, 118; and religion, 92-
    93, 106; at sea, 97, 99–102, 104;
    and sex, 92, 100–101, 104, 106,
    110–111, 118; sources, 240; and
    violence, 97–99, 104; and women,
    95, 100, 104, 111, 119
Melville, Herman, works: 'In a
    Church in Padua', 93; 'The Lake',
    237; Mardi, 107; Moby-Dick, 92,
    104, 108, 111–113, 118; Redburn,
    98; Timoleon, 93; Typee, 100,
    104–106; White-Jacket, 108. See
    also Pierre
Melville, Malcolm (HM's son), 108,
    118
Melville, Maria (HM's mother), 94,
    96
Melville, Thomas (HM's uncle), 94–95
Merle, Joseph, 66, 69
Moby-Dick (Melville), 92, 104, 108,
    111–113, 118
Moore, Henry, 155
Moore, Tom, 88
Moravia, Alberto, 230–231
Morse, Dr Eliakim, 159
Mozier, Joseph, 180
Murray, John, 90–91, 106, 108

Naplas, Louis, 204
Napoléon (Gance), 210
The Necessity of Atheism (Shelley and
    Hogg), 65
Niccolini, Giovanni Battista, 173
Nin, Anaïs, 213–215
Nouvelle Revue Française, 206–207,
    213
Nukahiva Island, Melville on, 100–103

Oenone (Hosmer), 172
L'Ombilic des Limbes (Artaud), 208
Oxford University, Shelley at, 62–63,
    66

Palmerston, Henry John Temple,
    Lord, 175
Parisot, Henri, 224
La Passion de Jeanne d'Arc (Dreyer),
    210, 213, 228
Paulhan, Jean, 213, 224
Peabody, Elizabeth, 135
Pequot War (1637), 123
Pericles (Shakespeare), 3
Petroni, Lucrezia. *See* Cenci, Lucrezia
Picasso, Pablo, 205, 224
Pictures from Italy (Dickens), 186–
    187; editions, 242
Pierce, Franklin, 131, 139–141, 152
Pierre (Melville), 90–92, 113–118;
    BC portrait in, 92, 115–116;
    editions, 241; female characters,
    107; incest in, 92, 113–114, 236
Pindar, xi, 238
Pius V, Pope, 24
Pouey, Fernand, 226–227
Prometheus Unbound (Shelley), 79
Provincial Tales (Hawthorne), 134
Puck (Hosmer), 172

Queen Zenobia (Hosmer), 138, 178–179
Queneau, Raymond, 208

Recchia, Beatrice. *See* Arias, Beatrice
Redburn (Melville), 98, 108
Regnier, Henri de, 204
Reni, Guido: BC portrait, 6, 46;
    Dickens on, 186–187; Hawthorne
    on, 142–143, 145; and Hosmer,
    174; and Shelley, 49–50, 53;
    Stendhal on, 189
Renoel, Robert, 200
Reynolds, Jeremiah N., 99
Ricci, Corrado, 7–10, 238–239
The Ring and the Book (Browning),
    184–185

Rinieri de' Rocchi, Giulia, 190
Rivière, Jacques, 206–207
A Roman Scandal (Kircher), 233
Rome: artistic and literary
    community, 142, 144, 166;
    Colosseum, 188; Hawthorne on,
    120; Hawthornes in, 142–144,
    166, 176; Hosmer in, 164–177,
    179–181; Melville on, 92
Rosalind and Helen (Shelley),
    79
Rousseau, Jean Jacques, 63, 69

Sade, Marquis de, 191, 219, 222
St. Louis Mercantile Library, 173,
    241
Salem witch trials, 122, 125–126
San Tommaso ai Cenci, Church of,
    21, 25
Sartre, Jean-Paul, 224
The Scarlet Letter (Hawthorne), 108,
    136–139, 236
Schramme, Cécile, 223
Sedgwick, Elizabeth, 159–161
Seneca, 213
Shakespeare, William, 3
Shand, William, 232
Shaw, Elizabeth. *See* Melville,
    Elizabeth
Shelley, Elena Adelaide (PBS's
    daughter), 81
Shelley, Elizabeth (PBS's sister), 59–
    61, 64
Shelley, Harriet (PBS's wife):
    character, 68; death, 77–78; and
    PBS, 67–68, 73–74, 78
Shelley, Hellen (PBS's sister), 59–61,
    70
Shelley, Mary (née Godwin; PBS's
    wife): background, 72; children,
    76, 79, 81; depression, 81, 82–83,
    85; *Frankenstein*, 74, 91, 170;
    influences, 170; and PBS, 72–74,
    76, 79, 81–83, 88; sources, 240;
    Valperga, 80
Shelley, Mary (PBS's sister), 59, 70

Shelley, Percy Bysshe, 49–89; and
  atheism, 80, 63, 65–67; and BC,
  56–59, 234–235; and Browning,
  185; and Byron, 52–53, 76;
  children, 73–74, 76–77, 79, 81;
  and Claire Clairmont, 72–76;
  death, 87–88; education, 60–65;
  and fathers, 64, 67, 85; funeral,
  121; and Hawthorne, 132; and
  Hosmer, 173, 175; and madness,
  53, 60, 66–67; marriage, first, 67–
  68, 70–74, 77; and Mary, 72–74,
  76, 79, 81–83, 88; and Melville,
  93, 99; and Murray, 91; portraits,
  56–57; and sisters, 59–61, 65, 70;
  and social reform, 63, 71; sources,
  239–240; and violence, 60–62,
  234
Shelley, Percy Bysshe, works: 'Julian
  and Maddalo: A Conversation',
  53–56, 79; Laon and Cythna, 78;
  Prometheus Unbound, 79;
  Rosalind and Helen, 79; 'To the
  Moon', 87. See also The Cenci
Shelley, Sir Timothy (PBS's father),
  64–65, 67, 70
Shelley, William (PBS's son), 76, 81–
  83
Sismondi, Jean-Charles, 173
slavery: and Hawthorne, 139–140;
  and Kemble, 161
Southey, Robert, 79, 86–87
The Spurt of Blood (Artaud), 202
Stead, Christina, 233–234
Stendhal (Henri Marie Beyle), 184,
  189–192, 242
Stephenson, Peter, 161
Stockdale, John James, 64
Story, William Wetmore, 142, 166–
  167
The Story Teller (Hawthorne), 130–
  131
Strindberg, August, 210–211
Supervieille, Jules, 225
Surcouf (Luitz-Morat), 206
Surrealist movement, 205, 208–211

Syon House Academy, Shelley at, 59–
  61

Tennyson, Alfred, Lord, 172, 196
Tennyson, Frederick, 120
Théâtre Alfred Jarry, 209–210
The Theatre and its Double (Artaud),
  213
'The Theatre and the Plague'
  (Artaud), 214–215
Théâtre des Folies-Wagram, 221
Thoreau, Henry, 136
The Threepenny Opera (Brecht), 212
Timoleon (Melville), 93
To Be Done with God's Judgement
  (Artaud), 226
'To the Moon' (Shelley), 87
The Token, 134
Toulouse, Dr. Edouard, 204
Trollope, Anthony, 120, 132
Twice-Told Tales (Hawthorne), 135
Typee (Melville), 100, 104–106
Tzara, Tristan, 225

Valéry, Paul, 213
Valperga (Mary Shelley), 80
'Van Gogh and the Suicide of Society'
  (Artaud), 226
Velli, Lodovica. See Cenci, Lodovica
Victor or Children in Power (Vitrac),
  211–212
Vilar, 225
Vinton, Alfred, 173
violence: and Artaud, 216; and
  Francesco Cenci, 18–26; and
  Melville, 97–99, 104; and Shelley,
  60–62, 234
Vitrac, Roger, 208, 211, 226–227

Watertown, Massachusetts, 157
Westbrook, Harriet. See Shelley,
  Harriet
White-Jacket (Melville), 108
Winthrop, Governor John, 123–124
Wollstonecraft, Mary, 72
Woolf, Virginia, 195